FINANCE

Third Edition

Michael Fardon B.A. M.Phil. A.C.I.B. Cert. Ed.
David Cox F.C.C.A. F.C.I.B. Cert. Ed.

Osborne Books

First published 1986.
Reprinted 1986, 1987, 1988, 1989, 1990.

Published by Osborne Books Limited,
Gwernant, The Common,
Lower Broadheath, Worcester, WR2 6RP.
Tel 0905 333691

Printed by Ebenezer Baylis & Son Limited,
The Trinity Press,
London Road, Worcester, WR5 2JH.

British Library Cataloguing in Publication Data

Fardon, Michael, *1951-*
  Finance. - 3rd ed.
  1. Great Britain. Finance
  I. Title II.   Cox, David, *1946-*
  332'.0941

ISBN 0-9510650-8-4

foreword to the third edition

This book is written specifically for students of the BTEC National Diploma/Certificate 'Finance' Core Unit. It is designed as a practical guide which covers the aims and objectives specified by BTEC; it is divided into three subject areas:

- personal finance
- business organizations
- social and public sector organizations

Personal finance is the logical starting point for any study of finance. It relates most directly to the student's immediate experience and establishes principles - the raising of funds, recording of data, financial planning - which are also essential to business, social and public sector organizations.

Business organizations form the second and major section of this book. A detailed analysis of the types of business organizations, of the way they raise money, record and plan and take decisions, is accompanied by a close study of accounting practice. This section is intended as a firm foundation for the 'Accounting' Unit in the second year of the BTEC course, for which Osborne Books has produced its *Accounting* textbook.

Social organizations, the public sector, and the social implications of business decisions are dealt with in the third section. It is intended that this area will be particularly useful for Public Administration students, as well as providing a bridge with the Core Unit, 'The Organization in its Environment'.

The material forming this third edition has been fully updated and revised by the authors to reflect the ever-changing 'financial' scene. There have been significant tax reforms since the last edition: the introduction of the Community Charge in England and Wales, and the separate assessment for taxation of husbands and wives. A number of Assignments and Case Problems within the text have been amended to take account of these changes and also the inevitable advance of inflation.

Lastly, we would like to stress that this text has been written by lecturers for lecturers, and is intended to be an essentially *practical* book. The publishers will always welcome your views, criticisms and suggestions.

Michael Fardon and David Cox
Worcester

Spring 1990

acknowledgements

The authors wish to thank Jean Cox for her invaluable assistance in the production of the text in its present form. They are also grateful to the following for their advice and expertise: Chris Bush, George Johnston, Peggy Rossiter, and Paul Russell. Thanks are also due to the following for permission to reproduce material: BTEC, Barclays Bank plc, National Westminster Bank plc, The Controller of Her Majesty's Stationery Office, and Hereford and Worcester County Council.

the authors

Michael Fardon, was born and educated in Worcester. After completing academic studies at London University, he worked for Midland Bank plc, where he was involved in the areas of personal and small business finance as well as specialising in International Corporate Finance for a number of years. His publications include banking textbooks and other titles from Osborne Books. He currently writes and lectures on a freelance basis.

David Cox is a Senior Lecturer in the Business Studies Department at Worcester Technical College. He worked for Midland Bank plc for a number of years, and has considerable full-time teaching experience, having taught students over a wide range of levels. He is also a qualified accountant and the author of a number of accounting and banking textbooks. He is co-author with Michael Fardon of *Accounting* and *Business Record Keeping* from Osborne Books.

contents

introduction to assignments

Assignment work forms a major part of BTEC teaching. In order to assist lecturers and students, fourteen fully developed assignments have been included in the text, printed on tinted paper. These assignments are ready for use, but as always, a certain amount of negotiation will have to take place between lecturer and students over issues such as group size, length of written work specified, time scale and resources which are available.

Skills development and skills assessment are central to current BTEC philosophy and, to assist lecturers, the assignments have been designed to develop the whole range of business-related skills. Each assignment includes in its headings a list of the skills specifically developed within its various tasks. The General Objectives covered are also stated in the headings, letter coded for convenience in accordance with the BTEC guidelines.

It is hoped that the assignments should not be seen by the students as staged 'exercises' as such, but as a part of the whole learning process, complementary to the Student Activities at the end of each Chapter.

section one
personal finance

Chapter One
Sources of Personal Finance:
Short Term Borrowing

"Where shall I get the money to buy the things I need?
Can I borrow for what I want to buy?
What happens if I can't repay what I borrow?
How can I cope with all the bills when they come at once?"

Questions such as these are often asked by people who are concerned or worried about personal finance. What is required is a systematic way of evaluating one's financial resources and a method of managing those resources, in other words, *financial planning:*

Personal financial planning may be defined as a method of making the most efficient and sensible use of financial resources which are earned, saved and borrowed.

This method takes into account the following factors:

• the amount of money available from earnings or social security benefits
• the ability of the individual to borrow
• the cost of the borrowing
• the choice between saving and borrowing
• the process of deciding on the priority of needs
• the need to plan for future requirements

In this Chapter we will examine the factors which relate to short term sources of finance, and see in a typical Case Problem how a simple method of financial planning can solve a potentially serious problem. Borrowing for a specific purpose will be dealt with in Chapter 2, the choice between saving and borrowing in Chapter 3, and the need to plan for future requirements in Chapter 4.

Sources of Personal Finance: Earnings

A part time job is often the first experience a person will have of earning money. The job is likely to be paid by the hour, by commission, or by the number of items dealt with (piecework). Whatever the nature of the job, it provides a useful source of income in addition to any parental allowance. The extra money will make it necessary for the person earning to make a number of straightforward financial and personal decisions.

Take for example a student working during the holidays in the telephone answering department of a busy Mail Order firm. He or she will work, say, six hours a day during the week on a basic hourly rate. This provides extra cash which can either be spent or saved. The decision will not be difficult to make.

A complication might arise, however, if the student is offered the option of a four hour shift on a Sunday at double the normal hourly rate. A number of questions will then need to be asked:

"Do I need the extra money?

What shall I do with the money? Save it or spend it?

Do I work the extra unsociable hours? Is it worth it? Will it spoil my social life?"

For anyone who works full-time, whether as a shop assistant or as a Managing Director, the same basic questions have to be answered. The following underlying principles will then apply:

- the harder the person is prepared to work, generally speaking, the more he or she earns

- the more the person earns, the more choices he or she has for spending or saving

- if a person works excessively hard, the greater the cost to health, social and family life

- the more the person earns, the more will be payable in tax (see Chapter 5, *Personal Taxation*)

Clearly, the individual needs to make a number of choices to dictate his or her lifestyle. Character and circumstance will play a part in the making of these decisions, but in the end it is up to the individual to decide.

Another factor which is part of the financial planning process is the ability of the individual to borrow.

Sources of Personal Finance: Borrowing from Institutions

A wide range of commercial organizations offers finance to the individual:

- **banks:** overdrafts, personal loans, revolving credit, mortgages
- **building societies:** mortgages, personal loans, overdrafts
- **Finance Houses:** personal loans and hire purchase
- **credit card companies:** extended credit on credit cards
- **retail stores:** credit cards, hire purchase (through Finance Houses), credit terms

Students are strongly recommended to obtain leaflets from these organizations describing the various schemes on offer.

Capital and Revenue Expenditure

Borrowing is normally carried out for two types of expenditure:

Capital Expenditure
If you buy a specific item for use in the long term (a car or a house), this is *capital expenditure*. Normally you would borrow by means of a loan with fixed repayments over a long period of time (a personal loan, a mortgage). We will deal with this type of finance in the next Chapter.

Revenue Expenditure
You buy many items which you will use up in the short term (food, travel, entertainment); this is *revenue expenditure*. At times of heavy spending you may need to borrow in the short term. We will examine this form of finance in this Chapter.

Before looking at how and in what circumstances money may be borrowed, it is useful to look at *who* can borrow and also examine the *cost* of borrowing in terms of *interest* and *APR* as defined by the Consumer Credit Act 1974.

A Legal Note: Borrowing by the Under-18s

An important legal point is that under the Minors Contracts Act 1987, any person under the age of 18 (a 'minor') is not legally bound by contracts for money borrowed; these contracts are unenforceable, although in certain cases a minor could be taken to court to enforce restitution of the money or goods bought with it. This is the reason why documents offering loans and credit often exclude applicants under the age of 18. If you are a minor and wish to borrow, your parents may need to sign a formal legal document, *a guarantee,* accepting liability for your debt. If this is done, the institution can then rely on your parents if you do not repay the borrowing.

Interest: The Cost of Borrowing

Any commercial organization lending money or granting credit (i.e. allowing you to repay what you owe over an extended period) will charge you for the use of the money. This charge (which will include a profit element) is achieved by the addition of an *interest* amount to the sum that you repay. Any loan or credit therefore involves:

- the *principal,* i.e. the amount of the finance provided
- the *interest,* i.e. the added cost of providing that finance

The amount of interest is dependent on the prevailing *rate of interest.*

An interest rate is the amount of interest expressed as a percentage of the amount borrowed over a period of time, usually a year ('per annum', often abbreviated to 'p.a.').

The formula for calculating an interest amount from a given interest rate is as follows:

$$\text{Interest} = \text{Amount borrowed} \times \frac{\text{interest rate}}{100} \times \text{period in years}$$

For example, if you borrow £1 000 for a year at an interest rate of 10%, the calculation will be:

$$\text{Interest} = £1\,000 \times \frac{10}{100} \times 1 = £100$$

Clearly, the higher the interest rate, the higher the cost of borrowing.

Annual Percentage Rate: the Cost of Borrowing

The Consumer Credit Act 1974 states that loans and credit (excluding house mortgages and overdrafts) up to £15 000 to individuals must be documented in the form of a *Regulated Agreement,* i.e. a loan or credit agreement which clearly sets out the terms of the finance granted, and which does not mislead the individual by using obscure language or, quite literally, small print.

The Act also requires that the cost of borrowing must be clearly stated as an *APR* to enable the consumer to compare the cost of credit from different institutions.

APR or Annual Percentage Rate, is the total annual cost to the borrower in interest and fees, expressed as a percentage of the amount borrowed.

It is important to note that *APR is not an interest rate.* The reason for this is that it also includes, as a cost, the fees which are sometimes payable when a consumer first signs a loan or credit agreement.

The Circumstances in which Short Term Finance is needed

The need for finance can be over differing periods of time and for large or small amounts. In this Chapter we will look at the needs for short term borrowing.

Borrowing for a short period of time may be needed

- in an emergency (if your car breaks down)
- at a time of heavy spending (Christmas)
- at the end of a month before a salary is received
- when money is needed but not available immediately (e.g. in a building society fixed term deposit)

The two most important sources of short term borrowing are a *bank overdraft* and the use of a *credit card.* Another bank scheme, a *revolving credit account,* is also described below.

Forms of Short Term Borrowing

❏ Bank Overdraft

An overdraft is borrowing on a bank account up to an agreed limit; interest is only charged on what is borrowed.

Overdrafts are very useful for occasional or periodic borrowing on current account. Overdrafts for personal (as opposed to business) customers are charged at a rate of approximately 5% added to the bank's *Base Rate.* Base Rate is an advertised fixed rate, set and varied periodically by the major banks, who use it as a *base* for working out their interest rates for borrowers, who are charged an agreed percentage above Base Rate. *No-one ever borrows at Base Rate.* Overdraft interest is normally calculated on a daily basis on the amount that is borrowed and charged to the borrower's *current* account quarterly. Some building societies offer overdrafts charged at an interest rate fixed by the individual society.

How to apply for an Overdraft
If you need a bank overdraft, you should apply to your bank for an interview. If the bank is happy that you will be able to repay the borrowing, they will mark a *borrowing limit* on your current account, i.e. an amount up to which you can overdraw. You are then free to issue cheques as and when you wish, subject only to the agreed limit. An agreement letter setting out the terms of the overdraft will be drawn up and signed by the bank A building society overdraft is normally part of a cheque account package and will be made available when the account is opened.

❏ Credit Cards

Credit cards are plastic cards issued by companies owned by the major banks, or by retail stores through these companies. Credit cards enable the holder to purchase goods and services and pay for them at a later date.

Cards issued by bank-owned companies include Visa and Access; these cards may be used to make purchases at numerous outlets including shops, garages, restaurants and theatres. The many store cards, for example, a Habitat card issued through Storehouse plc and Citibank Savings, enable the holder to make purchases only in that store or group of stores.

A person uses a credit card to make purchases of goods over a period of time up to a total maximum amount, or credit limit. This limit is determined by the card company, and is often initially 10% of the card-holder's salary. The element of credit enters because the user does not have to pay straightaway. He or she will, in due course, be sent a monthly statement by the card company detailing all the purchases made, and asking for a payment to be made within 25 days. Payment may be made either by post, by means of a bank giro credit attached to the bottom of the statement, or by direct debit (automatic transfer) from the card holder's bank account. Interest is normally charged on the card, and an annual fee is also sometimes payable. Credit cards are an easy and flexible way of obtaining credit: 'Buy now, pay later'.

How to apply for a Credit Card

Obtain from a bank or a store an application form similar to that illustrated in fig. 2.1 (see page 13). Complete the form and hand it to the appropriate bank or store. If the credit card company considers you creditworthy - it will judge this from details of your salary, status, and bank record on the form - you will be sent a card by post after about three weeks.

❏ Revolving Credit Account

A Revolving Credit account is a separate account (operated either by a bank or by a retail store through a bank) to which the customer transfers a regular monthly payment, normally by standing order (automatic transfer) from his or her current account.

The customer is able at any time to borrow on the Revolving Credit account up to a limit of (usually) thirty times the monthly transfer. A transfer of £10 a month will therefore enable the customer to have a maximum borrowing of £300 outstanding at any one time. Thus a bank revolving credit account will enable you to buy what you want, and a retail store revolving credit account will enable you to obtain credit at that store.

How to apply for a Revolving Credit Account

Obtain and complete an application form similar to that illustrated in fig. 2.1 (see page 15). The bank or store will assess your creditworthiness and, if you are suitable, will agree to a Revolving Credit limit. It should be noted that different banks give different names to this type of account, e.g. Midland Bank's 'Save and Borrow Account'.

Case Problem: Christmas Shopping

Situation

You are a parent in a family unit of four. There are five shopping days left before Christmas. It has been a month of exceptionally heavy expenditure. The balance of your bank current account is £5.20 and you have only £25 in cash left in your pocket. There is a gas bill of £45.60 outstanding, and today you have received the red final demand notice. You estimate that you need £150 to complete your Christmas shopping, which includes Christmas decorations £25, Christmas meal £35, and a present for your wife/husband £25. You have an Access Card with a limit of £500 and £50 due payable on 13th January. You have no other borrowing facilities and your income, which is paid at the end of the month into your bank account, covers your normal monthly expenses, usually with £50 to spare. What should you do?

Solution

There is no simple answer, but the following options show how sensible short term borrowing can solve a potentially distressing problem.

Option One: The Scrooge Alternative

It would be possible to cut down drastically on your spending: you could leave the house undecorated, abandon the idea of a Christmas lunch and buy no presents. You could approach the Gas Board, negotiate an extension and/or make a part payment with your cash. You would achieve your saving, but at what cost?

Option Two: Living on Credit

It would be possible to throw caution to the winds, using your available Access credit of £450, or negotiating an overdraft with the bank. You could then spend all you need (and possibly more) and pay off the Gas Board. But what would happen in January or February when the borrowing had to be repaid and, in addition to the principal borrowed, considerable interest had mounted up?

Option Three: Financial Planning

It is possible to tailor your spending to enable you to have a festive time but also to raise finance *which you know that you will be able to repay*. Firstly you should decide on priorities and then make reasonable economies.

	previous estimate	revised estimate
Gas Bill (must be paid)	£45.60	£45.60
Decorations (do you need to spend £25?)	£25.00	£5.00
Christmas Lunch (you can economise here)	£35.00	£25.00
Present for wife/husband (an agreed reduction)	£25.00	£5.00
Remaining expenses	£65.00	£40.00
TOTAL	£195.60	£120.60

You have saved nearly £80 without prejudicing your Christmas. How will you raise the short term finance? An overdraft of £120 might be negotiated with the bank. As it appears that there is normally a monthly surplus of £50, you could agree with the bank manager to make monthly reductions to the overdraft when your salary is paid into the account at the end of the month.

The free credit offered by the Access Card until 13th February (the payment date for your *Christmas* purchases) could be an attractive alternative, but the interest costs thereafter, if the full amount was not repaid, would be high compared with those of an overdraft. It is up to the borrower to work out *how much* he or she can afford to repay, and *when,* and then to decide the least expensive way of raising finance.

Chapter Summary

❑ The sources of personal finance include earnings and borrowing.

❑ Personal borrowing involves an interest cost to the borrower measured in terms of an interest rate.

❑ The cost of personal borrowing schemes may be compared by examining the Annual Percentage Rate (APR).

❑ Forms of short term personal borrowing include:
  • overdrafts
  • credit cards
  • revolving credit accounts

❑ Short term finance is normally for day-to-day expenditure known as *revenue expenditure*.

In Chapter 2 we will examine fixed repayment finance, a longer term borrowing comitment which can be entered into for an item we particularly want and intend to keep. Expenditure of this type is known as *capital expenditure*.

 Student Activities

1. A friend, aged 18, wishes to borrow money to buy a stereo system costing £750, but she is confused by the references in publicity material from lending institutions to interest rates and 'APR'. Write down what you understand by the relationship between interest rates and APR, giving examples from publicity material for credit schemes. Would there by any further points to consider if your friend were aged 17?

2. You are changing jobs and find that instead of being paid weekly you are going on to a monthly payroll. As a result you will be very short of money during your first month in the new job. You estimate that you will need £100 to see you through. What sources of finance are available, and how would you apply for credit?

3. Calculate the interest you will pay if you borrow:

   (a)   £1 250 @ 12% for 2 years
   (b)   £1 650 @ 9% for 3 years
   (c)   £1 000 @ 17% for 6 months
   (d)   £22 000 @ 11% for 25 years

   Suggest the types of items (e.g a car, a house) which could be purchased by these borrowings.

4. **Subject for discussion**
   Investigate the salaries earned by a solicitor, an accountant, a bank manager, a teacher, a clerical worker, an unskilled worker, all at the age of 35. Discuss in your group:

   (a) the reasons for the difference in salaries
   (b) the disadvantages of being highly paid
   (c) any evidence that the highly paid save more, or borrow less

   Information for the above could be obtained from newspaper advertisments or from your local careers library.

5. Calculate how much you spent last month under two headings: 'revenue expenditure' and 'capital expenditure'. Analyse the sources of finance which enabled you to make this expenditure. If you are familiar with pie charts, construct two: one for revenue and capital expenditure and one showing the sources of finance.

6.

> *18 Manorford Close*
> *Wichenfield*
> *Worcester WR5 4RD*
>
> 30 March 1988
>
> Dear Mr Stirling,
>
> I have just left College in Worcester and have got a job working at Intermail, a local mail order company. I have also left home and am staying with a friend (address as above). I have found the last two months quite a strain and I am finding difficult to cope with paying for everything, which is why my bank account has gone into the red occasionally. I do earn a reasonable wage, which is paid into the bank, as you will see from my statement. Can you suggest any ways the bank can help me?
>
> Yours faithfully,
>
> *F MacPherson*
>
> Fiona MacPherson (Miss)

You work in the local branch of the National Bank plc, and are handed the above letter by Mr Lionel Stirling, the branch manager. He asks you to draft a reply for his signature, mentioning that he thinks that the best schemes for Miss MacPherson would be a credit card and a revolving credit account. He suggests that you explain these two schemes in your reply .

He also asks you to make sure that Miss MacPherson is over 18. Why should he be interested?

Chapter Two
Borrowing for a Specific Purpose

We have seen in the last Chapter that individuals borrow to finance short term spending (revenue expenditure). They can also borrow over a long period of time for specific items which they intend to retain (capital expenditure). Such borrowing normally involves fixed repayments.

There are two forms of fixed repayment finance:

• instalment credit
• mortgage finance

Instalment Credit is available for the purchase of *specific items* such as consumer goods (e.g. cars, hi-fi equipment), holidays, and for home improvement schemes. An amount is borrowed to finance the item and repaid in equal monthly instalments over a period of up to five years. The borrowing is normally unsecured: the borrower does not have to mortgage his or her house to obtain the finance.

Instalment Credit is of two types:

• *personal loan* (from banks and building societies)

• *hire purchase* or 'point of sale' credit, arranged by the supplier of the goods (often a shop), but funded by a Finance House

Mortgage Finance is the granting of a loan, usually for a house purchase, secured on that property. Mortgage Finance is long term, often for 25 years, and repayable by monthly instalments which will vary as interest rates alter.

Instalment Credit: Personal Loan

A personal loan is

• for a fixed amount (normally up to £10 000)
• over a fixed period (normally up to five years)
• at a fixed interest rate for the life of the loan
• repaid by fixed monthly instalments
• used to buy items which the borrower then owns

The main characteristic of the personal loan is that the repayments are *fixed:* the borrower knows exactly *how much* he or she has to repay and *when*. To help the borrower, lending institutions usually provide repayment tables setting out the amount of the monthly instalments for loans of differing amounts and periods. On the following two pages are set out an application form for a personal loan (fig. 2.1), and repayment tables (fig .2.2).

To National Westminster Bank PLC
Personal Loan Proposal
(Please complete all sections in **block capitals**)

NYCHAVON Branch

Surname _JONES_	Mr/Mrs/Miss/Ms Forenames _ANNE CATHERINE_
Surname —	Mr/Mrs/Miss/Ms Forenames —
Address _102 ONSLOW GARDENS WOODBURY WORCS._ Postcode _WS2 8PZ_	Date of Birth/s _9 JULY 1957_
	Home Telephone Number _WOODBURY 691_

Period at present address — _5_ Years

Marital status — Married/Single/Other

Residential status — Owner/Tenant/With Parents/Other

If you own your residence give — Date of purchase _20.1.85_ Cost £ _49,500_

Mortgage outstanding £ _29,500_

Occupation — _TEACHER_

Name and address of employer — _HEREFORD & WORCESTER COUNTY COUNCIL COUNTY HALL, SPETCHLEY ROAD WORCESTER_

Length of service with present employer — _12_ Years _9_ Months

If less than 3 years with present employer give time with previous employer — — Years — Months

Is your job pensionable? — Yes/No

Net Income (include overtime) after deduction of PAYE, National Insurance Stamps etc

Monthly		Weekly	
Self	Spouse	Self	Spouse
£ _850_	£ —	£ —	£ —

Is your salary paid direct to a bank? — Yes/No

Cheque Card held? — Yes/No

Give the name of Credit Cards held if any — _ACCESS_

Details of existing Bank Account(s)
(a) Type of account held — Current/Deposit/Other/None

(b) Bank/Branch where account maintained — _NAT. WEST._ Bank _NYCHAVON_ Branch

(c) Period account maintained — _16 YEARS_

The total cost of the transaction will be approximately — £ _6000_

and the balance is to be found from — _PERSONAL SAVINGS AT WESTMID BUILDING SOCIETY_

Amount of loan required — £ _2,000_

I/We require a loan for the purchase of (give brief details). — _FORD FIESTA — NEW VEHICLE. (PRESENT VEHICLE NO LONGER SERVICEABLE)_

Repayable by _36_ monthly instalments

I/We require Personal Loan Protector Cover to apply to the first-named person above. (Delete if not required.)

I/We confirm that the above information is correct to the best of my/our knowledge and undertake to furnish the Bank if required, with evidence of expenditure.

Signature(s) of applicant(s) — _A. C. Jones_

Date _4 JULY 1990_

For Bank use only	
PNL	
C/A	
S	
I/V	

Fig 2.1 A Personal Loan Application Form

Loan Repayment Table at APR 20%

A Amount of Loan £	500	1,000	3,000	5,000
Repayment Term 12 months				
B Total Payable £	570.96	1,141.92	3,425.88	5,709.84
C Insurance Premium £	18.00	36.00	108.00	180.00
D Monthly Repayment £	47.58	95.16	285.49	475.82
B Total Payable £	551.16	1,102.32	3,306.84	5,511.36
D Monthly Repayment £	45.93	91.86	275.57	459.28
Repayment Term 18 months				
B Total Payable £	600.12	1,200.06	3,600.18	6,000.30
C Insurance Premium £	21.00	42.00	126.00	210.00
D Monthly Repayment £	33.34	66.67	200.01	333.35
B Total Payable £	575.82	1,151.64	3,455.10	5,758.38
D Monthly Repayment £	31.99	63.98	191.95	319.91
Repayment Term 24 months				
B Total Payable £	631.20	1,263.84	3,791.52	6,319.20
C Insurance Premium £	25.00	51.00	153.00	255.00
D Monthly Repayment £	26.30	52.66	157.98	263.30
B Total Payable £	601.20	1,202.40	3,607.44	6,012.48
D Monthly Repayment £	25.05	50.10	150.31	250.52
Repayment Term 30 months				
B Total Payable £	663.60	1,328.70	3,986.10	6,643.50
C Insurance Premium £	29.00	59.00	177.00	295.00
D Monthly Repayment £	22.12	44.29	132.87	221.45
B Total Payable £	627.30	1,254.60	3,764.10	6,273.30
D Monthly Repayment £	20.91	41.82	125.47	209.11
Repayment Term 36 months				
B Total Payable £	697.32	1,395.72	4,187.52	6,979.32
C Insurance Premium £	33.00	67.00	201.00	335.00
D Monthly Repayment £	19.37	38.77	116.32	193.87
B Total Payable £	654.12	1,308.24	3,924.72	6,540.84
D Monthly Repayment £	18.17	36.34	109.02	181.69
Repayment Term 48 months				
B Total Payable £	770.88	1,541.28	4,624.32	7,706.88
C Insurance Premium £	43.00	86.00	258.00	430.00
D Monthly Repayment £	16.06	32.11	96.34	160.56
B Total Payable £	709.44	1,419.36	4,258.08	7,096.80
D Monthly Repayment £	14.78	29.57	88.71	147.85
Repayment Term 60 months				
B Total Payable £	849.00	1,698.60	5,095.80	8,493.00
C Insurance Premium £	53.00	106.00	318.00	530.00
D Monthly Repayment £	14.15	28.31	84.93	141.55
B Total Payable £	768.00	1,536.00	4,607.40	7,678.80
D Monthly Repayment £	12.80	25.60	76.79	127.98

NOTES

Loan Protector Plan
The borrower has the option of taking out insurance with the Personal Loan. This insurance, known as a "Loan Protector Plan" covers the following risks:

• sickness
• accident
• death

The insurance premiums will be paid along with the loan repayments.

Repayments
The Repayment Tables show repayments made for loan periods of up to five years in sections headed "Repayment Terms".

• with insurance
The first three lines of each Repayment Term section refer to a loan taken out *with* insurance cover.

• without insurance
The last two lines of each Repayment Term section refer to a loan taken out *without* insurance cover.

Fig 2.2 Personal Loan Repayment Tables

A Note: APR and the Interest Rate for Personal Loans

A borrower may be puzzled by the fact that an APR for a Personal Loan is usually about twice the fixed interest rate.

The interest rate is fixed for the duration of the loan, and will not vary with other rates such as Bank Base Rate. Interest for the *whole loan* for the *whole period* is calculated at the fixed rate and added to the amount borrowed (the principal) before the first repayment is made. This interest is then repaid as part of the monthly instalments, along with the principal amount. As the amount of the loan remaining to be repaid *reduces* over its life but interest is charged on the *whole* amount for the *whole* period (i.e. the interest calculation assumes the loan does not reduce monthly), the APR may be *twice* as much as the fixed interest rate.

For example, £1 000 borrowed at a fixed rate of 10% over two years will be charged interest as follows:

$$\text{Interest} = £1\,000 \times \frac{10}{100} \times 2 = £200$$

The total amount to be repaid will be the principal £1 000 plus interest of £200 = £1 200. There will be 24 monthly repayments of £50. The *fixed* rate will be 10%, but the *APR* will be approximately 20%.

Remember, APR measures the *cost* of the loan but is not, in itself, an interest rate. It is the APR which the prospective borrower must look at in order to compare a Personal Loan with other similar schemes.

How to apply for a Personal Loan

It is necessary to complete a Personal Loan application form (see fig. 2.1), obtainable, for example, from a bank or a building society. The form will ask for details such as occupation, salary, property owned (if any) and other credit commitments. These details will be processed ('credit-scored') by the lender's staff (or by computer) to decide whether or not you are suitable for the granting of a loan. You will be seen to be more creditworthy if you:

- own your house
- are in a stable job
- have a regular salary paid to the bank

You may or may not have an interview with a manager or senior clerk. You will be given a decision very rapidly (often the same day) so that you may, if successful, buy the item you want without delay. The agreement to lend will be documented in a formal Loan Agreement required by the Consumer Credit Act, and signed by both lender and borrower.

Instalment Credit: Hire Purchase (H.P.)

A Hire Purchase credit, like a Personal Loan, enables an individual to obtain consumer goods, and to repay the cost of the item over a period of time, normally up to five years. The difference with Hire Purchase is that ownership of the goods does not pass to the borrower until repayment is complete.

A deposit is payable when the finance is arranged. If you fall behind with your repayments, but have paid off a third of the amount owed, the goods by law cannot be repossessed. Hire Purchase is available from retail outlets with an arrangement with a Finance Company to offer 'point of sale' credit.

How to apply for Hire Purchase

The purchaser applies for credit to the Finance House via the supplier of the goods, who also processes the paperwork. In this triangular relationship of purchaser, supplier and Finance House, the borrower rarely comes into contact with the lender.

Case Problem: Purchasing a Video Camera

Situation

You wish to buy a video camera and recorder to enable you to make home movies. You have no savings but think that you may be able to afford some money out of your income each month towards the machine. By shopping around you discover that the price for a reasonable set of equipment is £1 000. Where could you obtain finance, and what considerations would you bear in mind when arranging it?

Solution

Assuming that you will take out some form of fixed repayment finance, the following steps should be taken:

- estimate the amount you can afford to repay each month for repayments
- by comparing the APRs of bank, building society and shop H.P. schemes, find the lowest APR, the cheapest source of finance.
- examine the repayment tables provided and find out if you can realistically repay the £1 000 within three to five years.
- if you can afford the repayments, apply for the credit and get the agreement signed as soon as possible
- buy the equipment while the price of £1 000 still holds

Long Term Finance: Mortgages

The personal finance we have looked at so far has been *unsecured*. The lending institutions have provided finance on the basis of the borrower's ability to repay, i.e. his or her *creditworthiness:* usually the fact that there is a salary or other funds to meet repayments.

A borrower may also raise *long term* finance (up to 25 years), normally for the purchase of a house, by pledging the house purchased as security for a loan by means of a *mortgage*.

A mortgage is a formal legal document signed by the borrower

- *pledging his or her property*
- *giving the lender legal rights over the property, including a power of sale if the borrower is unable t to repay the loan*

The word 'mortgage' is consequently used to describe a long term loan which provides money for the purchase of a property. Mortgages are available from banks, building societies and specialist companies. People who borrow by means of a mortgage should appreciate the fact that if they fail to repay, the lender can sell the house and make the borrower homeless.

There are three methods of repaying a mortgage loan:

- repayment mortgage
- endowment mortgage
- pension mortgage

The difference between them is the way in which the principal amount is repaid.

❑ Repayment Mortgage

A fixed amount is borrowed at the outset: normally up to 90% of the purchase price of the house (although it may be a higher percentage). Repayments, which are monthly, are made up of two elements: the principal (fixed amount) and the interest on whatever principal remains to be repaid.

The interest rate, set by the lending institutions, varies in line with interest rates in the economy, and so therefore does the amount of the monthly repayments. By the end of the loan (usually after 25 years) principal and interest have both been fully repaid; the house belongs to the borrower.

❏ Endowment Mortgage

The loan will be treated in the same way as a Repayment Mortgage, except for the repayment of the principal amount borrowed. An *endowment life assurance policy* on the life of the borrower is taken out to repay the principal at the end of the loan. An endowment policy is a life assurance policy which will pay out a sum of money on a fixed date (in this case at the end of the loan) or on the death of the borrower, whichever occurs earlier. Assuming the borrower remains alive, which is hopefully the case, he or she will make monthly payments, normally in one amount, which cover *interest on the loan* and *premiums* to the Life Assurance Company. These mortgages have proved popular because the insurance policy often pays an added bonus when the loan is repaid (say after 25 years) which is an extra benefit for the borrower. The bonus comes out of the profits of the insurance company.

❏ Pension Mortgage

A pension mortgage acts in exactly the same way as an endowment mortgage except that the loan is repaid in one amount at the end of the loan period from a lump sum payment from a *personal pension scheme* on the retirement of the borrower. The pension scheme will also, of course, provide pension payments for the rest of the borrower's life. During the loan the borrower makes monthly repayments covering interest on the loan and pension contributions. Pension mortgages are popular with the self-employed and people with private pension plans because they enable the borrower to save tax.

How to apply for a Mortgage

The procedure for applying for both types of mortgage and some of the problems encountered and decisions required can be well illustrated in a Case Problem.

Case Problem:
The Jones Family - Raising a Mortgage

Situation

Benjy and Lou Jones are planning to buy a home of their own and are examining the options. They have building society savings of £5 000 between them. The husband, Benjy, earns £12 000 per year and Lou does part-time work bringing in £5 000 per year.

Lending institutions, such as banks and building societies, each have their own *two* formulae for calculating the maximum amount that can be borrowed. These formulae are commonly:

1. maximum amount of loan = 90% of valuation of property

2. maximum amount of loan = 2.75 x the major wage-earner's salary plus the secondary salary

The lending institution will only lend the *lower* of the two amounts calculated.

The Jones couple have seen in a local development a flat on which they have set their hearts. The asking price is £50 000. They calculate the maximum amount they can borrow as follows on the two formulae given them by their Building Society:

1. The building society will lend them a maximum of 90% of the valuation = £45 000.

2. The amount they can borrow based on the earnings formula is lower:

2.75 x Benjy Jones' salary of £12 000 =	£33 000
Lou Jones' income of £5 000 =	£5 000
Total	£38 000

The maximum that they can borrow is therefore the *lower* of £45 000 and £38 000.

They clearly have a number of problems:

* If the flat costs £50 000 and they can only borrow £38 000, they need £12 000. They have only £5 000 saved. They obviously cannot, on the face of it, afford the flat.

* Repayments on a loan of £38 000 over 25 years would normally be approximately £400 per month. Can they afford this?

* When they have resolved the problem of which flat to buy, do they choose a repayment, endowment or pension mortgage?

Solution

It appears that the couple must either raise further finance, which may be difficult, or rethink their ideas.

Further sources of finance might include:

* a loan from the family with low interest and deferred repayment
* increased income from earnings - is the husband due for promotion or a rise - can the wife take a full-time or more remunerative job?

A more sensible solution, bearing in mind the likely additional cost of fitting out and running a new home would be to reconsider the situation:

* to find a cheaper flat in the same or similar development, priced at about £40 000
* to find a second-hand flat of a similar type - the seller of the flat may be prepared to drop the price

In any event, the couple must work out how much they can afford to repay each month. Once a reasonable figure is established for a purchase price and the monthly repayment, the couple must approach one or a number of lending institutions for quotations for repayment, endowment and pension mortgages. These institutions might include:

* the building society which which they have their savings
* banks (including foreign banks in the UK) and other building societies
* mortgage brokers and specialist companies offering endowment mortgages
* the company operating the development (if they want to buy a new flat) - such companies often associate with building societies to offer attractive mortgage terms

The couple will then decide on the best terms, submit a formal written mortgage application and, if successful, receive an offer of finance. The lending institution will often help to arrange surveys, legal services and insurance. The whole transaction, from application to moving in, will often take six weeks or more.

Chapter Summary

❏ In this Chapter we have examined personal finance in terms of the sources of fixed repayment finance which is used for specific purposes.

❏ Fixed repayment finance can take the form of instalment credit (up to five years) or mortgage finance (up to 25 years).

❏ Instalment credit includes personal loans and hire purchase.

❏ Mortgage finance includes repayment, endowment and pension mortgages.

❏ Raising finance is a complex matter, presenting a number of problems to be solved and decisions to be made.

❏ These problems lead by implication to the subjects dealt with in Chapters 3 and 4:

- Is it better to save rather than to borrow?

- How can one plan one's spending patterns (i.e. budget) to allow for future needs?

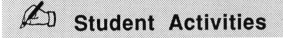 **Student Activities**

1. You work in the Westmidlands Building Society, 2 The Parade, Pershore, Worcs., WR8 9OE and receive the following letter from John Nuttall. Write a reply for signature by your branch manager, John Grant, explaining the three types of mortgage available and your lending formula. (Assume you will lend 90% of the value of the house and 2.75 x major salary + whole of second salary).

> 12 *Magnolia Walk*
> *Worcester*
>
> 1 July 1988
>
> Dear Sir,
>
> I am considering the possibility of buying a property valued at £50,000. I earn £12,000 a year and my wife earns £6,000 a year. I shall be grateful if you would let me know how much we could borrow, and also what is the difference between a repayment, endowment and pension mortgage.
>
> I look forward to hearing from you.
>
> Yours faithfully,
>
> *J. Nuttall*
>
> John Nuttall

2. You want to buy a dining room suite of furniture for £1,000 from a major retail store. Investigate the different types of finance that are available. Write down a description of each scheme, detailing its terms, the cost of borrowing and the likely repayments over three years. Recommend the scheme which you consider to be the best. Obtain an application form for the recommended scheme and complete it, assuming that you are 25, married, a house owner and working for the local authority.

3. If a building society will lend on mortgage up to 90% of the value of a house and works on the formula 2.75 x the major salary plus the whole of the second salary, what is the most expensive house the following couples can afford? Remember that the savings figure quoted will form the couple's 10% contribution in each case.

(a) Hugh and Anne, salaries £7,000 and £5,000, savings £3,000.
(b) Rodney and Jan, salaries £8,000 and £7,000, savings £5,000.
(c) William and Sue, salaries £17,000 and £6,000, savings £10,000.
(d) Mike and Anne, salaries £25,000 and £8,000, savings £5,000.

4. You work as an enquiry clerk at the National Bank plc and are asked what is the difference between the interest rate of 10% and the APR of 20% quoted on a bank personal loan. Write down how you would answer this enquiry making sure that you distinguish clearly between the two rates and state why the APR has to be quoted.

Chapter Three
The Decision to Save or to Borrow

Money is a resource. If you have money in your possession, or the expectation of money in the form of future earnings, you have purchasing power which you can use for your benefit.

A number of questions have to be asked to determine how the money can be *efficiently* used. The answers will often depend as much on your preferences as on your circumstances:

"Shall I spend my earnings on something I want now and not bother to save for something I might need in the future?
Shall I save so that I can buy what I really want in the future?
Shall I borrow now for that item, knowing that it will cost me more to borrow in the long term?"

These questions involve what is known as *Opportunity Cost*.

Opportunity Cost

The questions we have just asked involve a choice. If we want an item badly enough, we will be willing to go without other items which we would also like:

* *in the present,* e.g. buying a motorbike instead of going to the Canary Islands on holiday
* *in the future,* e.g. repaying a loan for an item that we want now *or* saving up for an item we want in the future; both saving and repaying consume future income which could be used to buy other things that we want

Opportunity Cost is the cost of obtaining something you want in terms of what you have had to give up in order to obtain it.

Opportunity Cost is the sacrifice you have to make in order to obtain what you want. If it involves repaying a loan or saving, you will also have to bear in mind such variables as inflation and interest rates in order to calculate how you can make most *efficient* use of your money.

The Decision to Save for a Future Purchase

If you decide that you do not want to spend your money at present, and consequently have to go without certain items (clothes and records, for instance), you will be able to save to buy something you really want in the future. The 'opportunity cost' will be the clothes and records. In making this decision you will have to examine how the rates of inflation and interest affect your decision.

Return on your savings: Interest received

Money under the mattress earns nothing. Money invested in a bank or a building society earns interest, representing the cost to you of being without your money for a period of time. You should maximise this return, as it represents future purchasing power.

Interest earned = Amount invested x $\frac{\text{interest rate}}{100}$ x period in years

The real rate of interest

The inflation rate is the percentage by which money loses its purchasing power over the period of a year. For example, if you have £100 at the beginning of the year and the inflation rate is 5%, you would need £105 at the end of the year in order to maintain the same purchasing power.

Inflation can clearly erode the value of your savings. A *real interest rate* is the rate of return on your savings adjusted for inflation. It is calculated by the simple formula:

Real interest rate = Actual interest rate *less* inflation rate.

If the real interest rate is positive, your savings are at least maintaining their purchasing power; if it is negative, your savings are declining in real value and you may wish to reconsider your decision to save.

Inflation and the cost of the item for which you are saving

If there is inflation, the cost of the item will normally *rise* during the year; you may wish to buy sooner rather than later. On the other hand if the item is a high-technology item, such as a computer or compact disc player, the price may be expected to *fall* as production becomes more efficient and volumes of sales rise. In this case you would be well advised to wait, unless the opportunity cost is so great that you are willing to pay the higher price and make sacrifices accordingly.

The Decision to Borrow rather than to Save

If you place an opportunity cost premium on an item, i.e. you must buy it whatever the cost, then you could borrow to obtain it. The costs here are:

- loss of future spending power because of having to make repayments

- the fact that the interest rates for borrowing are far higher than the interest rates paid on your savings, e.g. it costs you more in interest to borrow £1 000 over a period of time than you would receive in interest if you saved £1 000 over that period

Case Problem: Buying a Microcomputer

Situation

You would like to buy a microcomputer. The one in which you are interested has just come onto the market, priced at £500. You have £250 already saved in a building society account, and have £25 a month available out of your income over the next twelve months for saving or repaying borrowing. Inflation is running at 5% and your savings are earning 7%. You have read in a magazine that the microcomputer's price may well drop to £300 in a year's time. The two options are obviously to borrow and buy now, or to save and buy later.

Solution

The solution all depends on the opportunity cost, or, basically, what you are willing to sacrifice in order to obtain the machine. You must first ask yourself:

- How badly do I want the machine?
- Is it worth my waiting for it to fall in price over the next twelve months?

You might calculate the cost in monetary terms as follows:

❑ Buy the machine now with your savings of £250 and borrow £250

You find that the £25 you have available monthly will repay a loan of £250 over 12 months at an APR of 20%. The total eventual monetary cost, including interest paid, will be approximately £550, calculated as follows:

	£
Machine cost £500 funded by • savings	250
• loan principal	250
Cost of borrowing £250 over one year at 20% APR	50
Total eventual cost	550

❑ Buy the machine at the end of the year for £500 (or even £300) by saving £25 out of income.

Saving is clearly a viable proposition because the real rate of interest is 2% (actual rate 7% less inflation rate 5%). The purchasing power of your savings at the end of the year will be:

	£
Amount already saved	250.00
Interest received on £250 at 7%	17.50
Amount saved during year (12 x £25)	300.00
Approximate interest on monthly savings of £25 at 7%	10.50
Amount available at end of year	578.00
Less 5% for inflation (approximately)	29.00
Total purchasing power at year end	549.00

This second option shows that to wait a year and save £25 per month allows you to buy the microcomputer and still have purchasing power of £49.00 (£549 less £500) to spare. It is clearly cheaper in monetary terms to save and wait rather than to borrow and buy, the cost being £500 compared with £550.

If the magazine prediction that the price of the microcomputer will fall to £300 by the end of the year proves to be correct, the difference between buying now or waiting until the year-end is quite dramatic. Instead of paying £550 at the outset you will only pay £300 and have £249 purchasing power available (£549 less £300) at the year-end. This situation will, of course, be the exception rather than the rule.

It is purely personal choice, however, to decide whether the opportunity cost will allow you to purchase *now,* and sacrifice £550 worth of other items. If you need the machine badly now, there is little choice.

The decision is entirely up to you; it is your *opportunity choice.*

Savings and Investments: An Economic Viewpoint

So far in this Chapter we have considered *savings* in general terms, but it is important in any study of finance to consider how and why people save and invest. If an individual or an organization wants to make a return on its money it can be done by:

- **saving** - the regular setting aside of money with a financial institution

- **investment** - placing a lump sum of money with a financial institution to achieve an increase in value of that money ('capital growth') or the receipt of a regular income

Many financial institutions compete for savings and investment and it is therefore advisable to 'shop around' for the best interest rate and return on investment.

Financial Intermediaries

Financial institutions treat savings and investments placed with them as a *source of finance* which they in turn re-invest and on-lend; these institutions are known as *financial intermediaries*.

Financial intermediaries include banks and building societies and the government-owned National Savings. In the diagram below you can see how the money flows from the public through the financial intermediaries as a *source of finance* to other sectors of the economy. Banks and building societies mostly on-lend deposits placed with them, whereas National Savings raises money from savers and investors for use by the Government in its public spending programme (see also Chapter 24 'Public Sector Finance').

Savings and Investment: The Flow of Funds

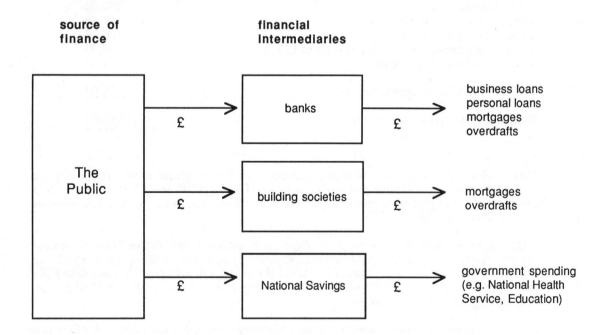

Savings and Investment: The Individual's Viewpoint

Motives for saving and investment
An individual normally saves or invests for one of two reasons:

- for a specific item, as already mentioned in this chapter
- for a 'rainy day', for the unforeseen event

In both cases it is in the individual's interest to find out the highest return, either in the form of interest paid or the capital growth of the investment scheme.

Schemes paying interest
The financial services industry is always bringing out new schemes which pay interest and you are advised to investigate:

- bank deposit and savings account schemes
- building society share accounts
- National Savings Ordinary and Investment Accounts and Income Bonds

When examining the interest paid on these schemes you will note that the interest rate payable may be quoted in a number of different ways, because of the income tax that is normally payable by individuals on interest received (see Chapter 5 for further details about income tax). The two common ways of referring to interest rates are:

- gross interest rate - interest rate *before* deduction of tax
- net interest rate   - interest rate *after* deduction of tax

Bank and building society schemes normally deduct Income Tax before you receive the interest. If you are not liable to pay income tax you can arrange with the institution to receive interest gross (without deduction of tax). This is advisable if you are a full-time student not paying tax!

National Savings schemes, on the other hand, do not deduct the tax from the interest, and leave you to settle with the tax authorities the amount (if any) that you owe. Clearly, if you are a student and do not pay tax, the National Savings schemes are particularly attractive.

All the above schemes are suitable for money which will be deposited for a short time, or may be needed at short notice; they are said to be *liquid* deposits, and are quite unsuitable if you are looking for *capital growth*.

Capital Growth Schemes
If you wish to invest your money for a long period of time you may well be looking for a scheme which will make your money grow in value over the years. Examples of this situation include parents investing money for their young children which the children can use when they leave home, and married couples saving for their retirement.

Many financial institutions and National Savings offer longer term investment opportunities. You should investigate the following:

- *stocks and shares* (including the popular "new issues" such as British Gas and Abbey National)
- *unit trusts* (look at the Saturday issues of The Times, Financial Times and The Independent)
- *National Savings Certificates and Capital Bonds* (information available at Post Offices)
- *endowment life assurance policies* (information from insurance brokers and the financial press)
- *TESSAs (Tax Exempt Special Savings Accounts)* available from 1991 from banks and building societies, offering five year, tax free saving

In each case consider how the institutions involved act as financial intermediaries, channelling funds from the public back into the economy.

Chapter Summary

❑ Opportunity Cost is the cost of obtaining something in terms of what you have had to give up in order to obtain it.

❑ Factors affecting opportunity cost include:

- inflation
- the degree of your need and your personal preferences
- fluctuations in the price of the item in question

Savings and investment enable the individual and the organization to accumulate wealth.

❑ Savings and investment institutions are often known as 'financial intermediaries' because they enable money deposited to be reintroduced into the economy.

❑ A distinction must be drawn between savings (gradual accumulation of wealth) and investment (the setting aside of a lump sum). A wide variety of schemes is available for both.

In the next Chapter we will consider spending decisions in the light of the need for any individual or household to budget for future needs.

Student Activities

1. (a) You have £2 000 to invest for a year. Investigate savings schemes offered by institutions such as banks, building societies and National Savings (available through Post Offices). Construct a schedule listing all the schemes, the interest rates applicable, and a projection of how much each investment will be worth in 12 months' time after interest has been added. Assume that you are a standard (lowest rate) taxpayer.

    (b) Find out the current rate of inflation and on a separate schedule adjust the interest rates you have recorded to produce a 'real' interest rate for each scheme. Write a brief comparison of all the schemes and give, with reasons, your recommendation for the best one.

2.   A friend of yours wants to buy a new type of camera, which currently costs £300, although the photography magazines state that the price may come down to £200 in a year's time. Your friend has £30 a month available out of income. Investigate the current interest rates for savers, the current APR for borrowers, and the rate of inflation. Write down the points you would consider when advising your friend.

3.   You have been given a cheque for £5 000 by your uncle, who has won £100 000 from a Premium Savings Bond. As a class, divide (if possible) into pairs and then:

Both write a 'thank-you' letter to the uncle stating precisely how you are going to spend and/or save the money.
Hand the letter to your partner and write a reply (as the Uncle) to the other's letter, evaluating the way the money is to be used. The uncle has been renowned in the family for being miserly and never enjoying himself, and has been nicknamed 'Uncle Scrooge'.

4.   (a)   Compile a list, in note form, of the major items which you have purchased over the *last* twelve months. Arrange these in order of priority as you see it. Would you in retrospect change your mind about purchasing any of the items?

(b)   Compile a list of items which you would like to purchase over the *next* twelve months, and again arrange these in order of priority. Given the situation that you are legally able to borrow money, find out the cost of borrowing, the return on savings and the rate of inflation, and decide whether you would prefer to save or to borrow for those items. Justify your decision.

5.   You work as an assistant in the firm of Severnside Financial Advisers who are brokers dealing in stocks and shares, unit trusts, and primarily in life assurance. You receive the following memorandum form your boss Robert Kirk who is advising a client, Mrs Sonia Cooper, who wishes to invest the sum of £10,000 over 15 years to achieve maximum capital growth. Find out the necessary information for him and send it to him with a suitable covering memorandum.

Memorandum

to Miss J Bristow

from R Kirk   **date** 2 April 19-9

Client: Mrs Sonia Cooper

Mrs Cooper is seeing me on 10 April at 11.00 a.m. She has
£10 000 to invest over 15 years. Please find out

(a)   5 recommended "safe" shares (let me know their price)
(b)   5 capital growth unit trusts (prices please)
(c)   any National Savings schemes that are suitable
(d)   recommendations for an endowment life policy

I need the information by 9 April at the latest. Thanks.

RK

Chapter Four
Personal Budget Planning

People sometimes get into financial trouble because of factors beyond their control, such as redundancy and illness. These circumstances are, understandably, distressing. Equally distressing are two other frequent causes of financial problems: a lack of control over personal spending and a lack of forward planning by the individual or family. Charles Dickens' Mr. Micawber set out two basic formulae:

Income greater than expenditure = happiness

Expenditure greater than income = misery

The problems often encountered are:

• *deficiencies in personal accounting:*

How much money do I have?
How much money have I spent?

• *the inability to budget for future needs:*

How am I going to manage when all the bills arrive at once?
How am I going to pay the car tax and insurance after I have paid for the holiday I have just booked?

The solution is one of simple housekeeping and basic common sense:

• know how much you have, and work out *what* you spend, and *when*
• if you are spending too much, cut down where you can
• if you have a surplus, save it for a time when expenditure is heavier
• borrow if you need to, but only if you know you can repay

Fig. 4.1 on the facing page gives you an idea of what items a family will have to pay for, or consider paying for. It also includes a pie chart showing the items making up the expenditure of an average household, and the percentages of those items.

If you are a single person household, the total cost worked out on a "per person" basis will be proportionally higher, as certain costs (e.g. TV licence) are charged per household, and not per individual. If you do not take account of these costs you could run into financial problems, as the case study on page 30 demonstrates.

HOUSEHOLD AND PERSONAL EXPENDITURE

This summary sets out the items of household and personal spending undertaken by a typical household of four: two parents and two children of school age. The sections are set out in order of priority.

Regular essential spending for the household

- mortgage payments/rent • Community Charge • water rates • gas bills
- fuel (oil or coal) • electricity • telephone • insurance (house, contents)
- food • household maintenance and repairs • TV licence • schooling expenses

Regular essential expenses for members of the family

- travelling expenses • car tax, insurance and maintenance • life assurance
- personal loan and credit card repayments • medical and dentists fees • basic clothing

Less essential items of personal expenditure

- books, magazines and newspapers • cinema, discos, entertainment • drinks
- cigarettes • records, tapes, videos • presents • holidays • fashion clothes
- hobbies and sports activities

SPENDING BY THE AVERAGE FAMILY

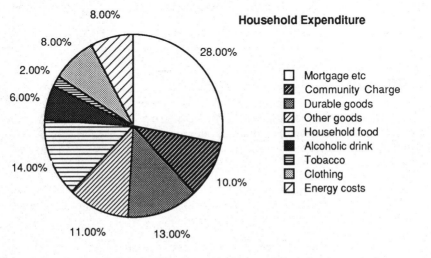

Source: Central Statistical Office Monthly Digest of Statistics (amended)

Fig 4.1

Case Problem: Miss Florence Cash

Situation

This young lady has recently left home in rural Herefordshire where she has lived comfortably with her parents. She qualified as a bilingual secretary at the local Technical College, and has now moved to London, having been fortunate to obtain a job with the comparatively high salary of £12 000 a year.

Miss Cash, however, has been in financial difficulties. She has just received another letter from her bank manager, this time asking her to return her cheque card and cheque book, and requesting that she restore her bank account to credit, the balance being £250 overdrawn. The bank is threatening legal action if she doesn't repay.

What has happened? From the pile of unopened bank statements to be found in her recently purchased flat, it will be seen that she earns £725 net a month but, out of that, she pays each month, on average:

• mortgage (£290) and Community Charge (£30)	£320
• electricity and gas bill	£50
• telephone	£20
• car (insurance, petrol)	£50
• TV and video rental	£20
• travel (season ticket)	£40
Total average monthly expenditure	£500

She also has to pay car tax (£100) and TV licence (£71) annually; the remainder of her income (and more) is spent on food, clothes and entertainment. Further investigation into her pile of mail reveals outstanding bills to Access (£250) and to a leading store credit card (£175), both of whom are pressing her for repayment of the money.

It appears that Miss Cash has been earning enough to pay for her basic expenditure, but despite this she has obviously been overspending. How can she remedy the situation?

Solution

The adoption of a personal accounting system

Miss Cash should develop a simple system to record her payments so that, at any time, she will know how much money she has left in the bank to spend. She should:

- record all payments by cheque (details to be written on the counterfoils)
- record all withdrawals of cash with her cash card
- keep a record of all standing orders and direct debits, i.e. automated computer payments of bills from her bank account
- retain her payslip
- retain sales receipts from credit card and store card transactions

She might find a notebook or a personal organiser a useful means of recording some of these details.

The use of the bank statement to estimate spending power

When each monthly bank statement arrives she can estimate how much remains before the next pay day by carrying out some simple checks and calculations:

- checking the statement to make sure her salary has been received
- ticking off on the statement each item paid out, either against cheque counterfoils or against her own separate record of standing orders and direct debits
- deducting from the final statement balance any outstanding cheques written out but not yet deducted from the account
- deducting from the final statement balance any items to be paid before the next pay day (such as standing orders and direct debits)

The total of this calculation will give her the amount she will have available for food, clothes, entertainment and other expenses. As we have seen from opportunity cost, the choice is hers entirely, but it would be sensible to allow enough money for food for the month before spending out on other items. As we will see in Chapter 10, this checking of the bank statement against records of payments, the *bank reconciliation,* is essential for all organizations, whether public sector, business or social.

The use of budget planning to calculate future needs

'Reconciliation' is also what Miss Cash has to achieve with her bank manager: it is clear that they are going to have to work out between them how much she owes, how she is going to repay her borrowing, and how she is to continue to meet her commitments.

Her present borrowing is:

Bank overdraft	£250
Access card debt	£250
Store credit card debt	£175
Total borrowing	£675

The bank manager is sympathetic and will allow Miss Cash to repay the overdraft by an agreed amount each month. He also appreciates that she will repay the credit card debts over a period of time. Before reaching his decision the bank manager has asked her to complete a 'Budget Planner' provided by the bank. This printed set of forms sets out a schedule of an estimate of monthly expenditure (fig. 4.2) and a Cash Flow Forecast (fig. 4.3). Both of these forms are illustrated on the following pages.

The Budget Planner: Monthly Expenditure Schedule and Cash Flow

Miss Cash has set out on the schedule marked 'Monthly Expenditure'
- her monthly expenses
- her annual expenses
- a weekly equivalent (for her information) of these expenses.

It should be noted that in addition to a cheap *annual* holiday break costing £100 she has budgeted for the following *monthly* payments:
- Access and store card debt £30
- clothing and shoes £20
- housekeeping £80
- sundry expenses ("pocket money") £40

The section marked 'Cash flow month-by-month' is of great use to Miss Cash and the bank, as it shows how and when her overdraft is repaid, and, of equal importance, when she may need to borrow again. The instructions for completing the Cash Flow form are set out on page 34.

Monthly Expenditure

FLORENCE CASH, 118 THE CREST, PALMERS GREEN, LONDON N13

EXPENDITURE	Annual	Quarterly	Monthly/ 4 Weekly	Weekly Equivalent
Mortgage Rent			290	67
Rates & Water Rate				
Property Maintenance				
House Contents & Bldgs Insce		included with mortgage		
Life Insurance				
Other Insurance (excl. car)				
Credit Card Repayments			30	7
H.P. Commitments				
Personal Loan Repayments				
Heating (solid fuel/gas/oil)				
Electricity			25	6
Gas			25	6
Telephone			20	5
Car Expenses	100		50	14
TV	71		20	6
School Expenses				
Fares/Season Ticket			40	9
Clothing/Shoes			20	5
Housekeeping			80	18
Club/Society Subscriptions				
Newspapers/Mag Subscriptions				
Savings/Investments				
Holiday Expenses	100			
Presents				
Pocket Money			40	9
Other Expenses				
Community Charge			30	7
Total Estimated Expenditure	£ 271	£ —	£ 670	£ —

Fig 4.2 Monthly Expenditure Schedule

Cash flow month-by-month

How much is needed each month to meet your expenditure?
Simply carry forward the monthly figure calculated on the monthly
Expenditure page and add the Annual and Quarterly figures.

FLORENCE CASH

MONTH-BY-MONTH	1 JAN	2 FEB	3 MAR	4 APL	5 MAY	6 JUN	7 JUL
Balance from last month (±)	(250)	(195)	(140)	(85)	(130)	(146)	(91)
ADD Income	725	725	725	725	725	725	725
Total Available 'A'	475	530	585	540	595	579	634
Monthly Expenditure	670	670	670	670	670	670	670
ADD Quarterly Annual } Items due this month			100 (car tax)		71 (TV licence)		
Total Expenditure 'B'	670	670	770	670	741	670	670
A − B = Balance to next month (±)	(195)	(140)	(185)	(132)	(146)	(91)	(36)

MONTH-BY-MONTH	8 AUG	9 SEP	10 OCT	11 NOV	12 DEC	13 JAN	
Balance from last month (±)	(36)	(81)	(26)	29	84	139	
ADD Income	725	725	725	725	725	725	
Total Available 'A'	689	644	699	754	809	864	
Monthly Expenditure	670	670	670	670	670	670	
ADD Quarterly Annual } Items due this month	100 (holiday)						
Total Expenditure 'B'	770	670	670	670	670	670	
A − B = Balance to next month (±)	(81)	(26)	29	84	139	194	

Fig 4.3 Personal Cash Flow Forecast

Completion of the Personal Cash Flow Forecast

O   Start with Month 1 (January), insert 'Balance from last month' at the top of the column. This is the amount in the bank account at the *beginning* of Month 1. A figure in brackets denotes (as in this case) an overdraft.

O   Add the income (her salary) for Month 1 to give 'Total available A'.

O   Combine all the monthly and any quarterly or annual expenses incurred during Month 1 to give 'Total expenditure B'.

O   Deduct B from A to give the balance of the bank account at the *end* of Month 1. Note again that a minus figure is an overdraft, and is shown in brackets.

O   Carry forward this balance to the top of the next column as the balance for the beginning of Month 2 (February).

O   Repeat the process for the subsequent months.

This 'Cash flow' calculation simply measures the flow of cash as it is earned and spent. The bottom line of each month column shows clearly the *amount* of financial assistance that may be required, and *when* it will be required. In Chapter 23 we will see that this form of cash planning is just as important to the business as it is to the individual. In the case of Miss Cash we can see from the bottom line of the Cash Flow that the overdraft stands at £195 at the end of Month 1, and is repaid by the end of Month 10, when the account stands at £29 credit.

It is also important to appreciate that this calculation is an *estimate* only. The bank would not expect Miss Cash to finish Month 10 with *exactly* £29 in her account: they would hope that she will have a positive balance, and would no doubt wish to have words with her if she still had an overdraft. It is nevertheless a very valid exercise and can prove useful both to the individual and to the business in forecasting future flows of money.

Bank Budget Planning Schemes

Banks realise that personal finance involves peaks of spending, when all the bills tend to come at once and the bank customer is in danger of going overdrawn. Many of the banks promote 'budget' accounts, specifically for the payment of budgeted items, allowing the 'budget' account to go overdrawn at such times.

The procedure is for a customer to record on a schedule similar to the Monthly Expenditure sheet in fig. 4.2 all bills and irregular expenditure (e.g. holidays) expected over a year. All these items are totalled and divided by twelve, producing a monthly figure which is paid into the 'budget' account, normally from the current account. The bills are paid exclusively from the budget account, by cheque, standing order or direct debit, and the bank will allow this account to go overdrawn when the need arises.

Chapter Summary

❑ Planning of expenditure is essential for individuals and families.

❑ The planning process includes

- recording personal spending
- reconciling the records with the bank statement
- itemising personal spending on some form of a budgeted expenditure schedule
- planning cash flow if you consider there may be a cash shortage during the year

❑ As the Case Problem demonstrates, failure to plan can result in an individual running into severe problems even when all *necessary* expenditure can be met out of income.

As we will see in later chapters, accounting control and budget planning are also important to the efficient functioning of business, Public Sector and social organizations.

Student Activities

1. Examine the list of household and personal expenditure items illustrated in Fig. 4.1 on page 29. Compile a *monthly* expenditure estimate for an imaginary family of four, based on your own and your family's experience. Construct either two pie charts or a comparative table showing how the spending pattern corresponds with the national average set out in Fig. 4.1. Give reasons for any significant differences.

2. You are paid a salary of £500 on the 27th of each month. Your regular monthly outgoings by standing order and direct debit from your bank account (with dates) are:

    1st, mortgage of £200.00, Community Charge £30.00; 2nd, season ticket £20.50, telephone £20.75;   23rd, TV and video rental £20.50; 25th, H.P. payment £32.23; 28th, life insurance £12.12.

    On 22nd May you receive your monthly bank statement which shows a credit balance at 15th May of £155.71. You go through your records and find that the following items are not on the statement: 20th May, cash card withdrawal £30; 20th May, cheque issued to Sainsbury's for £35.93; 21st May, cheque issued to W.H. Smith for £41.50. You estimate that you will also need £50 to cover expenses before the receipt of your salary. How much money (if any) do you have available, and what are you going to do about your personal budgeting

    - in the short term
    - in the long term

3.   You have noticed that during the last year your bank charges have been high because you have from time-to-time gone overdrawn without realising it. You decide to draw up a Monthly Cash Flow for the 12 months from January 19-8, so that you can see what is happening to your finances.

- Your bank balance at the beginning of the year is £120 overdrawn
- Your net monthly income is £525

your outgoings are as follows:

- *monthly*   mortgage £170, Community Charge £31, car £35, housekeeping £160

- *quarterly*   telephone £52, electricity £67 (both paid in March, June, September, December)

- *annual*   car tax and insurance £280 (February), holiday £500 (August), Christmas shopping £200 (December)

When you have drawn up the Cash Flow,

- state whether you think you are living within your means

- suggest adjustments you might make to your spending pattern

- suggest ways you could get the bank to help you.

4.   Leslie Ball, a friend of yours, has recently moved away from home to a flat in St. Albans (3a Sumpter Place, St. Albans, Herts). He is finding it difficult to cope financially and mentions on the telephone that, although he has a regular wage of £85 per week, paid in cash, most of it seems to have gone by Monday evening, and he is unable to pay a number of pressing bills. In short, he is in a financial mess. Write a letter to him suggesting ways he can put his affairs in order.

Assignment One

Personal Financial Planning: Setting up Home

GENERAL OBJECTIVES COVERED
A, B.

SKILLS DEVELOPED
Working with others, communicating, numeracy, information gathering, information processing, identifying and tackling problems.

SITUATION
Robert Griffin and Catherine Jones are getting married and are setting up home in a town in East Anglia. They are fortunate in that their parents are jointly bearing the substantial cost of their wedding, and are providing £2 000 in total for the new home. The couple are otherwise responsible for planning how they use their savings and joint income, and deciding where they are to live, and what sort of lifestyle they are to adopt. Their circumstances are as follows:

Robert Griffin is a trainee Chartered Accountant, aged 22, who has been working for two years for a local firm, is studying for his professional exams, and is earning £10 000 p.a. gross (£630 net monthly - which will increase to £660 net monthly when he gets married). He is ambitious, and hopes after he qualifies in two years' time to move to London where he will be able to obtain a substantially higher salary. His audit work requires him to be mobile, so he runs a Citroen 2CV6, which is cheap to maintain; his employers pay a generous mileage allowance which amply covers his petrol costs. He has few other financial commitments as he lives at home with his parents, paying them a rental for his 'keep'. He is a keen rugby player, and regularly spends time and money 'out with the lads'. Largely because of his spending habits, Robert has negligible savings. His philosophy is to work hard and to spend hard, a view not entirely shared by his fiancée.

Catherine Jones is a newly qualified Home Economics teacher, aged 21, earning £9 000 p.a. gross (£575 net monthly). She has lived away from her parents since being at Teacher Training College, and currently rents a furnished flat in the town. Her landlord is responsible for the running costs, but Catherine has to pay for the gas, electricity telephone, and her Community Charge. She does not have a car, as she is a keep fit 'fanatic', and cycles to work. She has accumulated savings of £3 500 in a high interest share account at a Building Society.

THE OPTIONS
Robert and Catherine are going to have to decide whether to live in Catherine's flat or see whether they can afford to buy a house in the area, but they have to bear in mind the fact that Robert may want to move to London in two years' time.

To help them in their initial discussions, Robert has compiled some figures from Catherine's bills and his parents' household expenses file. His parents live in a three-bedroomed semi-detached house with a mortgage of £35 000 outstanding. These figures will enable the couple to compare the cost of living in a flat or a fairly typical house. Robert has adjusted them to reflect the expenses incurred by a married couple.

	Flat £	House £	Frequency
Mortgage	-	350	monthly
Rent	200	-	monthly
Community Charge	700	700	annually
Telephone	65	75	quarterly
Gas Heating	30	50	quarterly
Electricity	80	125	quarterly
TV	120	120	annually
Repairs	-	150	annually
Housekeeping	180	200	monthly

In addition they note that they will incur the following costs:

- Robert's car (insurance, tax, servicing) £300 p.a.
- repayment of any money they borrow in addition to the mortgage

One item relating to their monthly spending is unfortunately in dispute: Robert insists that he will need at least £40 a month for 'going out with the lads', whereas Catherine says that they ought to save at least £30 a month for future expenses; she is also emphatic on the point that Robert's place, once he is married, should be in the home.

They also discuss the following 'one-off' items which they may need:
- a honeymoon costing from £250 to £800 in total for the two of them
- furniture for the new house (if they buy one) £3 000 to £5 000
- a new fitted kitchen for £3 000, if they buy a house (Catherine has a rich uncle who has promised £2 000 if the couple contributes £1 000)

STUDENT TASKS

Form into groups of approximately four on the directions of your lecturer. Then subdivide each group into two, each 'subgroup' of two taking the part of either Robert or Catherine. Each group of four is then effectively an engaged couple. (It may be useful for two females to take the part of Catherine, and two male students the part of Robert!) The tasks are as follows:

1.   Each group will compile a 'household' file which should chart the progress of the negotiations required by the tasks in this Assignment. The file will include:

- a record of decisions taken
- a record of calculations made, including budget planners, leaflets and other information from lending institutions

2.   Each group will calculate from Robert's figures, using two monthly expenditure schedules

(a) the average monthly cost of running a flat,
(b) the average monthly cost of running a house

assuming a mortgage of £35 000 for the house and including the cost of running a car. This is a *basic* running cost which will exclude the cost of any other borrowing, saving or spending. It will enable the couple to decide whether the house is financially feasible when they get married. It will also give them an idea of monthly income which they will have spare for other purposes.

3. Discuss and decide in your group whether to retain the flat or to buy a house. Remember that the reasons will be personal as well as financial. Justify your decision and record your reasons in your household file. If you decide to buy a house you will need to find out from lending institutions how much they are willing to lend you on the basis of your salaries (see Chapter Two).

4. Bearing in mind the decision made in Task 3 you must now examine your present position and decide what to do with

    *   your savings
    *   money contributed from members of the family

    You will need to consider the cost of a honeymoon, and if you are buying a house, the amount to be spent on

    *   the house itself
    *   furniture and fittings
    *   the kitchen

    Remember that you may want to borrow for items other than the house. It will be useful to collect explanatory leaflets, application forms and repayment tables from lending institutions to assist you in your calculations.

    Also, if you are saving, research the different ways of investing your money, comparing interest rates and returns on investment, retaining the leaflets for your household file.

5. Having resolved the problem of Robert's spending requirements and Catherine's plans for saving, draw up a final monthly expenditure schedule incorporating all your planned running expenses. You will need to make sure that you are living within your means and can repay any borrowing. If you think it appropriate you may use the monthly expenditure schedule as a basis for a bank 'budget' account, in which case you should include a completed application form in your file.

6. Present your proposals orally to the class as a whole, and be prepared to justify your decisions. Bear in mind that there is no single right answer, there are only logically reached conclusions.

Chapter Five
Personal Taxation

Income is often referred to in terms of 'wages' or 'salary'. Wages are normally paid weekly, frequently in cash, to employees in the areas of production and service. A salary is the payment to employees working in administration and management; it is usually paid monthly, and often direct into a bank or a building society account. If you earn either wages or a salary, you will look at your income in two ways:

(1) You will be aware of the amount you earn before deductions, your *gross* earnings, when you say, for instance, 'I earn £10 000 a year'.

(2) You will know how much you receive each week or month after your employer has made certain deductions, as this is the amount you have available for the budgeting process. This is your *net* income.

Income can also include investment income: interest from savings accounts and dividends from shares. All forms of income may be liable to tax. In this chapter we will look in detail at the deductions of Income Tax and National Insurance. We will then examine the situation of an employee starting work for the first time and encountering unfamiliar forms and procedures.

Deductions from Gross Pay

There are a number of deductions from gross pay, some compulsory and some voluntary.

Compulsory Deductions
Your employer will deduct the following as a matter of course:

- Income Tax - money paid to the Inland Revenue to fund Government spending
- National Insurance Contributions - money paid to the State to fund retirement pensions and sickness benefit

Voluntary Deductions
Your employer will deduct the following at your request:

- Pension/Superannuation scheme payments
- Union subscriptions
- Payments to charity (if your employer operates a charitable giving scheme)

It is the responsibility of your employer to account to the various bodies concerned for the amounts deducted from your gross pay.

Taxation of Income: the Flow of Funds

The following diagram shows

- *on the left* the various sources of income received by the individual
- *on the right* the deductions made from that income

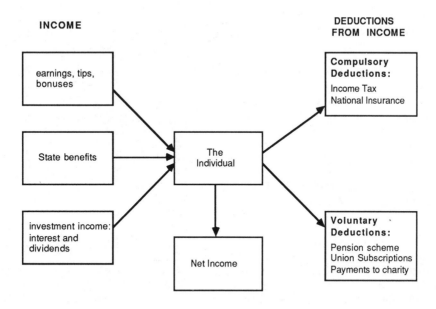

Income Tax

Income tax is a tax on income received by an individual.

'Income' for tax purposes includes pay, tips, bonuses, and benefits in kind (e.g. company car, cheap loans), pensions, most State Benefits, and interest and dividends from investments.

If you are in employment the Income Tax on your pay is deducted by the employer from your gross pay by means of a scheme known as PAYE (Pay As You Earn). This scheme, as its title suggests, enables you to spread out your taxation evenly over the year instead of having to pay it in one amount.

Taxable Income: the Personal Allowance

Income which is liable to tax is known as taxable income.

Taxable income is calculated by deducting the personal allowance from gross income.

You do not, fortunately, have to pay tax on all your income. In order to help the lower paid, the Government gives a **Personal Allowance**, an amount which you can earn during the tax year (6 April - 5 April), on which no tax is paid at all.

The personal allowance, which is announced by the Chancellor of the Exchequer in his annual budget, is normally increased in line with inflation each year, and is fixed for each tax year. The amount of the personal allowance varies, depending on factors such as whether you are single or married, or over a certain age. The allowances fixed for the tax year from 6 April 1989 to 5 April 1990 include the following:

The allowances fixed for the tax year from 6 April 1990 to 5 April 1991 include the following:

- personal allowance £3 005
- married couple's allowance £1 720

A single male or female may therefore earn up to £3 005 without deduction of tax . Married couples are taxed separately as individuals and each will receive a *personal* allowance of £3 005. Additionally a *married couple's allowance* of £1 720 will be given to the husband, or, if he is not earning enough to make use of it, to the wife, if she is.

Additional allowances are also given to the over-65's, widows, single parent families and the blind.

Income Tax Calculations

It is the responsibility of the employer to see to it that the employee pays the right amount of tax through the PAYE system.

There are two rates of income tax applicable to taxable income:

- 25%, charged on taxable income *up to* £20 700
- 40%, charged on taxable income *above* £20 700

If therefore you are fortunate to receive taxable income that exceeds £20 700, you have to pay income tax at 40% *on the excess* and income tax at 25% on the first £20 700 of taxable income.

If we take two employees of the same organization, an unmarried senior accounts clerk earning £10 000 gross p.a., and an unmarried sales director earning £30 000, it is a simple matter to work out how much income tax they pay each year. Remember that taxable income in each case is gross income less the personal allowance of £3 005. The figures are quoted to the whole £ (i.e. pence are ignored).

	Accounts Clerk	Sales Director
	£	£
Gross income	10 000	30 000
less personal allowance	3 005	3 005
Taxable income	6 995	26 995
Income tax @ 25%	1 749	£20 700 @ 25% = 5 175
Income tax @ 40%	nil	£6 295 @ 40% = 2 518
TOTAL INCOME TAX (to nearest £)	1 749	7 693

These tax calculations cannot, however, be taken in isolation, as the employer will also, as we will see, deduct National Insurance Contributions, and the Inland Revenue may make further adjustments by means of a *tax code*.

Tax Codes and Allowances

Additional Allowances

The Inland Revenue, as well as granting the personal allowance, gives additional allowances against tax. For the person in employment they could include expenses incurred in employment, professional subscriptions, and clothing and specialist equipment used when working.

The allowance system works so that earnings spent on these items up to the amount of the appropriate allowance will not be subject to income tax.

Calculation of the Tax Code

How does the employer know what allowances have been given to the employee and how much tax to deduct? How do the tax authorities make allowances, in practical terms, for clothing, equipment and subscriptions? The Inland Revenue gives each employee a *tax code,* a number which is used by the employer to calculate the taxable pay. The tax code incorporates *all* the tax allowances, including the personal allowance.

Typical allowances for an unmarried factory worker would be:

Personal allowance	£3 005
Allowance for work clothing	£50
Total allowances	£3 055

During the tax year the employee's tax code will be 305, the amount of the total allowances less the last digit. The code will be followed by a letter, the two most common of which are:

L = a code incorporating a single person's or wife's earned income allowance
H = a code incorporating a married man's allowance

In the case of this factory worker the full code will be 305L.

When the Inland Revenue has allocated the tax code to the employee, the tax is, in principle, easy to calculate. Take, for example, the factory worker referred to above who earns £8 000 a year.

Gross annual pay	£8 000
Less allowances (code 305L - see above)	£3 050
Taxable annual pay	£4 950
Tax payable for the year = £4 950 @ 25% =	£1 237.50

The employer's task of collecting the tax on a weekly or a monthly basis is less simple. What happens for instance if an unmarried employee starts work, for the first time, halfway through the tax year? No tax will be payable, unless the employee earns over £3 005 i.e. the personal allowance, in that year. How is the employer to know how much to deduct, and when? The Inland Revenue makes the calculation of tax on a *weekly or monthly* basis possible for the employer through the PAYE system.

PAYE: Calculation of Net Pay on a Weekly Basis

The Inland Revenue supplies the employer with tax tables and deduction sheets (P11) for working out an individual's net pay on a *weekly* (or monthly where appropriate) and *cumulative* basis. There are two sets of tables (illustrated in fig. 5.1):

- the Free Pay tables
- the Taxable Pay tables

The **Free Pay Tables** have a page for each week, telling the employer for that particular week, depending on the tax code of the employee, how much income since the beginning of the tax year is *not* subject to tax. This figure is the *Free Pay* of the employee.

The **Taxable Pay Tables** tell the employer how much tax at basic rate (currently 25%) is payable on the employee's taxable income since the beginning of the year.

TABLE A–FREE PAY

WEEK 31
Nov 2 to Nov 8

Code	Total free pay to date	Code	Total free pay to date	Code	Total free pay to date	Code	Total free pay to date	Code	Total free pay to date	Code	Total free pay to date	Code	Total free pay to date	Code	Total free pay to date
	£		£		£		£		£		£		£		£
0	NIL														
1	11·47	61	369·21	121	726·95	181	1084·69	241	1442·12	301	1799·86	361	2157·60	421	2515·34
2	17·36	62	375·10	122	732·84	182	1090·58	242	1448·32	302	1805·75	362	2163·49	422	2521·23
3	23·25	63	380·99	123	738·73	183	1096·47	243	1454·21	303	1811·95	363	2169·69	423	2527·12
4	29·45	64	387·19	124	744·62	184	1102·36	244	1460·10	304	1817·84	364	2175·58	424	2533·32
5	35·34	65	393·08	125	750·82	185	1108·25	245	1465·99	305	1823·73	365	2181·47	425	2539·21
6	41·23	66	398·97	126	756·71	186	1114·45	246	1472·19	306	1829·62	366	2187·36	426	2545·10
7	47·12	67	404·86	127	762·60	187	1120·34	247	1478·08	307	1835·82	367	2193·25	427	2550·99
8	53·32	68	410·75	128	768·49	188	1126·23	248	1483·97	308	1841·71	368	2199·45	428	2557·19
9	59·21	69	416·95	129	774·69	189	1132·12	249	1489·86	309	1847·60	369	2205·34	429	2563·08
10	65·10	70	422·84	130	780·58	190	1138·32	250	1495·75	310	1853·49	370	2211·23	430	2568·97

EXTRACT FROM FREE PAY TABLES

TABLE B

TAX DUE ON TAXABLE PAY FROM £7921 TO £8280

Total TAXABLE PAY to date	Total TAX DUE to date	Total TAXABLE PAY to date	Total TAX DUE to date	Total TAXABLE PAY to date	Total TAX DUE to date	Total TAXABLE PAY to date	Total TAX DUE to date	Total TAXABLE PAY to date	Total TAX DUE to date	Total TAXABLE PAY to date	Total TAX DUE to date
£	£	£	£	£	£	£	£	£	£	£	£
7921	1980.25	7981	1995.25	8041	2010.25	8101	2025.25	8161	2040.25	8221	2055.25
7922	1980.50	7982	1995.50	8042	2010.50	8102	2025.50	8162	2040.50	8222	2055.50
7923	1980.75	7983	1995.75	8043	2010.75	8103	2025.75	8163	2040.75	8223	2055.75
7924	1981.00	7984	1996.00	8044	2011.00	8104	2026.00	8164	2041.00	8224	2056.00
7925	1981.25	7985	1996.25	8045	2011.25	8105	2026.25	8165	2041.25	8225	2056.25
7926	1981.50	7986	1996.50	8046	2011.50	8106	2026.50	8166	2041.50	8226	2056.50
7927	1981.75	7987	1996.75	8047	2011.75	8107	2026.75	8167	2041.75	8227	2056.75
7928	1982.00	7988	1997.00	8048	2012.00	8108	2027.00	8168	2042.00	8228	2057.00
7929	1982.25	7989	1997.25	8049	2012.25	8109	2027.25	8169	2042.25	8229	2057.25
7930	1982.50	7990	1997.50	8050	2012.50	8110	2027.50	8170	2042.50	8230	2057.50

EXTRACT FROM TAXABLE PAY TABLES

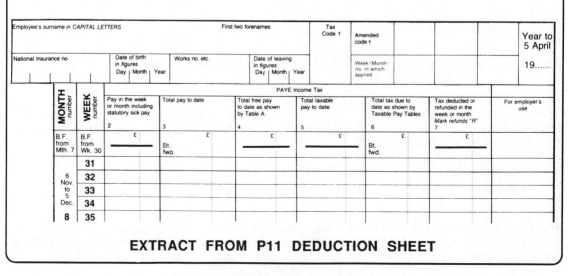

Fig 5.1 Tax Tables and Deduction Sheet
© Crown Copyright

The employer must therefore keep the following cumulative (running) totals for each employee from the beginning of the tax year (or when the employee starts work with him in that tax year) on his deduction sheets. The number in brackets below refers to the relevant column on the Inland Revenue's P11 standard deduction sheet (see fig. 5.1):

(a) The Total Gross Pay to date [3]
(b) The Total Free Pay to date (from the Free Pay Table) [4]
(c) The Total Taxable Pay to date, this is (a) minus (b) [5]
(d) The Total Tax due to date (from Taxable Pay Table) [6]

To work out an employee's tax for the week, all the employer has to do is:

- fill in the totals indicated above, and
- subtract *last week's* Total Tax due (Column 6) from this week's figure; the difference is this week's tax due, which is then recorded in Column 7 of the deduction sheet

The employer in this way collects Income Tax on behalf of the Inland Revenue and by means of the PAYE scheme enables the employee to pay tax as he or she earns. This scheme also allows for flexibility. If an employee moves job, the previous employer will simply provide the new employer with the cumulative totals for pay and tax to date on a form P45, so that tax may be correctly calculated from the first pay date in the new job. In all cases the employer will, after the end of a tax year, give the employee a P60 form which will state the amount of gross pay, the tax paid and National Insurance Contributions.

National Insurance Contributions

The employer will also have to account for the employee's National Insurance contributions by deduction from gross pay. Payment of National Insurance enables the employee in time of need to claim benefits from the State such as retirement pension and sickness benefits. The amount contributed depends on earnings. The employer also makes a contribution. The contributions of both employer and employee are recorded on the P11 deduction sheet (this section not illustrated).

The amounts payable, for example, for an employee earning between £46.00 and £79.99 per week are: employee 2% on earnings up to £46 and 9% on earnings from £46 to £79.99, employer 5% of gross pay. *No* National Insurance is payable by the employee if earnings are less than £46.00 a week and *no* National Insurance Contributions are payable by the employee on any earnings *above* £350 a week.

The National Insurance 'not contracted-out' rates (which are commonly used) are set out below. Tables for the calculation of the rates are available from the Department of Social Security.

National Insurance Contributions (1990/1991)

Total weekly earnings	Employee	Employer
Under £46	Nil	Nil
£46 to £79.99	2% on earnings up to £46, plus 9% on earnings between £46 and £350	5%
£80 to £124.99		7%
£125 to £174.99		9%
£175 to £350		10.45%
£350 or more	2% on £46 and 9% on £304	10.45%

The Tax Return

Occasionally, an employee's sources of income and the allowances claimed become complex and/or the employee is in the higher tax bracket. In these cases the Inland Revenue will ask for the completion, after the end of a tax year, of a Tax Return. the employee will list all sources of income and all allowances claimed. This will enable the Inland Revenue to assess either underpayment or overpayment of tax, and to adjust the Notice of Coding or to ask for a payment of arrears, or make a refund if tax has been overpaid.

Tax and Interest

❑ Tax due on interest received

Income tax is payable on most bank and building society interest received. You do not have to account for this tax to the Inland Revenue yourself. It is deducted by the institution concerned, which pays you the net amount of interest. Only if you are a higher rate tax payer will there be a further amount of tax to pay to the Inland Revenue. If you are not liable to pay income tax you can arrange with the institution to receive interest gross (without deduction of tax).

❑ Tax relief on interest paid

If you borrow to purchase your home, the interest payable each year on borrowings of up to £30 000 (for each house or flat) qualifies for tax relief. In other words the income you use to pay the interest is not subject to Income Tax.

How does this work in practice?

Adjustment of Coding

The usual method used to be for the amount of interest you paid each year to be included in the allowances in your PAYE tax code. You therefore did not pay tax on this amount of interest.

MIRAS

Many lending institutions have now adopted MIRAS (Mortgage Interest Relief at Source). This scheme enables the lending institution to work out in money terms the benefit to you of the tax relief. The formula is:

$$\text{Amount of interest paid} \times \frac{\text{tax rate}}{100} = \text{Tax Relief}$$

The tax relief on the interest contained in each repayment is then either paid separately to you whenever you make a repayment or, more usually, deducted from the repayment, so that you pay a net amount. Thus tax relief is given *at source*. The lending institution, which is then obviously out of pocket, will reclaim the tax relief from the Inland Revenue.

Note that only the interest on loans for the purchase of your home is eligible for tax relief; interest on other loans, e.g. to buy a car, go on holiday, or to improve your home, is not eligible.

Case Problem: Ted Ragle Starting Work

Situation

Ted Ragle is a newly qualified music teacher who is starting work for the first time. He has been given a contract by the local Education Authority and will receive his pay from the local County Council. His personal situation is as follows:

- his annual gross salary is £9 000
- he receives the personal allowance of £3 005
- National Insurance is paid at the not contracted-out rate
- 6% of his gross salary is paid into a pension scheme
- he himself pays £40 subscription to the Teachers' Union each year (direct from his bank account)

What are the forms and procedures he is likely to encounter during his first few months at work?

Solution

- His employer will give him a form P46 to sign; this is a declaration that he has not worked before or received unemployment benefit. His employer will send this form when signed to the Inland Revenue to tell them that he has started work with them.

- His employer will also give Ted a 'Coding Claim Form' to enable him to claim for additional allowances such as his £40 a year subscription to the teachers' union. Ted will have to send this himself to the local Inland Revenue office which will deal with his tax affairs.

Having worked for two months Ted has received his second pay slip from his employers and also a Notice of Coding from the Inland Revenue. These forms are illustrated and explained in the illustrations on the next two pages.

From this point onwards it is unlikely that Ted will have any further problems or queries. As he is a basic rate taxpayer it would be unusual for him to have to complete a tax return. All he will receive will be:

- monthly payslips from his employer
- an annual P60 from his employer setting out his total pay and deductions for the tax year
- an annual Notice of Coding from the Inland Revenue to advise code changes brought about by the annual personal allowance increase after the budget

He should check these documents, as the Inland Revenue and employers have been known to make mistakes with tax codes and payslips.

Ted Ragle's Payslip

WCC Wyvern County Council		Pay Statement May 1990	
	£		**£**
Pay	750.00	Tax (Code 304L)	112.75
Overtime	0.00	N.I. Non-Contr Out	53.50
		Superannuation	45.00
TOTAL GROSS PAY	750.00		
		TOTAL DEDUCTIONS	211.25
		NET PAY	538.75

CUMULATIVES

Taxable earnings	901.82
Tax to date	225.25
NI to date	107.00
Superannuation	90.00
NET PAY	1077.75

EMPLOYEE DETAILS

Mr E Ragle
Staff No 0178653425
NI No YT 77 77 01 A
Tax Ref 792/W1

Notes

- the Net Pay box shows the amount received by Ted Ragle in May
- the left hand side of the payslip (upper half) shows the gross amount earned in May
- the right hand side of the payslip (upper half) shows the income tax and National Insurance Contributions for May
- the superannuation payment is 6% of Ted's gross salary and is paid before tax is deducted
- the tax code shown (304L) is calculated as follows:

single person's allowance	£3 005
union subscription	£40
total allowances	£3 045

the final digit of 3045 is removed and the letter 'L' added (Ted is single) to give a code of 304L

- the cumulatives section sets out for Ted the running totals of earnings and deductions in the current tax year
- Ted's staff number, National Insurance number and reference number from the local tax office are shown in the Employee Details section
- figures for income tax and National Insurance can be taken from calculation tables, but are most likely produced by a computer payroll package

Ted Ragle's Notice of Coding

☐ [Inland Revenue crest] **Inland Revenue** **PAYE-Notice of coding** *Please keep this notice for future reference and let me know of any change in your address. The enclosed notes explain the entries.*	Issued by H.M. Inspector of Taxes WYVERN BLOCK A GOVERNMENT BUILDINGS STRATFORD ROAD WYVERN WV5 2LE

792

MR E RAGLE FIRS COTTAGE THE GREEN WELLINGTON WYVERN WV2 6RP	*Please use this reference if you write or call. It will help to avoid delay.* 792/W1

YT	77	77	01	A

Date   21.04.90

This notice cancels any previous notice of coding for the year shown below. It shows the allowances which make up your code. Your employer or paying officer will use this code to deduct or refund the right amount of tax under PAYE during the year shown below.
Please check this notice. If you think it is wrong please return it to me and give your reasons. If we cannot agree you have the right of appeal.
Please let me know at once about any change in your personal circumstances which may alter your allowances and coding.

COUNTY COUNCIL OF WYVERN

See Note	Allowances	£	See Note	Less Deductions	£
	SUBSCRIPTION	40			
	PERSONAL	3005			
				Less total deductions	
	Total allowances	3045		Allowances set against pay etc. £	3045

Your code for the year to 5 April 1991   is   **304L**   Please see Part A overleaf

P2 (T)

Notes

- the **allowances** section includes the Union subscription and the personal allowance
- the **deductions** section can be used to *reduce* the tax code to claim unpaid tax
- the **tax code (304L)** calculated will operate for the tax year April 1990 to April 1991

The Role of the Accountant as Adviser

Tax Advice

Many people find personal finance and personal taxation complex and demanding, but they are able to cope with the budgeting, planning and form filling. There may come a time, however, when these tasks become over-burdensome and outside help is required: an accountant is consulted.

This consultation could occur in situations such as when the individual or family unit is well off, has investment income from stocks and shares, receives a legacy or pools win, or simply does not have time to deal with the tax return. An accountant's fees are not low, and the advice may cost hundreds of pounds, but the expertise purchased should save money, as the accountant will work out the most *tax efficient* way of organising the client's financial affairs.

Types of Accountant

There are a number of different types of accountant:

- the public sector accountant, who works for government departments and local authorities
- the certified and cost and management accountants who usually work within industry and commerce
- the independent 'Chartered' accountant who operates on his or her own or in a firm, on the same consultative basis as a GP doctor or a dentist

The individual seeking tax advice is most likely to consult a qualified Chartered Accountant. If the individual also runs a business, the accountant will be able to assist with business planning and give advice on the books of the business.

If you are interested in finance, like working with figures and with people, and are looking for a varied and rewarding career, you may wish to consider a career in one of the branches of accountancy. Further information may be found in careers libraries and also the Careers Appendix in Osborne Books' *Accounting*.

Chapter Summary

❑ Personal taxation is often seen as a problem area associated with complex form filling.

❑ Once the basic principles have been grasped - the assessment for tax, the allowance system and its administration through PAYE - personal taxation should present few problems, either when you have to pay tax, or if you work in an office and have to calculate deductions from wages and salaries.

❑ So far we have looked at *personal* taxation. It should be noted that any individual in *business,* as a sole trader or partner, is equally liable to Income Tax, but directly liable, i.e. tax is generally payable in lump sums rather than through PAYE.

❑ Limited Companies are not subject to Income Tax, but instead pay *Corporation Tax.* on their taxable profits

❑ For the individual, however, Income Tax remains the largest deduction from gross pay; for the State, as we will see in Chapter 24, it forms a major source of Revenue.

Student Activities

1. You are employed by a large insurance company. Your young cousin, Tom Hardy, is about to start work full time for the first time in a building society. He writes to tell you that he will be earning £6 000 a year, or £500 a month. Write a reply telling him what his actual net salary is more likely to be by explaining the deductions that are likely to be made from his monthly pay. His address is Jasmine Cottage, Orchard Close, Weatherbury, Dorset.

2. Using the tax rates and personal allowances quoted in the Chapter, and ignoring National Insurance and other deductions, work out the monthly pay received by the following, after tax:

   - Henry Eliot, unmarried, earning £5 500 a year
   - Charles Kingsley, married, earning £12 000 a year
   - Francis Bacon, married, earning £27 000 a year
   - Rebecca Mills, unmarried, earning £6 000 a year
   - Michael Idas, unmarried, earning £40 000 a year
   - Andrew Brown, married, earning £29 000 a year
   - Christopher Williams, unmarried, earning £19 000 a year

   Note: assume that if the employee is married that he <u>or she</u> has the married couple's allowance.

3. You are a wages clerk working for Premier Designs, a recently established business. Obtain a set of Tax Tables and work out the net weekly pay (ignoring National Insurance) for the first week of the tax year for the following employees (you are to assume that the only allowance granted is the personal allowance):

   - Neil Carter, single, gross weekly pay £75.10
   - Wendy Smith, single, gross weekly pay £57.90
   - Peter Watson, married, gross weekly pay £81.35
   - Emma King, married, gross weekly pay £88.34
   - Paul Downes, married, gross weekly pay £93.21
   - Mike Hardy, unmarried, gross weekly pay £83.92
   - Tina Davies, married, gross weekly pay £72.81
   - John Payne, married, gross weekly pay £88.92

4. You are a wages clerk working for Saxon Burgers, a fast food store. Obtain a set of Tax Tables and work out the net weekly pay (ignoring National Insurance) for Jane Willis (who is single and works irregular hours) for the first eight weeks of the tax year.
   The gross weekly wages are as follows:

   Week 1 £59.00
   Week 2 £52.00
   Week 3 £58.50
   Week 4 £53.25
   Week 5 £60.00
   Week 6 £58.90
   Week 7 £52.35
   Week 8 £61.50

5. A fellow student has started a holiday job earning £70 per week. He only expects to work 12 weeks during the year and has no other income. He says that his employer has deducted tax from his earnings for the first two weeks, and he does not think that this is right. Advise him accordingly.

Assignment Two

Personal Taxation: the Wages Clerk

GENERAL OBJECTIVE COVERED
A

SKILLS DEVELOPED
Information gathering, information processing, numeracy, communicating, design and visual discrimination.

SITUATION
You are a wages clerk in a medium-sized engineering firm, Technocomponents Limited. In preparation for an influx of new employees joining the firm in September, your supervisor has allocated to you the task of preparing an explanatory leaflet containing details of how wages will be paid, and what deductions will be made. The reason for this leaflet is that normally when new employees join the firm, the accounts department is overwhelmed with small queries such as:

"How can my wages be paid to my bank account?"
"How do I pay tax?"
"How much tax do I have to pay, and when?"
"How do I know that I am paying the right amount of tax?"
"Who pays my National Insurance?"
"Do I get a pension, and who pays for it?"
"Do I pay my Union subscription through you?"
"Can I give money to charity through you?"

Your supervisor hopes that a suitable leaflet will save the accounts department a great deal of time.

Technocomponents Limited, which operates on the PAYE system, has a computerised payroll producing bank giro credits which the firm passes through the bank clearing system. Some employees are still paid in cash; in their case the pay details and payslip are processed on the computer, and a wage packet is then made up manually. The company also runs a pension scheme which takes 5% of employees' gross pay, and has an arrangement with the Union to deduct the subscription of £36 p.a.

STUDENT TASKS
1.   Individually, you are to design a leaflet for new employees to explain:
   * how wages can be paid into a bank account, or in cash
   * what 'personal allowances' are
   * how taxable pay and tax is calculated by using the personal allowance - give examples
   * how income tax and National Insurance are deducted by the employer by PAYE
     (a mock-up of a wage slip would be useful here)
   * what a Notice of Coding is, and where it comes from
   * what a P60 is, and where it comes from
   * the situation regarding Pension and Union payments
   * what to do if the payslip or Notice of Coding seem to be incorrect

2.   Divide into groups of three or four and give a talk entitled 'Your Tax and You' to the rest of the class, who will play the role of new employees. Your lecturer will be able to help with visual aids such as charts and overhead projector slides.

Assignment Three

Adam Smith: Starting Work

GENERAL OBJECTIVE COVERED
A

SKILLS DEVELOPED
Numeracy, information gathering, information processing, identifying and tackling problems.

SITUATION
Adam Smith, aged 19, has just left College in Worcester where he has been studying Business Studies full time. He has obtained a management trainee post in Brentfield plc, a fast growing household products retailing company which offers a wide variety of goods, including food, D-I-Y products and garden accessories. Adam will be based in Greenham, a new town in Wiltshire. He has been given a starting salary of £12 000 gross per annum, and will be paid monthly, at the end of the month. He starts work next Monday.

At present he lives at home in Worcester and will initially stay at Greenham during the week, Brentfield paying his travel and accommodation expenses. In three months' time they will cease to pay his keep, and he will have to fend for himself. He is an ambitious individual and has a number of plans:

- to buy, with the help of a mortgage, a new small semi-detatched fully furnished house (Greenham, being a new town, has a number of low cost housing developments, with units starting at £45 000)
- to buy a car, with the help of a personal loan or on H.P, to enable him to travel home at weekends and to take girlfriends out

His present financial situation is as follows:

- he has building society savings of £15 000, largely from a legacy
- he has lived at home, and has only had to pay £5 a week from part-time earnings for his keep

He discusses his plans with his parents, who point out that he will soon be incurring a great deal of expenditure, including:

- *household expenditure:* mortgage, Community Charge, telephone, electricity, TV, housekeeping (food, repairs)
- *car expenditure*: repayments on loan/H.P., tax, insurance, servicing, petrol
- *personal expenditure:* clothing, entertainment, holidays

His parents have generously offered to provide him with all the necessary basic household items (such as linen and pots and pans) to enable him to set up home.

Adam is a sensible individual, and realises that he will have first to calculate his income, and then plan his expenditure.

STUDENT TASKS

You are to assume the role of Adam Smith (or Alice Smith if you prefer) and undertake the following tasks. You are to write an individual assignment answer, but may work in groups to gather and process the information.

1. ### Calculate the net monthly pay Adam will receive by drawing a mock-up of his payslip
   Assume that he has the single person's allowance and pays National Insurance. His pension is non-contributory, i.e. his employer pays. He intends to join the Union, which charges £7.50 a month for its subscription; this will be deducted by his employer.

2. ### Calculate the monthly cost of living in Greenham
   Assume that Adam will live in a semi-detached house, runs a small car and allows for personal expenditure. A budget planner form should be used in this exercise. Note: *pencil in* the total monthly expenditure for the time being (this will have to be amended after Task 3 has been completed)

3. ### Calculate the cost of borrowing for the house and car
   The differences between the totals arrived at in Tasks 1 and 2 will give the amount available each month for repayment of any borrowing. This will enable Adam to decide whether or not he can afford either a house or a car (or both), and if he can, what price brackets he will be looking at. Students should look at personal loan and mortgage application forms and repayment tables; these are normally available from banks and building societies, who will also advise on the proportion of the purchase price of the house or car which can be borrowed (normally 90% of the house price, 70% of the cost of the car). When the monthly repayment figures have been decided upon, they can be entered into the budget planner used in Task 2, and the total monthly expenditure can then be inked in.

4. ### Consider how to manage during the first month
   Adam will be paid at the end of the first month. Bearing in mind that he will incur costs during this period (new clothes £150, spending of £20 per week), but no further "keep" payments to his parents, he will need to raise the finance from somewhere. You are to consider and list the various sources of funds (parents, savings, bank borrowing) and decide on the option which you think most sensible. Write down your justification for this choice.

n two
ess organizations and
ce

Chapter Six
Business Organizations: Sources of Finance

In previous Chapters we have looked exclusively at the decisions which need to be made by the individual in running his or her financial affairs. We have looked at earnings, savings, borrowing and taxation, and examined the problems of individuals in a variety of stiuations. In this Chapter we will turn to the person setting up in business and deal with the two basic questions which have to be answered before business can commence.

"What form should my business take - do I trade on my own, form a partnership, or set up a limited company?

Where will the money come from - do I have sufficient myself, or will I have to borrow?"

We will turn first to the choice of different types of business organization and outline their advantages and disadvantages.

Business Organizations

❑ Sole trader

If you set up in business, you may do so for a number of reasons: redundancy, dissatisfaction with your present job, or developing a hobby or interest into a business operation. The majority of people setting up in this way do so on their own. If you decide to do so, you become a *sole trader*.

A sole trader is an individual trading in his or her name, or under a suitable trading name.

There are a number of *advantages* in being a sole trader:

- **freedom** - you are your own boss
- **simplicity** - there are none of the statutory returns necessary, for instance, for limited companies
- **cheapness** - there are none of the legal costs of drawing up partnership agreements or limited company documentation

There are also *disadvantages*:

- **risk** - you are on your own, with no-one to share the responsibilities of running the business
- **time** - you will need to work long hours to meet tight deadlines
- **expertise** - you may have limited skills in such areas as finance and marketing

You must also bear in mind the following *financial* considerations:

- **capital** - do you have sufficient money to start the business?
- **tax** - as a self-employed person you will be subject to Income Tax and will have to pay National Insurance Contributions
- **providing security** - if you borrow for setting up in business you will invariably incur the liability of having to pledge valuable assets (such as your home) or obtain the guarantee of someone you know

- **liability for debt -** you will be solely liable for all debts of the business; if the business fails you will have to repay all its debts, and may have to sell your personal assets; you may be taken to Court and be made bankrupt if you cannot do so.

It is clear that setting up in business as a sole trader involves total commitment in terms of your capital, your time, your home, and the risk involved. Setting up as a sole trader is often the first step. When the business is successful and needs to expand you will need help in running it. The question then arises: should you form a partnership or a limited company?

❑ Partnerships and Limited Companies

A partnership is a group of individuals working together in business with a view to making a profit.

A limited company is a separate legal body, owned by shareholders, run by directors.

It should be noted that a company can be referred to either as a

- *private limited company* (abbreviated to *Ltd.*) or as a
- *public limited company* (abbreviated to *plc.*)

Most small or medium-sized businesses which decide to incorporate (form companies) become private limited companies. If, however, they are larger, with a share capital of over £50 000, they can become public limited companies. A plc *can* be quoted on the Stock Exchange or Unlisted Securities Market, but not all take this step. Students should refer to Chapters 19 and 20, for details of the accounting statements of partnerships and limited companies.

The following Case Problem highlights the advantages and disadvantages of partnerships and limited companies.

Case Problem: Output Services - Partnership or Limited Company?

Situation

James Curry has been running a computer bureau as a sole trader for two years. His business, 'Output Systems', has involved managing the accounts and payroll for a number of local firms on his computer. He has worked from home and made a handsome profit in the first two years. He realises however that he must diversify to develop the business and he has proposed to a Joe Harvey, a friend of his, that they join forces. Joe Harvey's interest is also in computers and he has been specialising in producing promotional literature for local firms and organising mailshots for them under the name 'Intermail Services'. Joe has agreed that they could pool their resources and offer a useful package of computer services, trading under the name of 'Output Services'. On the advice of their bank manager, they seek professional advice from a solicitor and an accountant as to whether they should form a trading partnership or a limited company.

❑ The Solicitor's Advice

Their solicitor, Mr Sykes, makes these points:

Liability

If they form a *partnership,* they are both individually and collectively responsible for all the debts of the partnership. If they form a *limited company* it is a separate legal entity, responsible for its own debts. They will become directors, i.e. employees of the company, and not strictly speaking liable for its debts, but ...

Security

If a partnership borrows from the bank, the partners will invariably have to pledge their homes as security. If they become directors of a company and the company borrows, the directors may be asked to guarantee the borrowing and support the guarantee with a mortgage over their homes - i.e. the position of personal liability with respect to *security* is little changed whether they are partners or directors.

Documentation

A *partnership* is often (not always) formalised in a written Partnership Agreement which the solicitor can draw up for them. The formation and registration of a *limited company* require much more documentation (including the Memorandum and Articles of Association) and are therefore more expensive in terms of legal fees. Running a limited company also involves more paperwork such as maintaining the minutes of meetings, filing accounts and annual returns.

The solicitor suggests that on the face of it a partnership would be the cheaper and simpler alternative, subject to their being able to get on with each other (the Partnership Agreement could cover cases of disputes) and also subject to the tax position, which is the province of the accountant.

❏ The Accountant's Advice

Their accountant, Mrs. Harris, makes these points:

Taxation

Partners are liable for personal Income Tax on profits divided between them and also liable for National Insurance Contributions. A limited company is subject to Corporation Tax on its profits and the directors are additionally liable on their salaries to Income Tax and National Insurance Contributions (also payable by the company). If the partners pay *higher* rate tax it will be more tax efficient to set up a limited company.

Audit and Accounts

A partnership is not required to have its accounts audited, but a company's accounts must, by law, be audited and sent each year to Companies House where they are available for public inspection, although smaller companies can submit abridged accounts. The accountant's fees for a limited company will generally be higher.

Raising of finance

It is often easier for a limited company to raise funds as there are institutions ready to take shares in a small company as a form of investment. This form of finance is not available to partnerships which rely more heavily on the introduction of money (capital) by the partners.

Solution

James and Joe decide that as they work well together they will choose the simpler and cheaper option of forming a partnership. They bear in mind that, if the business expands further, they may in the future form a limited company, but only if their personal tax bills justify the action, and if they need to raise further finance from bodies which will want a proportion of the shares of the company.

The Business Plan and Sources of Finance

❑ The Business Plan

If you are starting up a business, whether it be as a sole proprietor, a partnership, or a limited company, you will need finance. It is normal, if you are applying to an outside body for finance, to prepare a written plan, normally referred to as a *Business Plan*. This sets out your product, expertise, market, your pricing policy and financial requirements. The Business Plan will be dealt with in detail in Chapter 23 following our explanation in intervening chapters of how differing business organizations prepare and finalise their accounts, projections of which normally appear in the Business Plan. It is sufficient for the purposes of this Chapter to note that the financial requirements of a business are calculated by means of a *Cash Flow Forecast* (see the Case Problem "Software Stores" in Chapter 23), a form similar to the Budget Planner form used by the individual to forecast expected income and expected expenditure on a monthly basis (see the Case Problem "Florence Cash" in Chapter 4). If there is a shortfall between income and expenditure, particularly in the early months of operations when large costs are incurred, then this difference is the amount of external finance required by the business.

How much External Finance is Needed?

You will need external finance if you do not have enough money to start the business from your own resources. This need causes problems: a provider of external finance will need reassuring about your commitment to the business. This commitment is often reflected in the amount of money you are able or willing to put in yourself. The potential lender will therefore ask:

"What percentage of the total needed by the business are you putting in yourself?"

"If you are putting in less than 50%, is it possible for you to raise more from private sources?"

The provider of finance will rarely lend more than half of the start-up cost, unless it will be repaid quickly. If the proprietor puts in less than 50%, a lender may quite rightly ask the question: "whose business is it?"

Over what Period is Finance Required?

There are three time scales for finance:

Short-Term	1 to 3 years:	day-to-day and seasonal requirements
Medium-Term	3 to 10 years:	purchase of large items, e.g. machinery
Long-Term	10 to 25 years:	purchase of land and premises

As you will see, the longer the life of the item purchased, the longer the loan that will be made available. A lender will obviously be unwilling to lend money over 10 to 25 years to finance an ice cream salesman for his summer stocks, but will provide funds over that period to enable a company to purchase a factory unit.

❑ Sources of Finance

We will now consider the various sources of finance. It should be noted that some of the sources listed here only provide finance to limited companies: this will be made clear in the text.

The Banks

The Clearing Banks are the largest providers of finance to *all* types of businesses. Bank facilities include:

Overdraft

An overdraft is short-term borrowing on current account. It is relatively cheap: the banks charge typically 4% to 6% over Base Rate for a new business, 2.5% to 5% over Base Rate for an existing business. Interest is normally charged quarterly, but you only pay interest on what you actually borrow. A 'limit' up to which you can borrow will be granted by the bank, and renewed annually, when an arrangement fee will also be charged (typically £10 per £1 000 of overdraft limit).

Medium-term loan
This is a fixed period loan (3 to 10 years) to cover the purchase of capital items such as machinery or equipment. Interest is normally 2% to 3% over Base Rate and repayments are by instalment. Repayment of principal may be postponed during the first two years of the loan (a 'repayment holiday') when only interest payments are made.

Long-term loan
This is similar to a medium-term loan but is repaid over up to 25 years.

The banks will invariably require security for business lending, either in the form of a mortgage of personal assets or a guarantee. In the case of limited companies, directors' guarantees (supported by mortgages) and/or a mortgage over the company's assets (a fixed and floating charge) are common forms of security. The reason that security is required is that business lending, from the banks' point of view, carries a greater element of risk than most personal lending.

Hire Purchase
Available to all types of business from finance houses, the majority of which are controlled by the banks. A hire purchase agreement enables a business to acquire an asset on the payment of a deposit and pay back the cost plus interest over a set period. At the end of the period ownership of the asset passes to the borrower. Hire purchase can be expensive when compared with a bank overdraft. It is often used to acquire vehicles and machinery.

Leasing
Leasing arrangements are also provided by finance houses. With a leasing agreement, the business has use of assets bought by the finance house. Title to the goods remains with the leasing company and the business pays a regular 'rental' payment. The title of the goods never passes to the business. A common form of lease is a *pay back lease* in which the business will pay back the cost of the item plus finance costs over the period of the lease. Clearly a lease is not a loan, but it can substantially reduce a business' financial requirements when it needs to make a capital purchase. Computer equipment is commonly leased.

Finance for Limited Companies: Equity Participation

Ownership of a limited company is in the form of shares (see Chapter 20), known as equity capital, held by the investors. In the case of a small company such as that contemplated in the Case Problem earlier in this Chapter, the shares may be held solely by the directors. Certain financial institutions may view such companies as ripe for investment and will inject money either in the form of loans or by the purchase of shares, or commonly both. In return, they may expect an element of control over the company and will possibly insist on having a director on the board of the company. Substantial amounts of money can be raised in this way, and limited companies interested in the concept will make application to any of the institutions or types of institution listed below:

Investors in Industry Group plc (3i)
A company 85% owned by the major banks, offering 5 to 20 year loans and requiring an equity stake in the borrowing company.

Merchant banks
Specialist banks serving the needs of companies, offering medium and long-term loans often in return for equity investment.

Venture Capital Companies

Non-banking commercial organizations investment money from private investors, often through the government's Business Expansion Scheme (BES), offering loans and requiring equity and a substantial element of control over the borrowing company.

Financial Assistance from Government Bodies

The government offers considerable assistance directly and indirectly to all types of new and established businesses in a variety of forms.

The Department of Trade and Industry (DTI) "Enterprise Strategy"

The DTI has divided the UK into two types of area, the 'assisted' areas (development, intermediate and urban programme areas [see fig. 6.1]), and the rest of the country (non-assisted areas). The following schemes are available:

Assisted Areas
- Regional Selective Assistance (discretionary grants for companies creating new jobs)
- Investment grants for firms with under 25 employees (Development Areas only)
- Consultancy grants: two thirds of the cost of approved business consultancy

Non-Assisted Areas
- Consultancy grants: half of the cost of approved business consultancy

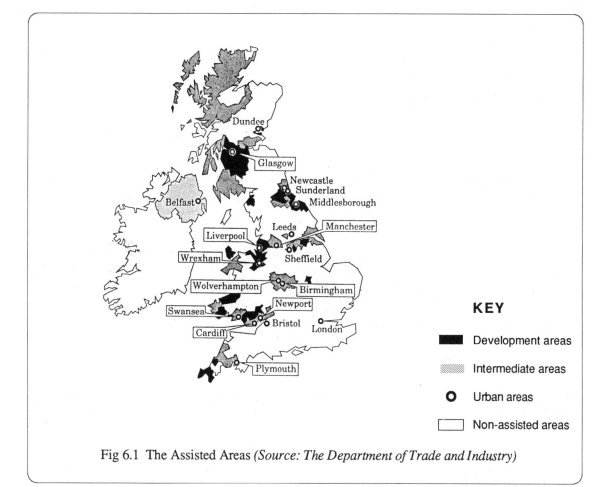

Fig 6.1 The Assisted Areas *(Source: The Department of Trade and Industry)*

The Department of Employment: Loan Guarantee Scheme

The government offers a guarantee for 70% (85% for Inner City Areas) of a bank medium-term loan (2 to 7 years) up to £100 000. This security enables banks and other financial institutions to lend money for projects which would be too risky by normal criteria. Borrowing under this scheme is not cheap because a premium of 2.5% p.a. is charged to the borrower on the guaranteed amount of the loan, effectively adding 1.75% p.a. to the cost of borrowing. The scheme has been very successful, however, and has enabled many businesses to expand.

The Manpower Services Commission: Enterprise Allowance Scheme

A weekly payment of £40 for a period of a year is available to people who wish to start up a new business. This sum is granted provided that the person

- has been on unemployment or supplementary benefit (or under a redundancy notice) for at least 8 weeks
- has £1 000 available to invest in the business
- will work full-time in the new business
- has not already started the business

The scheme has helped many people who, without the living wage of £40 per week, would not have been able to survive the early months of setting up a business when normally the income is slow in arriving and all resources are spent on stock and other setting-up expenses. The initial £1 000 required is sometimes a stumbling block, but some clearing banks are willing to lend for this purpose.

Local Government Grants and Loans

Assistance to new business is often given at low rates of interest by local authorities.

Other Sources of Government Assistance

Information and free advice may be obtained from the local Enterprise Agencies and Small Firms Services which the government has set up in a number of regional centres.

Chapter Summary

❏ An individual setting up in business can operate either as a sole trader or join forces with others to form a partnership or set up a limited company.

❏ A partnership is simpler and less expensive to establish than a limited company, but the directors of a limited company have limited liability, unlike the partners of a firm who are all fully liable for the total debt of a partnership.

❏ An individual setting up in business will often produce a Business Plan which will, among other things, estimate the financial needs of the business by means of a Cash Flow Forecast.

❏ A business will need to decide how much money is to be contributed by the owner(s), and for what period external finance will be required.

❏ Some sources of finance are commercial and some Government funded. The businessman should investigate as many sources as possible, with the help of the local Enterprise Agencies.

In the following Chapters, before returning to the Business Plan, we will examine the forms of accounts of different business organizations, the documents used, and the computerisation of those accounts and documents.

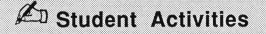 **Student Activities**

1. Brian Richards was made redundant six months ago, and has, since then, been drawing Unemployment Benefit. He has £2 000 redundancy money left, and wishes to start up in business restoring antique furniture, a hobby he has practised for some time. He knows there is a market for his work, as he can sell to the local antique shops, making a good profit. Write down your advice to him about:

    (a) Government and local authority schemes which can help him
    (b) Commercial organizations which can advise and assist him

2. You work in the Worcester branch of the National Bank (124 High Street, Worcester) and receive a letter from Mrs. Stella Nelson who runs a bakery, 'Upper Crust'. She has not needed financial assistance in the past, but now asks about the different types of bank finance that are available. She has heard that overdrafts are a cheap way of borrowing, but needs money to buy new ovens and freezers. Write a suitable reply for signature by your manager, Mr. L. Stirling. The letter should explain the different forms of finance available and be addressed to Mrs. Stella Nelson, 'Upper Crust', Cathedral Walk, Worcester, WR1 25EZ.

3. Your father in Anthony Page, Finance Director of Page Construction Ltd., a prosperous building company. The company needs to raise further capital to finance expansion of its activities, and your father is interested in the concept of issuing shares to investing 'venture capital' companies active in 'equity participation'. He asks you to help him. Write a memorandum to the Board of Directors explaining this concept and listing the various sources of 'venture capital'. You should highlight the advantages and disadvantages of such schemes.

4. John Simpson and Helen Jones are interested in setting up in business jointly to operate river cruises under the business name of 'Sabrina Cruises'. They have £30 000 between them to invest and need a further £25 000 to buy and equip their first boat. They are not sure

    (a) whether to form a partnership or a limited company
    (b) where the extra £25 000 will come from

    As the local Enterprise officer, set out your advice to them in writing.

Assignment Four

Setting up in Business:
Tudor Catering

GENERAL OBJECTIVES COVERED
B, C.

SKILLS DEVELOPED
Learning and studying, working with others, communicating, information gathering, information processing, identifying and tackling problems.

SITUATION
Jenny Day and Kate Melbury both work full-time in an insurance office in Melchester. They both have an interest in catering, and in their spare time they have been cooking and selling their products to pubs, hotels and restaurants in the area. Their operations have been independent, and as such they have been 'sole traders'. They have operated from home, baking at the weekends and in the evenings, stocking their freezers, and supplying their customers on demand. They are both interested in traditional English fare: Jenny makes pies with fillings such as turkey, game, steak, and rabbit; Kate specialises in desserts such as fruit pies, syllabub, sorbets, and meringues.

Recently both Jenny and Kate have experienced a considerable increase in demand for their products and have found it difficult to keep up with the orders. They reckon that the point has been reached where they can safely give up their jobs - they earn approximately £14 000 p.a. between them - and set up in business together as 'Tudor Catering', a name chosen to reflect the traditional nature of their food. They have the added security that their husbands are in full-time employment, and can support them while they start their new venture. They know that they can trade as a partnership or as a limited company, but they have a number of questions that need answering before they can make up their mind:

1.   What is the difference between a partnership and a limited company? How do you form a partnership and and a limited company?

2.   Where are they going to get the necessary finance for their business? They will need four additional freezers at £250 each, and more importantly, a delivery van, which they can obtain second-hand for £3 500.

3.   They have between them savings of £2 000 at Building Societies. Should they use these funds?

4.   What will they do about their banking arrangements? Will they need a separate account?

They clearly need professional advice. They consult their bank manager and, on his recommendation, a solicitor, an accountant and also, for general advice, the local Enterprise Agency.

STUDENT TASKS

1.   Divide into groups of approximately three students. You will take the role of advisers to the business. Between you (ideally individually) draft a series of letters, having first undertaken the necessary research. The letters should be addressed to Mrs. Jenny Day, Willow Cottage, Greenwood Regis, Wiltshire. The letters required are as follows:

A letter from the solicitor, Mr. D. Sykes, explaining the difference between a partnership and a limited company, and outlining the formalities that are required when forming each type of business entity.

A letter from the accountant, Mrs. S. Harris, setting out in *basic* terms the difference between taxation of a partnership and taxation of a limited company. You are to assume that Jenny and Kate are basic rate taxpayers, and are likely to remain so after the formation of the business.

A letter from the bank manager, Mr. D. Guest, setting out the different types of finance available, the likely security requirements, and the formalities that will have to be complied with when a business account is opened.

2.   In your groups from Task 1 you now take the role of an advisory panel from the local Enterprise Agency. You read and discuss the letters with the two businesswomen, who could be 'played' by your lecturer(s), and plan out how the business will operate. You then write a report addressed to 'The Management, Tudor Catering'. The report will include a recommendation for the formation of a partnership or a limited company. It should cover:

• a description of the operation of the new business as you see it
• a comparison of a partnership and a limited company in terms of costs and the liability of the owners
• the sources of finance and the extent to which personal savings should be used

3.   Present your report orally to the class and be prepared to answer any questions.

Chapter Seven
Commercial Documents

Whenever you or I buy goods from a shop there is usually very little documentation involved: if we pay in cash or by cheque most shops record the transaction by entering the amount on a till or cash register which often prints a receipt. Payment by credit card will cause the shop, in addition, to complete a credit card slip or voucher. It is only if we buy a major item, such as a car, furniture, or a house, that more formal documentation is produced.

Business and public sector organizations, however, need more involved documentation to cover the purchase of their requirements. The reason for this is that most organizations buy goods on credit: that is, payment is not made immediately; settlement is often made at the month-end, or some later date. This type of trading is not confined solely to such organizations: for example, many individuals have a newspaper delivered each day and agree to settle at the end of the week or month. Equally, not all purchases made by business and public sector organizations are on credit: low value items are usually paid for straightaway out of *petty cash* (see Chapter 9), but these are exceptions to the normal credit trading arrangements.

Debtors and Creditors

Before we start to consider the various documents involved in a commercial transaction, we need to define two terms that are used frequently in Finance: these terms are *debtors* and *creditors*.

Debtors are people who owe money to you or to your organization.

Creditors are individuals or organizations to whom you or your organization owe money.

For example, if I sell goods to you on credit, until you make payment, you are my debtor. From your point of view, I am your creditor because you owe the money amount of the goods to me. Debtors are *assets,* while creditors are *liabilities*.

*Assets are items **owned** by a person or organization, including amounts due to be received, e.g. from debtors.*

*Liabilities are amounts **owed** by a person or organization, e.g. creditors.*

Most organizations have, at any one time, both debtors and creditors, i.e. they are owed money (assets) while, at the same time, they owe money (liabilities).

The Flow of Documents

When purchases are made on credit, a number of documents form the 'paperwork' of a transaction. The principal documents are:

Purchase order (see fig. 7.1)

This is prepared by the organization that wishes to buy certain goods and is sent to the firm that is to supply the goods. The details to be found on a purchase order are:

- name of organization issuing the purchase order, i.e. the buyer
- name of organization that is to supply the goods, i.e. the seller
- description of the goods, unit price, and quantity required
- date of issue, and signature of person authorized to issue the order

Most purchase orders are numbered; also, only certain people within an organization are authorized to sign purchase orders. By these means, control can be maintained; without such control different people would be placing orders and, inevitably, duplication of orders, waste, and even fraud would take place. However, not all organizations use a purchase order system, but most of the larger ones operate such a system.

Delivery note

When the goods ordered are despatched to the buyer they will be accompanied by a delivery note prepared by the seller. A delivery note simply lists the goods being delivered, and acts as an advice to the buyer so that they can check they have received the goods listed. Often a copy of the delivery note is signed by the buyer and sent back, by means of the carrier, to the seller as a proof of delivery. A delivery note acts solely as a document which controls the physical movement of the goods - it forms no part of the accounting system.

Invoice (see fig. 7.2)

This is the most important document in any transaction. It is prepared by the seller and is sent to the buyer. It states the goods supplied and the money amount to be paid by the buyer. The following information is included on an invoice:

- name and address of seller
- name and, most probably, the address of buyer
- date of sale
- details of goods supplied
- details of any trade discount* allowed, and total money amount due
- terms of trade, e.g. date of payment, any cash discount* offered for quick settlement

* Note: Do not confuse trade discount, and cash discount. *Trade discount* is an amount sometimes allowed as a reduction in price when goods are bought by people in business, e.g. a plumber's merchant will often allow trade discount to a plumber, but not to the general public. *Cash discount* is an allowance off the invoice amount for quick settlement, e.g. 2.5 per cent cash discount for settlement within one week: the buyer can choose whether to take up the cash discount by paying promptly, or whether to take longer to pay, perhaps one month from the invoice date, without the cash discount.

Invoices are numbered and a copy will be kept by the seller. You can see invoice books for sale in most stationers' shops and, when invoicing is handled by computer (see also Chapter 12), blank invoice forms can be purchased in continuous stationery form.

When organizations are registered for Value Added Tax (VAT) - see also Chapter 11 - they must charge VAT at the appropriate rate (currently 15 per cent) on all taxable supplies. In addition the invoice must state the seller's VAT Registration Number, and the date for tax purposes (the *tax-point*) on which the sale passes through the accounts. You should note that, when VAT is charged, it is on the amount *after deduction of cash discount* (if any), whether or not the buyer takes advantage of the cash discount.

PURCHASE ORDER

STATIONERY STORES
FRIAR STREET
WORCESTER WR1 2EJ

Tel: Worcester (0905) 830282

To:

ABC Sales
Birmingham Road
Worcester   WR5 2BT

Date of order: 9 November   19-6   **Order No.**   7890
Date required: 31 November   19-6

Quantity	Description	Product No.	Price
20 10 reams	Pocket calculators A4 paper	A4215 P276	£3.00 each £4.00 per ream

Please quote Order No. on delivery note, invoice and other correspondence

For Stationery Stores

Jean Adams

MRS. J. ADAMS
BUYER

Fig. 7.1 An example of a purchase order

INVOICE

ABC SALES

To: Stationery Stores
Friar Street
Worcester, WR1 2EJ

Birmingham Road
Worcester WR5 2BT

Tel: (0905) 853344

VAT Reg. No. 941 1863 40

Sales Invoice No. 1234
Date/Tax Point 14 November 19-6

Your Order No. 7890

Quantity	Descriptions	Unit Price	Amount
20	POCKET CALCULATORS	£3.00	£60.00
10 reams	A4 PAPER	£4.00	£40.00
		SUB-TOTAL	£100.00
		VALUE ADDED TAX AT 15%	£15.00
		INVOICE TOTAL	£115.00

Terms: Net 30 days from Invoice Date

Fig. 7.2 An example of an invoice

CREDIT NOTE

ABC SALES

Birmingham Road
Worcester WR5 2BT

To: Stationery Stores
Friar Street
Worcester, WR1 2EJ

Tel: (0905) 853344

VAT Reg. No. 941 1863 40

Credit Note No. CN 456
Date/Tax Point 26 November 19-6

Quantity	Descriptions	Unit Price	Amount
2	POCKET CALCULATORS	£3.00	£6.00
		SUB-TOTAL	£6.00
		VALUE ADDED TAX AT 15%	£0.90
		TOTAL	£6.90

Reason for credit: Faulty

Fig. 7.3 An example of a credit note

For example:

	No cash discount offered	Cash discount of 2.5% offered
Selling price (excluding VAT)	£100.00	£100.00
Less cash discount of 2.5%	-	£2.50
	£100.00	£97.50
VAT at 15%	£15.00	*£14.62
Total amount payable	£115.00	£112.12

If cash discount is not taken the buyer will pay £100 plus VAT of £14.62 = £114.62.

* The total VAT on a tax invoice is *rounded down* to a whole penny, i.e. any fraction of a penny is ignored.

Credit note   (see fig. 7.3)

If a buyer has occasion to return goods, e.g. goods damaged, wrong goods supplied, the seller will prepare a credit note to record the amount credited to the buyer's account. A credit note is also used for correcting errors on invoices previously issued which have overcharged the customer.

Statement of account   (see fig. 7.4)

Few buyers make payment against an invoice; instead they wait for the supplier to send a statement of account. This is simply a statement of the transactions between buyer and seller showing how much is currently owed by the buyer. The details to be found on a statement are:

- name and address of supplier
- name and address of buyer
- details of transactions, i.e. invoices sent and payments received, since the last statement date
- balance owed by buyer

Most statements are prepared with three money columns: debit, credit, and balance. 'Debit' is used for invoices sent to the buyer, 'credit' for receipts, and credit notes. The balance column, usually with a debit balance, shows the amount now due. (A debit balance indicates the buyer is a *debtor* of the seller.) Statements can be handwritten, typed, or prepared by computer.

STATEMENT

ABC **SALES**

Birmingham Road
Worcester WR5 2BT
Tel: (0905) 853344

To: Stationery Stores
      Friar Street
      Worcester, WR1 2EJ

VAT Reg. No. 941 1863 40

Date	No.	Details	Debit	Credit	Balance
19-6					
14 Nov.	1234	Goods	£115.00		£115.00DR
26 Nov.	CN 456	Credit Note		£6.90	£108.10DR

Amount   now   due   ^

Fig. 7.4 An example of a statement of account

Cheque

Payment by the buyer is usually made to the seller by cheque. The recording of such payments is discussed further in Chapter 9.

Case Problem: Selling on Credit

Situation

Matthew has recently started up in business with a fruit and vegetable stall in the local market. Up until now all transactions for the purchases he has made have been settled either in cash or by cheque; similarly all his sales have been paid for by his customers in cash or by cheque (collectively known as 'cash sales'). He has today been approached by Goodfood, a firm of caterers who operate a number of works' canteens in the locality, to quote for all their fruit and vegetable supplies. The value of this potential contract is sales of about £250 each week; Goodfood require an invoice at the end of each week listing Matthew's sales to them for the week, and they agree to make payment not later than 30 days after the date of the invoice. As this is the first time that Matthew has sold goods on credit, and realizing the potential dangers of non-payment, he seeks your advice.

Solution

The steps that need to be taken by Matthew are:

• When approached by a previously unknown organization wishing to buy goods on credit, the seller should ask for two references. One of these should be the buyer's bank, and the other a trader with whom the buyer has previously done business.

• The seller, Matthew, must, before supplying goods on credit, take up both references, and obtain satisfactory replies. (Note that it is not possible to approach a bank direct for a reference on one of their customers. It can only be done bank-to-bank, and so the seller must ask his or her own bank to approach the buyer's bank.)

• Once satisfactory replies have been received, a credit limit for the customer should be established. (This is similar to the way in which credit limits are established by credit card companies.) The actual amount of the credit limit will depend very much on the expected amount of future business - perhaps £1 000 in this example. The credit limit should not normally be exceeded.

• Matthew should ensure that invoices and monthly statements are sent out promptly.

• If a customer does not pay within a reasonable time, procedures should be followed to chase up the debt promptly. These procedures may involve taking legal action to recover the debt.

Summary of the Flow of Documents

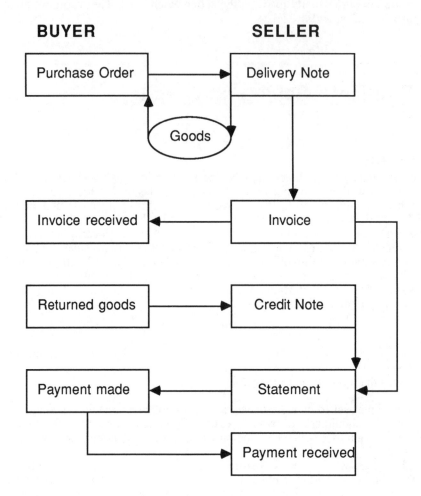

BUYER   **SELLER**

Purchase Order → Delivery Note

Goods

Invoice received ← Invoice

Returned goods → Credit Note

Payment made ← Statement

Payment received

Chapter Summary

❏ For business and public sector organizations, correct documentation is important in order that purchases and sales can be recorded correctly.

❏ The invoice is the most important document because it states the value of the sales and, hence, the amount payable by the buyer.

❏ In order to avoid potential bad debts, it is necessary to follow strict procedures before selling goods on credit to unknown organizations.

This Chapter has looked at the basic documentation; the next Chapter shows how the accounting information for purchases and sales is collected in the books of prime entry.

✍ Student Activities

1. Obtain a copy of an invoice used by either a business or a local authority. Taking this as a guide, you are to design an invoice for a new business. The details of name, address, etc., can be either your own, or those of a fictitious organization.

2. You are in business and, two-and-a-half months ago, sold goods for £125 to J. Smith of 281 High Road, York. An invoice was sent at the same time as the goods. Despite sending a statement of account at the end of month one, and again at the end of month two, no payment has been received. Draft an appropriate letter to this overdue debtor. *(Note: the £125 was the only item on the statement.)*

3. You have the following financial details about J. Wilson, a customer of your organization:

1 Mar.	Balance due, £145
3 Mar.	Goods sold to J. Wilson, £210, invoice number 8119
10 Mar.	Cheque received from J. Wilson, £145
23 Mar.	Goods returned by J. Wilson, £50, credit note number CN 345 issued.
28 Mar.	Goods sold to J. Wilson, £180, invoice number 8245

   You are to prepare the statement of account to be sent to the customer on 31 March. This should show clearly the balance due at the month-end.

4. When selling goods on credit to new customers it is important to follow certain procedures before goods are supplied. Explain the procedures to be followed, with reasons, to a new clerk who has joined the accounts department of your organization.

5. You work for Jane Smith, a wholesaler of fashionwear, who trades from Unit 21, Eastern Industrial Estate, Wyvern, Wyvernshire, WY1 3XJ. A customer, Excel Fasions of 49 Highland Street, Longtown, Mercia, LT3 2XL, orders the following:

   5 dresses at £30 each
   3 suits at £45.50 each
   4 coats at £51.50 each

   Value Added Tax is to be charged at the current rate on all items, and a 2.5 per cent cash discount is offered for full settlement within 14 days. Prepare invoice number 2451, under today's date, to be sent to the customer.

6. You work for Deansway Trading Company, a wholesaler of office stationery, which trades from The Model Office, Deansway, Worcester, WR1 2EJ. A customer, The Card Shop of 126 The Cornbow, Leamington Spa, Warwickshire, CV33 0EG, orders the following:

   5 boxes of assorted rubbers at £5 per box
   100 shorthand notebooks at £4 for 10
   250 ring binders at 50p each

   Value Added Tax is to be charged at the current rate on all items, and a 2.5 per cent cash discount is offered for full settlement within 14 days. Prepare invoice number 8234, under today's date, to be sent to the customer.

Chapter Eight
Data Collection in Accounting

In the previous Chapter we saw how documents are used by organizations for the purchase and sale of goods. These documents are then used as a means of recording transactions in the accounting system.

The two most common types of accounting transactions are:

- *the purchase of goods* with the intention that they should be resold at a profit, e.g. a shop buying groceries from a wholesaler or from a manufacturer

- *the sale of goods* in which the organization trades, e.g. a shop selling groceries to its customer

With both types, the transaction might be conducted on a *cash* or a *credit* basis, e.g. a shop will sell most of its goods for cash, but some customers might have an account which will be settled at regular intervals.

There are other, less common, accounting transactions and we shall look at how to deal with unsatisfactory/wrong goods later on in this Chapter. For the moment we will focus our attention on the two common accounting transactions of purchases and sales. You should note that, in finance, *'purchases'* and *'sales'* refer to the goods in which the organization trades, and *not* to the purchase or sale of items intended to be used *by* the business.

Purchases Day Book

The purchases day book is a collection point for accounting information on the credit purchases of a business and it takes the following form (with sample entries shown):

PURCHASES DAY BOOK

DATE	SUPPLIER'S NAME	INVOICE NO.	£
19-1			
3 Feb.	J. Smith	541	105.50
12 Feb.	I. Williams	A278	25.45
15 Feb.	G. Hall	3528	152.60
20 Feb.	E. Lewis	88/818	355.00
28 Feb.	Total for month transferred to		
	purchases account		638.55

The purchases day book is prepared from invoices received from suppliers. It is totalled at appropriate intervals - daily, weekly or monthly - and this total will tell the organization the amount of purchases for the period. The total for each day, week or month's purchases is recorded separately in a *purchases account* and, at the end of the organization's financial year, the annual total of purchases is used in the financial statements to calculate profit (see Chapter 13). At the same time it is necessary to keep a record of how much is owed by the organization to each individual supplier: this is done by maintaining a separate account in the name of each supplier (in the same way that banks keep records of individual customers' accounts). The amount of each purchase from a particular supplier is recorded as increasing the amount already owing, while payments to the supplier will reduce the amount owing. The individual suppliers' accounts are known collectively as the *purchases ledger,* while the total amount owing is referred to as the organization's *creditors*.

Sales Day Book

The sales day book works in the same way as the purchases day book but, as its name suggests, it lists the sales made by an organization. In its simplest form the total sales recorded by a shop till for the day, week or month acts as a sales day 'book'. For an organization that sells on credit terms, with the issue of an invoice to cover each transaction, the sales day book, which is prepared from the individual invoices, takes the following form (with sample entries shown):

SALES DAY BOOK

DATE	CUSTOMER'S NAME	INVOICE NO	£
19-1			
8 Mar.	I. Mills	281	225.00
14 Mar.	H. Sanderson	282	155.50
16 Mar.	M. Lloyd	283	250.00
20 Mar.	J. Adams	284	289.00
29 Mar.	P. Green	285	185.50
31 Mar.	Total for month transferred to sales account		1 105.00

The sales day book, therefore, provides a total of sales for the period which is recorded in *sales account*. The total of sales for the year is then used at the end of the organization's financial year to help in the calculation of profit (see Chapter 13). Also, an organization needs to keep accurate records of how much is owed to it by each customer. A separate account is kept for each customer with invoices issued increasing the amount owed by a particular customer, while payments received will reduce the balance. Collectively the customers' individual accounts are known as the *sales ledger,* and the total amount owing at any one time is the figure of the organization's *debtors*.

Case Problem: Mr. I. Lewis

Situation

Mr. I. Lewis runs a small engineering business and all his purchases and sales are on credit terms. He employs a clerk on a part-time basis to keep his accounting data up-to-date. Unfortunately the clerk was taken ill last week and Mr. Lewis, knowing nothing about finance, asks if you can help. On investigation you find an 'in-tray' with a number of invoices received from suppliers of goods, together with copies of invoices sent out to customers by Mr. Lewis' typist. The list is as follows:

19-1
8 Dec. Invoice no. 1234 received from MPF Metals for £108.75
8 Dec. Invoice no. A 340 sent to Johnson Bros. for £220.00
9 Dec. Invoice no. XYZ 678 received from A. Osborne for £85.50
9 Dec. Invoice no. A 341 sent to McGee's Metals for £180.25
10 Dec. Invoice no. A 342 sent to Wilson Trading Co. for £112.40
10 Dec. Invoice no. P 41 received from Murray Ltd. for £115.00
11 Dec. Invoice no. 1256 received from MPF Metals for £111.50
12 Dec. Invoice no. A 343 sent to Johnson Bros. for £121.00

You are asked to enter these transactions in the appropriate day books (VAT is to be ignored). If Mr. Lewis owed MPF Metals £325.55 before entering these transactions, what is the amount owed now? If Johnson Bros. owed Mr. Lewis £65.25 before these transactions, how much do they owe now? Where would this information be recorded?

Solution

PURCHASES DAY BOOK

DATE	SUPPLIER'S NAME	INVOICE NO	£
19-1			
8 Dec.	MPF Metals	1234	108.75
9 Dec.	A. Osborne	XYZ678	85.50
10 Dec.	Murray Ltd.	P41	115.00
11 Dec.	MPF Metals	1256	111.50
12 Dec.	Total for week transferred to purchases account		
			420.75

SALES DAY BOOK

DATE	CUSTOMER'S NAME	INVOICE NO	£
19-1			
8 Dec.	Johnson Bros	A340	220.00
9 Dec.	McGee's Metals	A341	180.25
10 Dec.	Wilson Trading Co	A342	112.40
12 Dec.	Johnson Bros	A343	121.00
12 Dec.	Total for week transferred to sales account		
			633.65

PURCHASES LEDGER
MPF Metals

19-1		£	£	Balance £
	Opening balance			325.55 CR
8 Dec.	Invoice no. 1234		108.75	434.30 CR
11 Dec.	Invoice no. 1256		111.50	545.80 CR

SALES LEDGER
Johnson Bros.

19-1		£	£	Balance £
	Opening balance			65.25 DR
8 Dec.	Invoice no. A340	220.00		285.25 DR
12 Dec.	Invoice no. A343	121.00		406.25 DR

Note: MPF Metals is a creditor of Mr. Lewis, while Johnson Bros. is a debtor.

Day Books and Value Added Tax

Most organizations of any size are registered for Value Added Tax (VAT). The topic of VAT and the way in which day books are used to account for VAT is covered in Chapter 11.

Returns Books

Whenever goods are bought and sold there are, inevitably, a number of occasions when they have to be returned. It might be that the wrong goods have been supplied, the wrong size or colour, or perhaps the goods are faulty. There are two aspects of returned goods to consider:

- **returns inwards** (also known as sales returns) - here goods which have been sold by the business to a customer are returned *to* the business, i.e. they are returned *in*

- **returns outwards** (also known as purchases returns) - goods which have been bought by the business are returned *by* the business to the supplier, i.e. they are returned *out*

Those businesses that have a reasonable number of returns transactions will use *returns daybooks,* one to record returns outwards and the other to record returns inwards. Returns daybooks are prepared from credit notes issued and received (see Chapter 7).

Example of a returns inwards day book
Returns inwards day book uses credit notes issued as the source documents and appears as follows:

RETURNS INWARDS DAY BOOK

DATE	NAME	CREDIT NOTE NO	£
19-1			
10 Aug.	L. Jones	RN240	15.00
17 Aug.	Midland Suppliers	RN241	25.50
30 Aug.	M. Green	RN242	48.00
31 Aug.	Total for month transferred to returns inwards account		88.50

As with the other day books, the total for the day, week or the month is transferred to the appropriate account: in this case it is *returns inwards account.* (We shall see, in Chapter 14, how this account and *returns outwards account* are used in the year-end financial statements.) At the same time it is necessary to record on the individual account of each customer (debtor) that they have returned goods and now owe a smaller amount than before, e.g. L. Jones, from the above day book, now owes £15 less than previously.

Example of returns outwards day book

RETURNS OUTWARDS DAY BOOK

DATE	NAME	CREDIT NOTE NO	£
19-1			
12 Sep.	H. Hughes	X414	60.50
20 Sep.	B. Lewis & Co.	123	10.00
27 Sep.	W. Thackeray	A456	12.00
30 Sep.	Total for month transferred to returns outwards account		82.50

This day book is prepared from credit notes received from suppliers in respect of goods that have been returned to them. As before, the total for the day, week or month is transferred - here it goes to *returns outwards account*. At the same time the record of how much is owed to each supplier is reduced in the purchases ledger by the amount of the credit note, e.g. a smaller amount is now owed to H. Hughes than before.

Books of Prime Entry

Day books are often described as *books of prime entry* (or books of *original entry*). This is because they are the first accounting books to record the details of business transactions from the commercial documents:

- Purchases day book is prepared from invoices received
- Sales day book is prepared from invoices issued
- Returns inwards day book is prepared from credit notes issued
- Returns outwards day book is prepared from credit notes received

Of course, as we have seen earlier, day books are not restricted solely to transactions on credit: for cash transactions a shop till provides a record of the total sales. We shall be looking at two other *books of prime entry* for cash transactions - cash book and petty cash book - in the next Chapter.

Division of the Ledger

For most organizations the accounting system (or 'ledger') is divided into four main sections:

- **Sales ledger:** as we have seen in this Chapter, this comprises the individual accounts of debtors

- **Purchases ledger:** this comprises, as we have seen, the individual accounts of creditors

- **Cash book:** as we shall see in the next Chapter, control of cash, in the form of cash itself *and* bank transactions, is a separate function of the accounting system

- **General ledger:** this section comprises all other accounting records, e.g. the accounts of sales, purchases, returns inwards, returns outwards, the owner's capital and all other accounts for assets and liabilities

In the days of fully handwritten accounting systems, a large book - known as the ledger - would be either divided into the four sections, or separate books would be used for each section. Nowadays, computer accounting programs can be purchased to handle each of the four divisions.

Chapter Summary

❏ Day books are often used as listing devices for purchases, sales, returns inwards, and returns outwards. An organization can prepare day books for other purposes to suit its own particular needs.

❏ Day books are books of prime entry because transactions are recorded in them first before being recorded elsewhere.

Cash book and petty cash book are books of prime entry for cash transactions: these are covered in the next Chapter.

✍ Student Activities

1. You are working for Wyvern Wholesalers and are required to enter up the purchases day book from the following details:

    19-1
    2 Apr. Bought goods from Severn Supplies £250, their invoice no. 6789
    4 Apr. Bought goods from I. Johnstone £210, her invoice no. A241
    10 Apr. Bought goods from L. Murphy £185, his invoice no. 2456
    12 Apr. Bought goods from Mercia Manufacturing £180, their invoice no. X457
    18 Apr. Bought goods from AMC Enterprises £345, their invoice no. AMC 456
    24 Apr. Bought goods from S. Green £395, her invoice no. 2846

    After entering the above in the purchases day book, explain to a junior clerk the following:

    (a) Whether the organizations from whom goods have been bought are debtors or creditors of Wyvern Wholesalers.

    (b) If the balance of the account of Severn Supplies was £262 on 1 April, what will it be on 30 April, assuming no payments have been made.

    (c) Where is the total of purchases day book transferred at the end of the month, and why?

2. The following details are to be entered in the sales day book of Wyvern Wholesalers:

    19-1
    2 Apr. Sold goods to Malvern Stores £55, invoice no. 4578
    4 Apr. Sold goods to Pershore Retailers £65, invoice no. 4579
    7 Apr. Sold goods to E. Grainger £28, invoice no. 4580
    10 Apr. Sold goods to P. Wilson £58, invoice no. 4581
    12 Apr. Sold goods to M. Kershaw £76, invoice no. 4582
    14 Apr. Sold goods to D. Lloyd £66, invoice no. 4583
    18 Apr. Sold goods to A. Cox £33, invoice no. 4584
    22 Apr. Sold goods to Dines Stores £102, invoice no. 4585
    24 Apr. Sold goods to Malvern Stores £47, invoice no. 4586
    27 Apr. Sold goods to P. Wilson £35, invoice no. 4587
    29 Apr. Sold goods to A. Cox £82, invoice no. 4588

Explain the following:

(a) If the balance of the account of Malvern Stores was £101 on 1 April, what will it be on 30 April, assuming that no payments have been received. Is Malvern Stores a debtor or a creditor of Wyvern Wholesalers?

(b) Where is the total of sales day book transferred at the end of the month, and why?

3.   The following transactions are to be entered in the *appropriate* day books of Wyvern Wholesalers for the month of May:

19-1
2 May	Bought goods from S. Green £180, her invoice no. 2901
3 May	Sold goods to P. Wilson £48, invoice no. 4589
6 May	Bought goods from Mercia Manufacturing £211, their invoice no. X495
8 May	Sold goods to Dines Stores £105, invoice no. 4590
10 May	Some of the goods, value £50, bought from S. Green are unsatisfactory and are returned to her; she issues credit note no. 221
12 May	Sold goods to D. Lloyd £105, invoice no. 4591
14 May	P. Wilson returns goods £18, we issue credit note no. CN989
17 May	Sold goods to M. Kershaw £85, invoice no. 4592
20 May	We return goods £35 to Mercia Manufacturing; credit note no. 811 received
22 May	Bought goods from AMC Enterprises £55, their invoice no. AMC 612
24 May	D. Lloyd returns goods £22, we issue credit note no. CN990
26 May	Sold goods to Pershore Retailers £75, invoice no. 4593

Total the day books at the month-end and indicate where the totals will be transferred.

(a) If the balance of P. Wilson's account was £108 on 1 May, what will it be on 31 May, assuming no other transactions have taken place? Is P. Wilson a debtor or a creditor of Wyvern Wholesalers?

(b) If the balance of S. Green's account was £264 on 1 May, what will it be on 31 May, assuming no other transactions have taken place? Is S. Green a debtor or a creditor of Wyvern Wholesalers?

4.   Enter the following transactions in the *appropriate* day books of Eveshore Engineering Suppliers for the month of August:

19-8
1 Aug.	Bought goods from Steel Suppliers £250, their invoice no. A83
3 Aug.	Bought goods from Howard Engineering £110, their invoice no. 2014
5 Aug.	Sold goods to Brown Bros. £95, invoice no. 5678
6 Aug.	Returned goods to Steel Suppliers £50; credit note no. 412 received
7 Aug.	Sold goods to G. Gregory £105, invoice no. 5679
10 Aug.	Brown Bros. return goods £20, we issue credit note no. CN771
12 Aug.	Bought goods from Howard Engineering £125, their invoice no. 2907
14 Aug.	Sold goods to Mereford Manufacturing £220, invoice no. 5680
17 Aug.	Bought goods from Birmingham Foundry £355, their invoice no. BM2841
20 Aug.	Mereford Manufacturing returns goods £25, we issue credit note no. CN772
21 Aug.	Sold goods to Brown Bros £250, invoice no. 5681
24 Aug.	Returned goods to Birmingham Foundry £75; credit note no. CN/BM 330 received
26 Aug.	Bought goods from Steel Suppliers £125, their invoice no. A107
28 Aug.	Sold goods to G. Gregory £158, invoice no. 5682

Total the day books at the month-end and indicate where the totals will be transferred.

Chapter Nine
Control of Cash

Cash, represented by cash itself *and* money in the bank, is the lifeblood of any organization. A person can be in business with an excellent product or service and making good sales, but a shortage of cash will mean that he or she will not be able to pay wages and day-to-day running expenses as they fall due: this will lead to a rapid failure of the business.

For all but the smallest organizations control of cash - including bank and cash transactions - takes place in two accounting records:

- Cash book
- Petty cash book

Cash Book

This is used for:

- all receipts by cheque
- all payments by cheque
- all receipts in cash
- most payments in cash, except for low value expense payments (which are paid through *petty cash book:* see later in this Chapter)

The cash book is usually controlled by a cashier who:

- records receipts and payments by cheque and in cash
- makes cash payments, and prepares cheques for signature by those authorized to sign
- pays cash and cheques received into the bank
- has control over the firm's cash float, either in a cash till or cash box
- issues cash to the petty cashier, as and when required

Layout of the cash book
Although a cash book can be set out in many forms to suit the requirements of a particular organization, a common format is the *two-column cash book*. This has two money columns on the left-hand side, and two on the right-hand side, as shown on the next page.

CASH BOOK

RECEIPTS					PAYMENTS				
Date	Details		Cash	Bank	Date	Details		Cash	Bank
			£	£				£	£

The left-hand side is used for receipts, with one column for cash receipts and the other for bank receipts. The payments side is on the right, with one column for cash payments and the other for bank (cheque) payments. Both the receipts and the payments sides have spaces for the date and details of each transaction.

Case Problem: A New Business

Situation

You have been appointed the cashier of a new business. The first month's transactions to be entered in the two-column cash book are:

  1 Jan. Started in business with capital of £1 250: £250 in cash and £1 000 in the bank
  3 Jan. Bought a typewriter for £300, paying by cheque
  7 Jan. Paid office rent of £150 in cash
  10 Jan. Bought office stationery for £75, paying in cash
  12 Jan. Withdrew £300 from the bank for business use
  16 Jan. Purchased goods for resale £200, paying by cheque
  19 Jan. Sold goods £125, receiving a cheque
  23 Jan. Sold goods £55, cash received
  27 Jan. Paid £100 of cash into the bank

All cheques received are banked on the day of receipt.

Solution

The cash book will record these transactions in the following way and, after they have been entered, is balanced on 31 January.

CASH BOOK

RECEIPTS					PAYMENTS				
Date	Details		Cash	Bank	Date	Details		Cash	Bank
19-1			£	£	19-1			£	£
1 Jan	Capital		250	1 000	3 Jan	Typewriter			300
12 Jan	Bank	c	300		7 Jan	Rent		150	
19 Jan	Sales			125	10 Jan	Stationery		75	
23 Jan	Sales		55		12 Jan	Cash	c		300
27 Jan	Cash	c		100	16 Jan	Purchases			200
					27 Jan	Bank	c	100	
					31 Jan	Balances c/d		280	425
			605	1 225				605	1 225
1 Feb	Balances b/d		280	425					

Note the following points:

The transactions on 12 and 27 January involved a transfer of funds between cash and bank. As each transaction is both a receipt and a payment within the cash book, it is usual to indicate both of them with a 'c' - this stands for *contra* and shows that both parts of the transaction are in the *same* book.

A cash book is balanced as follows:

* add the two cash columns and subtotal in pencil
* deduct the lower total from the higher (in this case payments from receipts) to give the balance of cash remaining
* the higher total is recorded at the bottom of both columns in a totals 'box'
* the balance of cash remaining is entered as a balancing item above the totals box (in this case on the right-hand side), and is also brought down underneath the total on the *other* side as the opening balance for the next period
* the two bank columns are dealt with in the same way

Notice that, in this example, the cash and bank balances have been brought down on the left-hand side. It might happen that the balance of the bank columns is brought down on the right-hand side: this happens where payments have exceeded receipts and indicates a bank overdraft.

It is very important to appreciate that the bank columns of the cash book represent the organization's own records of bank transactions and the balance at bank - the bank statement may well show different figures (see Chapter 10).

Checking the cash book

There is no point in keeping records of cash and bank transactions if we cannot, from time-to-time prove that the records are accurate. How can we check the cash book? For the cash columns the answer is easy - count the cash in the till or cash box. In the above example, at the end of January the business should have cash totalling £280; if this is wrong, the discrepancy needs to be investigated urgently. What about the bank columns? We could, perhaps, enquire at the bank and ask for the balance on 31 January, or we could arrange for the bank statement to be sent at the end of each month. However, as indicated previously, the balance of the account at the bank may well not agree with that shown in the cash book. There are several reasons why there may be a difference: for example, a cheque which has been drawn (written out) recently may not yet have been presented to the bank for payment, and so we have a difference of timing - it has been entered in our cash book, but is not yet on the bank statement. To agree cash book and bank statement, it is usually necessary to prepare a *bank reconciliation statement,* and this topic is dealt with fully in Chapter 10.

Cash discount columns

Often an additional column is introduced on each side of the cash book to incorporate cash *discount allowed* (on the receipts side) and cash *discount received* (on the payments side). Such a *three-column cash book* takes the following form:

CASH BOOK

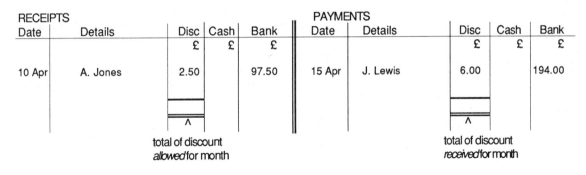

RECEIPTS						PAYMENTS				
Date	Details	Disc	Cash	Bank		Date	Details	Disc	Cash	Bank
		£	£	£				£	£	£
10 Apr	A. Jones	2.50		97.50		15 Apr	J. Lewis	6.00		194.00

total of discount *allowed* for month

total of discount *received* for month

In the cash book above, on the receipts side, A. Jones owed us a total of £100 but, in order to encourage prompt settlement, we have allowed him to deduct a 2.5 per cent *cash discount* and so he sends us a cheque for £97.50 in full settlement. On the payments side, we owe J. Lewis £200 but, provided we pay promptly, we are allowed to deduct cash discount of 3 per cent, and so the cheque sent is for £194.

Note the following points:

- The discount columns are used only to record the amount of *cash discount* for early settlement (see Chapter 7), and *not* trade discount.

- The discount amount is entered in the appropriate discount column, while the net amount (i.e. actual amount received or paid) is entered in the cash or bank columns.

- At the end of the month each discount column is totalled separately - no attempt should be made to balance them. The monthly total is then transferred from the receipts side to *discount allowed account* in the general ledger, while that from the payments side goes to *discount received account,* also in the general ledger. At the end of the year, the totals of discount allowed and discount received accounts feature in the financial statements (see Chapter 14).

- The cash and bank columns are balanced in the usual way and the balances carried down to next month.

Later on in this Chapter we shall look at a more detailed form of cash book, the *analysed cash book.*

Petty Cash Book

While a cash book is used to make payments in cash for fairly substantial amounts, a petty cash book is used to record low-value payments for various small purchases, e.g. to pay the window cleaner, bus fares, and small items of stationery. It would not be appropriate for such expenses to be entered in the main cash book, as a large number of small payments would clutter it up. Instead an amount of cash is handed by the cashier to a member of staff, the *petty cashier,* who will control the money and make payments as appropriate. When the petty cashier is running short of money, he or she will request a further amount from the cashier. Alternatively, many petty cash books operate on *the imprest system,* whereby the petty cashier starts each week or month with a certain amount of money - the imprest amount. As payments are made during the period, the amount of money will reduce and, at the end of the period, the float will be made up by the main cashier to the imprest amount. For example:

Started week with imprest amount of	£100.00
Total of petty cash amounts paid out during week	£78.45
Cash held at end of week	£21.55
Amount drawn from cashier to restore imprest amount	£78.45
Cash at start of next week, i.e. imprest amount	£100.00

If, at any time, the imprest amount proves insufficient, further amounts of cash can be drawn from the cashier. Also, from time to time, it may be necessary to increase the imprest amount so that regular shortfalls are avoided.

The petty cashier, who is likely also to have other tasks within the organization, is responsible for control of the petty cash, making cash payments when appropriate, keeping records of payments made, and balancing the petty cash book at regular intervals. Payments out of petty cash are made only against correct documentation - usually a petty cash voucher (see fig. 9.1) - duly signed by a person authorised to allow payments to be made. Any relevant documentation, e.g. a receipt, should be attached to the petty cash voucher.

Petty Cash Voucher

No 057

Date *11 May 19·6*

For what required	AMOUNT £	p
Envelopes	*1*	*55*
Parcel tape	*3*	*10*
	4	*65*

Signature *T. Lewis*

Passed by *D. Farmer*

Fig. 9.1 An example of a petty cash voucher

Layout of a petty cash book

PETTY CASH BOOK

Receipts £	Date	Details	Voucher No.	Total Payment £	Analysis columns			
					Postages £	Travel £	Stationery £	Meals £

This layout shows that receipts from the main cashier are entered in the column on the extreme left; then there are columns for the date and details of all transactions, together with the petty cash voucher number. The total payment is in the next column and then follow the analysis columns. An organization will use these to analyse each transaction already entered in the total payment column. The headings are at the discretion of the organization, and there may be more than the four columns shown here. At the end of the week the petty cashier will total the analysis columns, the sum of which should equal the total of the total payment column, and the amount of money needed from the main cashier.

Case Problem: Petty Cash Book - Imprest System

Situation

You are the petty cashier working in a small organization. There are a number of transactions for the week to be entered in the petty cash book:

19-1
10 Apr. Started the week with an imprest amount of £75.00
10 Apr. Paid postages £3.45 on voucher no. 47
10 Apr. Paid travel £1.25 on voucher no. 48
11 Apr. Paid stationery £0.75 on voucher no. 49
12 Apr. Paid travel £2.50 and meal £5.40 on voucher no. 50
12 Apr. Paid postages £4.40 on voucher no. 51
13 Apr. Paid travel £11.25 on voucher no. 52
14 Apr. Paid travel £5.50 and meals £12.30 on voucher no. 53
14 Apr. Paid stationery £3.65 on voucher no. 54
14 Apr. Cash received to restore imprest amount

Solution

PETTY CASH BOOK

Receipts	Date	Details	Voucher No.	Total Payment	Postages	Travel	Stationery	Meals
£	19-1			£	£	£	£	£
75.00	10 Apr.	Balance b/d						
	10 Apr.	Postages	47	3.45	3.45			
	10 Apr.	Travel	48	1.25		1.25		
	11 Apr.	Stationery	49	0.75			0.75	
	12 Apr.	Travel/meal	50	7.90		2.50		5.40
	12 Apr.	Postages	51	4.40	4.40			
	13 Apr.	Travel	52	11.25		11.25		
	14 Apr.	Travel/meals	53	17.80		5.50		12.30
	14 Apr.	Stationery	54	3.65			3.65	
				50.45	7.85	20.50	4.40	17.70
50.45	14 Apr.	Cash received						
	14 Apr.	Balance c/d		75.00				
125.45				125.45				
75.00	15 Apr.	Balance b/d						

Note the following points:

- The amount of cash received from the main cashier to restore the imprest amount is the same as the total paid out during the week.

- The total of each analysis column will be added to other payments which may have been made in cash and by cheque for each expense category. For example, petty cash postages are £7.85, and if payments for postages by cheque during the period amounted to £80, the organization has incurred a total cost of £87.85 for postages. (This is the amount that will eventually be charged as an expense in the financial statements for postages along with other payments for postages during the year: see Chapter 13).

Analysed Cash Book

Many smaller organizations use an analysed cash book to provide more information than the three column cash book looked at earlier in this chapter. An analysed cash book (which is used as an alternative to the three column cash book) divides both receipts and payments between a number of categories. For example, receipts might be divided between cash sales, sales ledger (receipts from debtors), and miscellaneous; payments might use cash purchases, purchases ledger (payments to creditors), and expenses - the latter can be divided into the main expenses headings.

Case Problem: Analysed Cash Book

Situation

James Brown runs a shop selling records, tapes, and compact discs. He uses an analysed cash book and the following transactions are to be recorded for the first week of April 19-1:

1 Apr.   Balances at start of week:
        cash   £55
        bank £275
1 Apr.   Cash sales £315
2 Apr.   Paid wages in cash £85
3 Apr.   Paid shop rent £100 by cheque
3 Apr.   Received a cheque for £97 from a debtor, T. Lewis, and allowed him £3 cash discount
3 Apr.   Cash sales £155
4 Apr.   Received a cheque for £125 from Wyvern School, a debtor
4 Apr.   Paid a creditor, Romulus Records, a cheque for £144, receiving £6 cash discount
5 Apr.   Cash sales £75
5 Apr.   Paid wages in cash £70
5 Apr.   Bought tapes, £175, paying by cheque
5 Apr.   Balanced the cash book at the end of the week

Solution

Receipts

Date	Details	Disc	Cash	Bank	Cash Sales	Sales ledger	Miscellaneous
		£	£	£	£	£	£
19-1							
1 Apr.	Balances b/d		55	275			
1 Apr.	Sales		315		315		
3 Apr.	T. Lewis	3		97		97	
3 Apr.	Sales		155		155		
4 Apr.	Wyvern School			125		125	
5 Apr.	Sales		75		75		
		3	600	497	545	222	
6 Apr.	Balances b/d		445	78			

Payments

Date	Details	Disc	Cash	Bank	Cash Purchases	Purchases ledger	Expenses Wages	Rent
19-1		£	£	£	£	£	£	£
2 Apr.	Wages		85				85	
3 Apr.	Rent			100				100
4 Apr.	Romulus Records	6		144		144		
5 Apr.	Wages		70				70	
5 Apr.	Purchases			175	175			
5 Apr.	Balances c/d		445	78				
		6	600	497	175	144	155	100

Notes:

- The analysed cash book simply analyses each receipt and payment between a number of headings. A business will amend the cash book and use whatever headings suit it best.

- For many small businesses an analysed cash book forms the main accounting record. However, as a business grows in size it will be appropriate to use a different system under which the total of each analysis column is, at the week or month-end, transferred to a separate account, e.g. sales account, purchases account, wages account, and rent account.

- Whenever receipts come in from debtors or payments are made to creditors, the appropriate personal account must also be amended in the sales ledger section or purchases ledger section.

Chapter Summary

❑ The cash book records receipts and payments, both in cash and by cheque.

❑ The petty cash book records payments for a variety of small expenses.

❑ An analysed cash book is used by many smaller businesses to analyse receipts and payments under a number of headings.

The bank columns of the cash book and the balance calculated are unlikely to agree with the bank statement: this leads us on to the next Chapter where we shall consider how to prepare bank reconciliation statements.

✍️ Student Activities

1. You are employed as an accounts clerk by Juliet Johnson, who operates a transport company. The cashier is on holiday and you are required to take on the task of keeping the two-column cash book. The following transactions take place (all cheques are banked on the day of receipt):

   19-1
   - 1 May   Balances: cash £72; bank £2 297
   - 3 May   Received cash from L. Williams £50
   - 3 May   Received a cheque from Status Superstores for £755
   - 5 May   Issued a cheque for £150 for office cash
   - 6 May   Paid cleaner's wages £84 in cash
   - 7 May   Received a cheque from J. Lewis & Co. for £1 354
   - 9 May   Paid telephone account £158 by cheque
   - 12 May   Received cash from P. Hardy £120
   - 13 May   Received a cheque from Iowa Transport for £862
   - 13 May   Paid Westland Garage £487 by cheque
   - 16 May   Paid cleaner's wages £80 in cash
   - 17 May   Received cash from H. Smithson £75
   - 20 May   Paid Lowland Tyre Co. £261 by cheque
   - 23 May   Paid Office Equipment Ltd. £176 by cheque
   - 24 May   Paid salaries by cheque £2 687
   - 24 May   Received a cheque from L. Carol & Co. for £347
   - 25 May   Paid Western Oils Ltd. £629 by cheque
   - 27 May   Issued a cheque for £150 for office cash
   - 31 May   Paid cash £64 to petty cashier
   - 31 May   Balanced the cash book and carried the balances down to 1 June

2. Walter Harrison is a sole trader who records his cash and bank transactions in a *three-column* cash book. The following are the transactions for June:

   19-2
   - 1 June   Balances: cash £280; bank overdraft £2 240
   - 3 June   Received a cheque from G. Wheaton for £195, in full settlement of a debt of £200
   - 5 June   Received cash of £53 from T. Francis, in full settlement of a debt of £55
   - 8 June   Paid the amount owing to F. Lloyd by cheque: the total amount due is £400 and you take advantage of a 2.5 per cent cash discount for prompt settlement
   - 10 June   Paid wages in cash £165
   - 12 June   Paid A. Morris in cash, £100 less 3 per cent cash discount
   - 16 June   Issued a cheque for £200 for office cash
   - 18 June   Received a cheque for £640 from H. Watson in full settlement of a debt of £670
   - 20 June   Paid R. Marks £78 by cheque
   - 24 June   Paid D. Farr £65 by cheque, in full settlement of a debt of £67
   - 26 June   Paid telephone account £105 in cash
   - 28 June   Received a cheque from M. Perry in settlement of his account of £240 - he has deducted 2.5 per cent cash discount
   - 30 June   Received cash £45 from K. Willis

   You are required to:
   - enter the above transactions in Harrison's three-column cash book, balance the cash and bank columns, and carry the balances down to 1 July

   - total the two discount columns and explain what these totals represent and where they will be transferred

3.   Prepare a petty cash book with four analysis columns for Postages, Travelling Expenses, Meals, and Sundry Office Expenses. Enter the following transactions for the week:
19-1
1 June   Balance of cash £100
1 June   Postages £6.35, voucher no. 123
2 June   Travelling expenses £3.25, voucher no. 124
2 June   Postages £1.28, voucher no. 125
3 June   Envelopes £4.54, voucher no. 126
3 June   Window cleaning £5.50, voucher no. 127
4 June   Travelling expenses £4.56, meals £10.85, voucher no. 128
4 June   Postages £8.56, packing materials £3.25, voucher no. 129
4 June   Taxi fare £4.50, meals £7.45, voucher no. 130
5 June   Marker pens £2.55, envelopes £3.80, voucher no. 131
5 June   Cash received from main cashier to restore imprest amount to £100

4.   Draw up a petty cash book with appropriate analysis columns and enter the following transactions for the month:
19-1
1 May   Balance of cash £150
1 May   Postages £7, travelling £2.85, voucher no. 456
2 May   Meal allowance £5.50, voucher no. 457
3 May   Taxi £4.50, voucher no. 458
4 May   Stationery £3.55, voucher no. 459
7 May   Postages £5.25, voucher no. 460
8 May   Travelling £6.50, voucher no. 461
9 May   Meal allowance £5.50, voucher no. 462
10 May   Stationery £8.50, voucher no. 463
14 May   Taxi £5.45, voucher no. 464
17 May   Stationery £4.60, voucher no. 465
21 May   Travelling £3.50, postages £4.50, voucher no. 466
23 May   Fares £3.80, voucher no. 467
26 May   Catering expenses £15.50, voucher no. 468
27 May   Postages £3.50, stationery £7.55, voucher no. 469
28 May   Travelling expenses £6.45, voucher no. 470
31 May   Cash received from main cashier to restore imprest amount to £150

5.   John Adams is a jobbing builder and, to help him keep his business records straight, he uses an analysed cash book. The headings used are *receipts:* cash sales, sales ledger, miscellaneous; *payments:* cash purchases, purchases ledger, and expenses, which are further subdivided between rent, van and wages. He asks you to write up his analysed cash book for the first week of July 19-2 for which the transactions are:

1 Jul.   Balances at start of week:
          cash £187
          bank £320
1 Jul.   Bought building materials £50, paying in cash
1 Jul.   Paid for van repairs £75 by cheque
2 Jul.   Received cash for completed job £125
2 Jul.   Received cheque from a debtor, Panton Parish Council, £145, after allowing them £5 cash discount
3 Jul.   Bought building materials £70, paying £65 in cash and receiving £5 cash discount
4 Jul.   Paid rent £35 by cheque
4 Jul.   Received cheque for completed job £175
5 Jul.   Paid a creditor, Builders Merchants (Wyvern) Ltd., £74 by cheque, receiving £6 cash discount
5 Jul.   Paid wages in cash £50

At the end of the week he asks you to balance the analysed cash book, and to carry the balances down to next week.

Chapter Ten
Bank Reconciliation Statements

We saw in the previous Chapter that the bank columns of a cash book represent an organization's own internal record of bank transactions, and the balance at the end of the week or month. As we noted, the bank statement may show a rather different balance and, assuming that there are no errors, both *are* correct. The problem is one of *timing*, e.g. when the cashier of an organization issues a cheque, the amount is immediately entered on the payments side of the cash book, even though it may be some days before the cheque passes through the clearing system and is recorded on the bank statement. Therefore, for a few days, the cash book shows a lower balance than the bank statement. When the cheque is recorded on the bank statement, the two will be in agreement. While we have looked at only one cheque here, an organization may be issuing many cheques each day - in fact large companies and Local Authorities will probably issue hundreds of cheques each working day.

Timing Differences

The two timing differences between the bank columns of the cash book and the bank statement are:

• cheques issued, not yet recorded on the bank statement (as described above)
• cash and cheques paid into the bank, but not yet recorded on the bank statement

With the second of these, the cashier will record a receipt in the cash book as he or she prepares the bank paying-in slip. However, the receipt may not be recorded by the bank on the bank statement for a day or so, particularly if the funds are paid in at a bank branch other than the one at which the account is maintained. So, for a few days, the cash book will show a higher balance at bank than the bank statement. When the credit is entered on the bank statement, the two will be in agreement.

These timing differences form the calculation known as a *bank reconciliation statement* - the organization's cash book *must not be altered* for these because, as we have seen, they will 'correct themselves' as time goes by. However, there may be other differences between the bank columns of the cash book and the bank statement, and these *do* need to be entered in the cash book to write it up-to-date.

Updating the Cash Book

The cash book needs writing up-to-date when certain items which appear on the bank statement should also appear in the cash book. It may be, for example, that the bank makes standing order payments on behalf of the organization - such items are correctly deducted from the bank account and should, at the same time, be entered as a payment in the cash book: the bank statement may serve to remind the cashier of the payment. Examples of items that show on the bank statement and need to be entered in the cash book include:

Payments

- standing order and direct debit payments deducted by the bank
- bank charges
- unpaid cheques debited by the bank (i.e. cheques paid in which have 'bounced' and will have to be deducted from the account)

Receipts

- standing order receipts credited by the bank
- bank giro credit (credit transfer) amounts received by the bank
- dividends received by the bank
- interest credited by the bank

For each of these items the cashier needs to check to see if they have been entered in the cash book; if not, they need to be recorded.

The Bank Reconciliation Statement

This forms the link between the balances shown in the cash book and the bank statement:

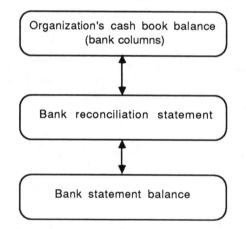

Upon receipt of a bank statement, reconciliation of the two balances should be carried out in the following way:

- tick off the items that appear in both cash book and bank statement
- from the bank statement, certain of the unticked items will need to be entered in the cash book to bring it up-to-date (see above)
- the bank columns of the cash book are now balanced to find the up-to-date figure
- the remaining unticked items from the cash book will be timing differences
- the timing differences are used to prepare the bank reconciliation statement, which takes the following format (with example figures):

JANE LEWIS

Bank Reconciliation Statement as at 31 October 19-1

	£
Balance at bank as per cash book	125
Add: cheques drawn, not yet presented for payment	55
	180
Less: cash and cheques paid in, not yet credited	20
Balance at bank as per bank statement	160

Note the following points:

- The above layout starts with the cash book balance and works towards the bank statement balance. There is no reason why it should not commence with the bank statement balance and finish with the cash book balance.

- If a bank overdraft is involved use brackets around the numbers to indicate this, and still add or deduct as appropriate, but be careful with the arithmetic!

- Once the bank reconciliation statement agrees, it should be kept because it proves that the cash book and bank statement were reconciled at a particular date. If, next time it is prepared, it fails to agree, the previous statement is proof that reconciliation was reached at that time.

Case Problem: A Question of Reconciliation

Situation

You are the cashier for Mrs. Jones, who runs a typing agency. The cash book (bank columns) for the month of January 19-6 are as follows:

CASH BOOK (BANK COLUMNS)

Receipts			£	Payments			£
19-6				19-6			
1 Jan.	Balance b/d		550	10 Jan.	J. Watt		60
9 Jan.	A. Roberts		125	18 Jan.	Typing Supplies		90
14 Jan.	Lewis' Ltd.		210	28 Jan.	N. Lowe		310
24 Jan.	P. Evans (Solicitors)		175	30 Jan.	Red Hill Garage		85
31 Jan.	J. Kenwright		165				
		Sub-total	1 225			Sub-total	545

The bank statement is received showing the following transactions for January 19-6:

	IN ACCOUNT WITH
	National Bank plc
	Branch..Bartown..............
TITLE OF ACCOUNT....MRS. M. JONES.........	
ACCOUNT NUMBER....67812318................	STATEMENT NUMBER 45

DATE	PARTICULARS	PAYMENTS £	RECEIPTS £	BALANCE £
19-6				
1 Jan.	Balance brought forward			550
9 Jan.	Credit		125	675
16 Jan.	Credit		210	885
17 Jan.	J. Watt	60		825
20 Jan.	Direct debit: A-Z Finance Co.	110		715
26 Jan.	Credit		175	890
27 Jan.	Typing Supplies	90		800
30 Jan.	Bank Giro Credit: MPF Industries		145	945
31 Jan.	Bank charges	10		935

Mrs. Jones asks you to reconcile the cash book with the bank statement.

Solution

The first step is to tick off the items that appear in both cash book and bank statement. This leaves the following items outstanding:

Cash Book:	Receipt on 31 Jan. for £165	)	each of these will appear in
	Payment on 28 Jan. for £310	)	the bank reconciliation
	Payment on 30 Jan. for £85	)	statement
Bank Statement:	Payment on 20 Jan. for £110	)	each of these needs to be
	Receipts on 30 Jan. for £145	)	written up in the cash book
	Payment on 31 Jan. for £10	)	

The next task is to write the cash book up-to-date, and calculate the balance:

CASH BOOK (BANK COLUMNS)

Receipts		£	Payments		£
19-6			19-6		
	Sub-total	1 225		Sub-total	545
30 Jan.	MPF Industries	145	20 Jan.	A-Z Finance Co.	110
			31 Jan.	Bank charges	10
			31 Jan.	Balance c/d	705
		1 370			1 370
1 Feb.	Balance b/d	705			

Reconciliation can now be made between cash book and bank statement:

MRS. JONES' TYPING AGENCY

Bank Reconciliation Statement as at 31 January 19-6

	£	£
Balance at bank as per cash book		705
Add: cheques drawn, not yet presented for payment	310	
	85	
		395
		1 100
Less: cash/cheque paid in, not yet credited		165
Balance at bank as per bank statement		935

The total of the bank reconciliation statement and the closing balance of the bank statement are reconciled, i.e. they agree. You can then be sure that neither the cashier nor the bank have made any errors, as they both inevitably do from time to time.

Chapter Summary

❑ A bank reconciliation statement agrees the bank columns of the cash book with the bank statement.

❑ Certain differences between the two are timing differences, e.g. cheques drawn, not yet presented for payment, and cash/cheques paid in, not yet credited.

❑ Other differences, correctly appearing on the bank statement, need to be entered in the cash book to bring it up-to-date: examples include standing orders and bank charges.

✍ Student Activities

1. The bank columns of F. Jones' cash book for December 19-5 are as follows:

19-5	Receipts	£	19-5	Payments	£
1 Dec.	Balance	280	9 Dec.	W. Smith	40
12 Dec.	P. Jones	30	13 Dec.	Rent	50
18 Dec.	H. Homer	72	18 Dec.	Wages	85
27 Dec.	J. Hill	13	20 Dec.	B. Kay	20
			31 Dec.	Balance	200
		395			395

He received his bank statement which showed the following transactions for December 19-5:

BANK STATEMENT

19-5		Payments £	Receipts £	Balance £
1 Dec.	Balance			280
12 Dec.	P. Jones		30	310
15 Dec.	W. Smith	40		270
17 Dec.	Rent	50		220
20 Dec.	H. Homer		72	292
23 Dec.	Wages	85		207

You are required to prepare a bank reconciliation statement to agree the cash book figure with the bank statement.

2.   The bank columns of J. Doyle's cash book for May 19-6 are as follows:

19-6	**Receipts**	£	19-6	**Payments**	£
1 May	Balance	300	2 May	P. Stone	28
7 May	Cash	162	14 May	Alpha Ltd.	50
16 May	C. Brewster	89	29 May	E. Deakin	110
24 May	Cash	60			
31 May	Cash	40			

She received her bank statement which showed the following transactions for May 19-6:

BANK STATEMENT

19-6		Payments £	Receipts £	Balance £
1 May	Balance			300
4 May	P. Stone	28		272
7 May	Cash		162	434
10 May	Dividend from investment		63	497
17 May	Standing order - insurance	25		472
17 May	Cheque		89	561
18 May	Alpha Ltd.	50		511
25 May	Cash		60	571
31 May	Bank Charges	10		561

You are required to:

• write the cash book up-to-date at 31 May 19-6
• prepare a bank reconciliation statement at 31 May 19-6

3.   Malvern Wholesalers requires the bank statement and cash book balances (bank columns) to be reconciled. You are given the following information as at 30 April 19-3:

• the bank columns of the cash book show a balance of £500 in the bank
• a payment of £200 has been recorded as a receipt in the cash book by mistake
• cheques for £120, £150 and £40 have been sent out in payment to various suppliers but have not yet been paid into the bank by those suppliers; they are recorded in the cash book
• a direct debit payment of £45 has been recorded by the bank, but has not yet been entered in the cash book
• a cheque for £500 has been recorded as a receipt in the cash book, but has not yet been paid into the bank account
• bank charges amounting to £20 appear on the bank statement, but have not yet been entered in the cash book
• a bank giro credit from a customer for £150 appears on the bank statement, but has not yet been entered in the cash book
• a cheque for £125 has been returned by the bank marked 'refer to drawer' (i.e. unpaid), but has not been written back in the cash book
• the bank statement shows a closing overdrawn balance of £130

You are required to:

• write the cash book up-to-date at 30 April 19-3
• prepare a bank reconciliation statement at 30 April 19-3

4. According to the cash book (bank columns) of a business, the bank balance on 30 April 19-2 was £1 784.20, but the bank statement on that date showed a balance of £1 714.90.

    An examination of the cash book and bank statement shows that:

    • a bank giro credit of £28.50 received direct by the bank had not been entered in the cash book

    • a cheque for £120 received and banked on 17 April 19-2 was unpaid (i.e. 'bounced'), but no entry recording that fact had been made in the cash book

    • a standing order (in favour of H.P. Insurance Co.) for £10 paid by the bank had not been entered in the cash book

    • £45 paid into the bank on 18 April 19-2 had been entered in the cash book as £54

    • cheques totalling £212.60 sent to suppliers and entered in the cash book had not yet been presented for payment to the bank

    • remittances from customers totalling £171.40 entered in the cash book and banked on 30 April 19-2 had not yet been credited by the bank

    You are required to:

    • write the cash book up-to-date at 30 April 19-2

    • prepare a bank reconciliation statement at 30 April 19-2

5. Explain to a person who has recently joined the firm where you work the reasons why the bank balance, as shown in the cash book, may not agree with that shown by the bank statement. Give examples of each, and distinguish between those that are timing differences, and those that need to be entered in the cash book.

Assignment Five

Cash Control:
the Cashier's Department

GENERAL OBJECTIVES COVERED
C

SKILLS DEVELOPED
Numeracy, information processing

SITUATION
You are working in the accounts department of ABC Electrical, a medium-sized electrical contracting firm that undertakes work for a range of private individuals, businesses, and local authorities. The cashier, who is responsible for both the firm's cash book and petty cash book, is away on holiday this week and you have been asked to carry out her work.

The following are the firm's cash/bank and petty cash transactions for the week:

19-6
8 May	Commenced the week with a bank balance of £420.50 and cash in hand of £125.25; the balance of petty cash is £50 (the imprest amount).
8 May	Sent cheque no. 123451 for £200 to Wiring Suppliers.
8 May	Paid £2.25 from petty cash for stationery: voucher no. 85.
8 May	Received a cheque for £138.50 from Bartown District Council.
9 May	Paid £2.80 from petty cash for travel expenses and £3.00 for postages: voucher no. 86.
9 May	Cash received from Mrs. Lewis for £27.50.
9 May	Withdrew £100 in cash from the bank (cheque no. 123452) for use in the business.
10 May	Received a cheque for £208.30 from J. Jones & Co.
10 May	Paid telephone account for £154.27 by cheque no. 123453.
10 May	Paid sundry expenses £1.82 and travel £2.50 from petty cash: voucher no. 87.
10 May	Paid stationery £1.60 and postages £2.00 from petty cash: voucher no. 88.
11 May	Paid wages £360.40 by cheque no. 123454.
11 May	Paid postages £2.68 from petty cash: voucher no. 89.
11 May	Paid Evans Ltd. £127.80 by cheque no. 123455.
11 May	Paid Building Supplies £54.50 in cash.
12 May	Paid £2.06 travel expenses and £1.50 sundry expenses from petty cash: voucher no. 90.
12 May	Received a cheque for £155.00 from Loamshire County Council.
12 May	Paid £1.66 for stationery from petty cash: voucher no. 91.
12 May	Restored petty cash imprest amount by transfer from the main cash book.

Note: all cheques received are banked on the day of receipt.

At the end of the week the following bank statement is received:

IN ACCOUNT WITH

National Bank plc

Branch..Bartown...............

TITLE OF ACCOUNT.....ABC Electrical.......

ACCOUNT NUMBER.....12345678.........................

STATEMENT NUMBER 38

DATE	PARTICULARS	PAYMENTS £	RECEIPTS £	BALANCE £
19–6				
8 May	Balance brought forward			420.50
8 May	Cheque		138.50	559.00
9 May	123452	100.00		459.00
10 May	Cheque		208.30	667.30
11 May	123451	200.00		467.30
11 May	Standing order: Midland Hire Purchase Co.	90.50		376.80
11 May	123454	360.40		16.40
12 May	Bank giro credit: Johnson Bros.		54.20	70.60
12 May	Bank charges	25.00		45.60
12 May	Balance carried forward			45.60

STUDENT TASKS

1. Rule up columns for a two-column cash book, and for a petty cash book with analysis columns for stationery, postages, travel and sundries.

2. Enter the above transactions for the week.

3. Balance the petty cash book and, at the end of the week, restore the imprest amount to £50 by transfer of the appropriate amount from the cash book.

4. Using the bank statement, write the cash book (bank columns) up-to-date.

5. Balance the cash book, and prepare a bank reconciliation statement.

Chapter Eleven
Value Added Tax

In Britain most organizations with a turnover, i.e. sales, of more than £25 400 a year, must be registered for Value Added Tax (VAT). This turnover figure is increased from time-to-time, usually as a part of the Chancellor of the Exchequer's budget proposals in March or April. The figure quoted was set in March 1990.

Once registered, an organization is issued with a VAT registration number which must be quoted on all invoices (see Chapter 7). It charges VAT at the current rate (15 per cent) on all taxable supplies, i.e. whenever it sells goods or supplies a service. From the supplier's viewpoint the tax so charged is known as *output tax*. A number of items are *zero-rated* and no tax is charged when they are supplied: for example, food and children's clothing are zero-rated.

Those who are registered for VAT must pay to the VAT authorities (H.M. Customs and Excise) the amount they have collected *(output tax)*, *less* the amount of VAT charged to them *(input tax)* on taxable supplies bought in. The payments are made usually after every three months, although some organizations submit a VAT return on a monthly basis. If input tax exceeds output tax, the organization claims a refund of the difference from H.M. Customs and Excise.

A Tax on the Final Consumer

It is the final consumer, who is not registered for VAT, that actually pays the tax. This, and the principles of VAT-collection, can be illustrated as follows:

Step 1 The manufacturer, who is VAT-registered, sells goods to a wholesaler for £100, plus VAT at 15 per cent, i.e.

Goods sold for	£100
VAT charged	£15
Invoice price	£115

The manufacturer will include the £15 of VAT collected on the next VAT return.

Step 2 The wholesaler, who is VAT-registered, adds his profit and sells the same goods to a retailer for £140, plus VAT, i.e.

Goods sold for	£140
VAT charged	£21
Invoice price	£161

The wholesaler owes the VAT authorities £6, i.e. £21 (output tax) less £15 (input tax), for this transaction, and these VAT figures for inputs and outputs will be included on the next VAT return. You should note that the only VAT paid over by the wholesaler is in respect of the value that has been added, i.e. £40 at 15 per cent = £6.

Step 3 The retailer, who is VAT-registered, adds his profit and sells the goods to a member of the public for £200, plus VAT, i.e.

Goods sold for	£200
VAT charged	£30
Invoice price	£230

The retailer will pay the VAT authorities £9 in respect of this transaction, i.e. £30 less £21, the figures for output and input tax, which will be included on the next return.

In all, therefore, the VAT authorities have received payments of tax wherever value has been added:

from manufacturer	£15
from wholesaler	£6
from retailer	£9
paid by final customer	£30

As you will see, it is the final customer who has had to provide the full amount of tax on the value added to the cost of the goods, while it is the manufacturer, wholesaler and retailer who have actually paid it over to the VAT authorities.

Accounting for VAT

Each VAT-registered organization must keep a *Value Added Tax account* as a part of their records in the general ledger. This records the VAT paid on *inputs* (purchases), and the VAT collected on *outputs* (sales). Every three months the VAT account is totalled and either a cheque is sent to Customs and Excise where tax on outputs exceeds tax on inputs, or a claim for repayment is made where the tax on inputs exceeds that on outputs. In both cases, all VAT-registered organizations have to submit a Value Added Tax Return, known as form VAT 100 (see fig. 11.1), usually every three months.

In order to obtain the information needed for an organization's VAT account, it is necessary to incorporate in the sales day book and purchases day book a column for VAT. The day books (see also Chapter 8) take the following form:

SALES DAY BOOK

Date	Customer's Name	Exclusive of VAT	VAT	TOTAL
19-1		£	£	£
15 Jan.	J. Smith	100	15	115
23 Jan.	H. Wilson	200	30	230
		300	45	345
		to Sales account (general ledger)	to VAT account (general ledger)	separate amounts to each debtor's account (sales ledger)

Value Added Tax Return

HM Customs and Excise

For the period
01 01 –1 to 31 03 –1

For Official Use

WRIGHT & CO LTD
WEST STREET
NORWICH
NR1 5DB

Registration Number	Period
316 1273 50	03 –1

You could be liable to a financial penalty if your completed return and all the VAT payable are not received by the due date.

Due date: 30 04 –1

For Official Use

Before you fill in this form please read the notes on the back. Complete all boxes clearly in ink, writing 'none' where necessary. Don't put a dash or leave any box blank. If there are no pence write "00" in the pence column. Do not enter more than one amount in any box.

		£	p
VAT due in this period on **sales** and other outputs	**1**	1,550	70
VAT reclaimed in this period on **purchases** and other inputs	**2**	650	25
Net VAT to be paid to Customs or reclaimed by you (**Difference between boxes 1 and 2**)	**3**	900	45
Value of **outputs** (pounds only) excluding any VAT	**4**	10,338	00
Value of **inputs** (pounds only) excluding any VAT	**5**	4,335	00

Retail schemes. If you have used any of the schemes in the period covered by this return please enter the appropriate letter(s) in this box.

If you are enclosing a payment please tick (✓) this box. ✓

DECLARATION by the signatory to be completed by or on behalf of the person named above.

I, DEREK JAMES WRIGHT
(Full name of signatory in BLOCK LETTERS)
declare that the information given above is true and complete.

Signature ... J Wright ... Date 20 April 19 –1

VAT 100   CD 1911/N1 (8.89)   F 3790(JANUARY 1990)

Fig. 11.1 Specimen Value Added Tax Return (form VAT 100)

PURCHASES DAY BOOK

Date	Supplier's Name	Exclusive of VAT	VAT	TOTAL
19-1		£	£	£
10 Jan.	M. Latcham	60	9	69
20 Jan.	L. Barber	100	15	115
		160	24	184
		to Purchases account (general ledger)	to VAT account (general ledger)	separate amounts to each creditor's account (purchases ledger)

If these were the only transactions during the quarter, the VAT will be settled as follows:

VAT collected on outputs (sales)	£45
less VAT paid on inputs (purchases)	£24
VAT due to H.M. Customs & Excise	£21

As can be seen, VAT charged on outputs exceeds that paid on inputs, and so a cheque for the difference, £21, will be sent to Customs and Excise together with the completed Value Added Tax Return (VAT 100).

Some VAT Calculations

It is easy to calculate the VAT amount when the price of goods before the addition of VAT is known: goods costing £100 plus VAT at 15 per cent incur VAT of £15 to give a total cost of £115. It is a little more difficult to calculate the VAT-exclusive amount if only the total cost including VAT is known. With VAT at 15 per cent the VAT fraction is 3/23, and the VAT-exclusive amount is 20/23:

$$\pounds 115 \times \frac{3}{23} = \text{VAT of } \pounds 15$$

$$\pounds 115 \times \frac{20}{23} = \text{VAT-exclusive cost of } \pounds 100$$

When calculating VAT amounts, fractions of a penny are ignored, i.e. the tax is rounded down to a whole penny.

Exempt Supplies

A few types of goods and services are neither standard-rated nor zero-rated for VAT: instead they are *exempt*. The effect of this is that the supplier of such goods cannot charge VAT on outputs (as is the case with zero-rated goods). However, unlike the supplier of zero-rated goods, the supplier of exempt goods cannot claim back all the tax which has been paid on inputs. Examples of exempt supplies include loans of money, sales or lettings of land or some property, and certain types of education and health care.

Chapter Summary

❏ VAT-registered organizations charge VAT on all taxable supplies.

❏ Certain types of goods are zero-rated, some are exempt; most are taxable.

❏ A VAT-registered organization must complete VAT form 100 at certain intervals, commonly every three months, and either pay over to Customs and Excise tax collected, or seek a refund where tax on inputs exceeds that on outputs.

Student Activities

1.   You work for Jayne Blake who operates a clothes wholesaling business. All the goods she buys and sells are subject to Value Added Tax at the standard rate (15 per cent). The following transactions are to be entered in the purchases day book or sales day book, as appropriate (in each case VAT is to be added):

19-6
1 Feb.   Bought goods from Flair Clothing Co. for £500 + VAT
2 Feb.   Sold goods to Wyvern Fashions for £200 + VAT
4 Feb.   Bought goods from Modernwear for £260 + VAT
10 Feb.   Sold goods to Zandra Smith for £160 + VAT
15 Feb.   Sold goods to Just Jean for £100 + VAT
18 Feb.   Bought goods from Quality Clothing for £800 + VAT
23 Feb.   Sold goods to Peter Sanders Menswear for £300 + VAT
24 Feb.   Sold goods to H. Wilson for £60 + VAT
26 Feb.   Sold goods to Mercian Models for £320 + VAT
28 Feb.   Bought goods from Flair Clothing Co. for £200 + VAT

You are required to:

• write up the sales day book and the purchases day book
• show how the Value Added Tax summary will appear for February

2.   The following is a summary of purchases and sales, excluding VAT, made by Mercian Computers for the three months ended 30 June 19-4:

Purchases   April £5 400,   May £4 800,   June £6 800.
Sales   April £8 200,   May £9 400,   June £10 800.

All purchases and sales are subject to Value Added Tax at the standard rate of 15 per cent.

You are required to:

• calculate the VAT amounts for each month and show the summary of Value Added Tax for the quarter
• explain the significance of the balance of VAT at 30 June 19-4 and how it will be dealt with

Assignment Six

Collection of Data; the VAT Return

GENERAL OBJECTIVES COVERED
C

SKILLS DEVELOPED
Numeracy, information processing, information gathering.

SITUATION
You are working in the accounts department of A-Z Ltd., a small wholesaling company which trades in glass giftware products. The company buys from a number of manufacturers, and sells to shops situated mainly in holiday areas.

Within the accounts department you are responsible for maintaining the purchases day book, sales day book, and the VAT summary (VAT is at the rate of 15 per cent). The following are the company's purchases and sales for the month:

19-1
3 Mar.   Bought goods from Glass Products Ltd. for £650 + VAT (at 15 per cent), invoice no. 1234.
4 Mar.   Sold goods to Sandy Cove Stores for £250 + VAT, invoice no. A456
6 Mar.   Bought goods from Trinket & Co. for £400 + VAT, invoice no. X174.
7 Mar.   Bought goods from Ash Ltd. for £300 + VAT, invoice no. C347.
10 Mar.   Sold goods to Regency & Co. for £360 + VAT, invoice no. A457.
12 Mar.   Sold goods to Eddies Emporium for £200 + VAT, invoice no. A458.
14 Mar.   Bought goods from R. Binns for £450 + VAT, invoice no. 3641.
16 Mar.   Sold goods to Sandy Cove Stores for £350 + VAT, invoice no. A459.
18 Mar.   Sold goods to Aladdin Stores for £180 + VAT, invoice no. A460.
21 Mar.   Bought goods from Glass Products Ltd. for £500 + VAT, invoice no. 1275.
24 Mar.   Sold goods to Spa Road Supplies for £600 + VAT, invoice no. A461.
28 Mar.   Sold goods to Aladdin Stores for £340 + VAT, invoice no. A462.
29 Mar.   Sold goods to Supergoods Ltd. for £520 + VAT, invoice no. A463.
31 Mar.   Sold goods to Sandy Cove Stores for £220 + VAT, invoice no. A464.

STUDENT TASKS

1.   Rule up a purchases day book and a sales day book with VAT columns.

2.   Enter the above transactions, and show the total purchases and sales for the month.

3. Prepare the summary of Value Added Tax for the quarter, taking note of the following transactions:

31 January	VAT on inputs for month	£300
	VAT on outputs for month	£375
28 February	VAT on inputs for month	£450
	VAT on outputs for month	£480

Show the net amount due to H.M. Customs and Excise for the quarter ended 31 March 19-1.

4. Complete the Value Added Tax Return (form VAT 100) below. There were no other transactions involving VAT during March.

Value Added Tax Return

For the period
01 01 -1 to 31 03 -1

HM Customs and Excise

For Official Use

A-Z LTD
STAFFORD STREET
PERRY BARR
BIRMINGHAM
B24 8AP

Registration Number	Period
417 2986 54	03 -1

You could be liable to a financial penalty if your completed return and all the VAT payable are not received by the due date.

Due date: 30 04 -1

For Official Use

Before you fill in this form please read the notes on the back.   Complete all boxes clearly in ink, writing 'none' where necessary. Don't put a dash or leave any box blank. If there are no pence write "00" in the pence column. Do not enter more than one amount in any box.

		£	p
VAT due in this period on **sales** and other outputs	1		
VAT reclaimed in this period on **purchases** and other inputs	2		
Net VAT to be paid to Customs or reclaimed by you (**Difference between boxes 1 and 2**)	3		
Value of **outputs** (pounds only) excluding any VAT	4		00
Value of **inputs** (pounds only) excluding any VAT	5		00

Retail schemes. If you have used any of the schemes in the period covered by this return please enter the appropriate letter(s) in this box.

If you are enclosing a payment please tick (✓) this box.

DECLARATION by the signatory to be completed by or on behalf of the person named above.

I, ...declare that the
(Full name of signatory in BLOCK LETTERS)

information given above is true and complete.

Signature ....Date ....19...........

VAT 100   CD 1911/N1(8.89)   F 3790(JANUARY 1990)

Chapter Twelve
Computers in Finance

The 1980s have seen a major growth in the use of computers in organizations of all sizes. In the 1970s and early 1980s, big mainframe computers were used by larger organizations such as local authorities, public utilities, e.g. gas and electricity, and major companies. Since then the age of the microcomputer, with powerful machines available at relatively low prices, has enabled smaller organizations to computerize some or all of their office routines.

Before the use of computers most aspects of accounting and finance, particularly in smaller organizations, were carried out by hand. However, larger firms and local authorities made use of mechanical accounting machines, but they were large, noisy and prone to breakdown. Now, twenty years after they started to be superseded by computers, such machines seem like the dinosaurs of the accounts department.

Computers, particularly microcomputers, are now used extensively by organizations of all sizes. They are probably at their best when used to handle large quantities of routine data, e.g. preparing invoices to send out to customers, or keeping the accounts of debtors and creditors up-to-date. It is to be hoped that, as part of your studies in Finance, you will have plenty of opportunity to use microcomputers to record transactions.

Computer Hardware

Any organization thinking of purchasing of a computer system has to consider the type of machine (the hardware), and the programs (software).

With regard to the computer itself, there is a distinction between a *mainframe* machine and a *microcomputer:*

- A mainframe computer is a very large machine with enormous capacity: it is likely to be installed as a central computer by organizations such as local authorities, banks, building societies and large companies.

- A microcomputer, a *micro,* is much smaller than a mainframe and is fairly portable; in fact some are designed to be portable and to be used when travelling. It is larger than the games machines that can be connected to a television set and, indeed, some manufacturers have developed games machines into acceptable micros for business use. A microcomputer is likely to be used by small and medium-sized businesses, although many larger businesses also install them for local use.

As it is more than likely that you will be using micros at college, work, or home, we will concentrate on these, although the basic principles also apply to mainframe computers.

The hardware of a computer system consists of:

Microprocessor
This is the heart of the computer, or central processing unit (CPU), where a network of electrical circuits store and manipulate data.

Keyboard
This enables the input of data and instructions to the computer.

Screen
The screen, or monitor, is similar to a television set but is designed specially to give a clear picture. Information contained in the computer is presented in a readable form on the screen.

Disc drive
This is a mechanism which reads information contained on magnetic discs and transmits it at high speed to the computer. Most microcomputers use small 'floppy' discs of 3 inch, 3.5 inch, or 5.25 inch diameter; some use hard discs which have a larger capacity. Mainframe computer systems use hard discs, and high-speed tapes. The cassette tapes used by games machines are considered to be too slow for professional use.

Printer
Most computer systems include a printer which enables information from the computer to be presented in a permanent form that can be read by the human eye. Printers vary in price and quality with, at the lower end of the scale, dot-matrix printers, extending through daisy-wheel printers, to laser printers.

Computer Software

Computer software comprises the programs, or packages, that give the operating instructions to the computer. Programs are contained in magnetic form on a disc which is inserted into the disc drive in order that the instructions can be read and passed to the computer. For accounting use, ready-made programs can be purchased and common applications include:

- stock control
- invoicing
- sales ledger (i.e. the debtors' accounts)
- purchases ledger (i.e. the creditors' accounts)
- general ledger
- payroll (i.e. details of wages and salaries)

Each of these common applications is considered in more detail below.

Other applications include word-processing, spreadsheets and financial planning (e.g. budgets) programs.

Often, nowadays, programs are fully integrated so that a business transaction can be recorded in a number of different accounting records at the same time. For example, when an invoice is prepared for the sale of goods, an integrated program will reduce the stock of goods held and will record, in the sales ledger, that an increased amount is owing by the debtor concerned. Most integrated programs can print out a trial balance and can also produce the financial statements (see Chapter 13) of trading, profit and loss account and balance sheet.

Using Computer Programs

When using computer programs it is usual to *batch* a series of transactions, e.g. to prepare a series of invoices; or to deal with a number of sales ledger transactions, or purchases ledger transactions. By batching there is less need to keep changing the program disc.

At first, entering transactions using a computer is relatively slow because it is necessary to set up a number of *data files*. For example, each customer to whom an organization sells goods needs a separate data file containing the name and address of the customer, credit limit, etc. The data file is usually held in magnetic form on a separate disc from that of the program and, as the computer will need to read information off both at various times, accounting transactions are best done on a computer system which includes twin disc drives. If a single disc drive system is used there will be some changing of discs required as the program is used.

In computer accounting much use is made of numbers to code items. For example, each customer's account in the sales ledger will be given a number; likewise each item of stock that a business sells will have a number. This makes for faster processing of transactions: by entering a number, the particular account or stock item can be displayed on the screen.

Stock Control

Control of stock is an important aspect for any business and the use of a computer program enables the records to be kept up-to-date as stocks are dispatched to customers and received from suppliers. At any one time, therefore, the computer system will be able to show the current stock position. At the same time a stock control system will give the minimum levels of stock that should be held, together with the quantities in which the stock item is re-ordered.

At the centre of a computer stock control program is the *stock file*. This maintains information on the:

- stock number allocated to a particular stock item
- description of the stock item
- name and address of supplier
- re-order level
- quantity of stock currently held
- allocation of stock to known future needs
- value of stock currently held

In addition, stock control programs can print out details of stock that need to be re-ordered and, in some cases, can print the purchase order. Also, the program can identify slow moving stock items, so that management can decide if it is worthwhile to continue stocking these items.

The main 'menu' for a stock control program will appear on the computer screen and will offer a number of choices, e.g.

```
Stock enquiry
Goods received
Goods issued
Reports
Stock updating
```

Selecting each item will take the user to further sub-menus which lead to each section of the stock control program. Thus, for example, a batch of goods received notes can be entered to each stock file.

The most common report to be produced from a stock control program is that showing the *stock status;* i.e. details of how many units of each stock item are in stock, the unit cost, and the total cost of stock held, as on the illustration on the next page:

STOCK STATUS REPORT

Date   30/08/-5   Page 1

Stock number	Description	Quantity	Unit cost (£)	Total value (£)
75001	Red paint: 1 litre tins	200	2.25	450.00
75002	Black paint: 1 litre tins	100	2.25	225.00
75003	Undercoat 1 litre tins	150	2.00	300.00

Other reports available include:

• details of items out-of-stock, or below minimum stock level
• slow moving stock items
• names and addresses of suppliers

Invoicing

Many organizations use a computerised accounting system to produce invoices. Two data files are required for the production of invoices: the first is the customer file, which contains the name, address and account number of the customer; the second is the product file, which contains product details, prices and unit quantities.

To produce an invoice, the computer operator builds up the invoice on the screen. Entered first is the customer's account number (this puts name, address, etc. on screen); then the product code and quantity of goods being sold is entered (these items then appear on screen). Trade discounts and Value Added Tax are calculated by the invoice program.

The on-screen invoice can then either be printed immediately, or it can be stored on disc for later printing of a batch of invoices. Specially prepared stationery is often used for computer-printed invoices; an example is shown in fig. 12.1.

Reports produced by an invoicing program include:

• sales analysis between different products
• sales analysis between customers in different sales territories, e.g. Northern customers, Western customers, etc.
• product lists
• customer lists, i.e. names, addresses, telephone numbers

A computerised invoice program can also be used for the production of credit notes.

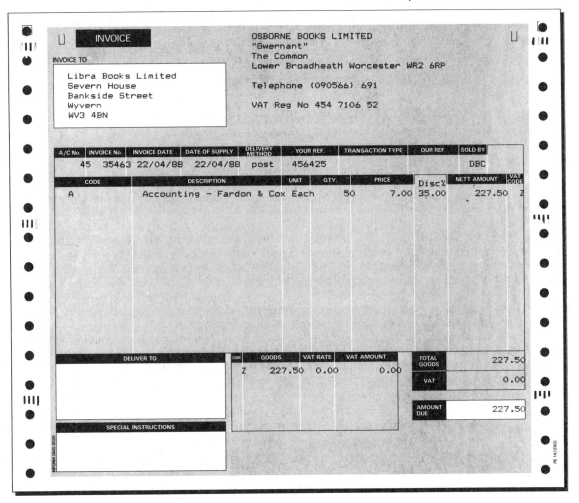

Fig. 12.1 Computer-printed invoice

Sales Ledger

A computerised sales ledger handles all the debtors' accounts, i.e. the customers of the organization. A customer file is maintained for each customer which contains details of name, address, account number, and credit limit.

The main menu for sales ledger opens up by displaying on screen a list of options such as the following:

> Amend customer details
> Insertion of new records
> Deletion of records
> Post transactions
> Reports

Selecting the first of these choices enables amendment of existing customer details, e.g. change of address, increase in credit limit, etc. The second and third choices allow the opening of accounts for new customers or the closing of accounts. Selection of 'post transactions' will lead to a further menu which will be similar to the following:

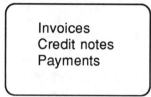

Selecting one of these will enable a batch of invoices, credit notes, or payments to be entered to the sales ledger accounts.

'Reports' from the main menu enables information to be printed from the sales ledger program. This information may be sent out to customers in the form of statements of account, or may be for use of the management of the organization, e.g. aged debtors schedule (see below). Most sales ledger programs can produce the following reports:

- day book listing, showing transactions posted during the day
- statements of account, to be sent to the customer at regular intervals
- aged debtors schedule, showing each debtor balance analysed over the current month and each of the previous two or three months - an example of such a schedule is shown in fig. 12.2
- debtors' letters, printing reminder letters to those customers whose accounts are overdue
- customer lists, giving names and addresses of customers

Osprey Books Ltd

AGED ANALYSIS OF DEBTORS

As at 25/04/-8

Account No.	Customer Name	Balance	Up to 30 days	Over 30 days	Over 60 days	Over 90 days
5	A–Z Books	121.00	0.00	41.00	0.00	80.00
16	Borth Booksellers Ltd.	63.00	20.00	0.00	43.00	0.00
28	The Fladbury Flyleaf	10.40	0.00	5.20	5.20	0.00
33	Lower Broadheath Books	29.96	0.00	3.16	0.00	26.80
58	Northern Books	441.00	68.00	84.00	289.00	0.00
75	Sansome St. Stationers	302.50	168.70	133.80	0.00	0.00
87	Technical Books Supplies	89.90	0.00	0.00	63.20	26.70
97	Wyvern County Books	284.50	143.50	0.00	141.00	0.00
Totals		1 342.26	400.20	267.16	541.40	133.50
Percentage			29.8%	19.9%	40.3%	10.0%

Fig. 12.2   Aged Debtors Schedule

Purchases Ledger

The operation of a purchases ledger is very similar to that of sales ledger, except that it deals with the creditors of the firm or organization. The supplier file maintains for each account details of the name, address, and credit terms allowed by the creditor. As with sales ledger, accounts are updated from batches of invoices and credit notes received, and payments made. Purchases ledger programs can print remittance advices and, for larger organizations, can also print payment cheques and bank giro credits.

Reports include:

* day book listing, showing transactions posted
* ageing creditors' schedule, showing amounts owing to creditors analysed between current month, and each of the previous two or three months
* supplier lists, giving names and addresses of creditors

Payroll

Payroll programs enable the speedy processing of employees' salaries, sick pay, and expenses. The static data held for each employee includes details of name, employee number, National Insurance number, tax code, salary and overtime rates.

The main menu on a payroll program will be similar to the following:

```
Employee details
Parameters
Payroll processing
Reports
```

Selecting the first option enables a new employee to be added or a person who has left to be deleted; also salary and wage rates, tax code, etc. can be changed. The second option 'parameters' includes details of tax codes, National Insurance rates, Statutory Sick Pay figures, that will apply when the program is run - this information changes each year, and the program will need updating. 'Payroll processing' allows information for the current pay period to be inserted, e.g. hours worked, overtime, etc. 'Reports' enables printouts and other information to be obtained from the program.

To process the payroll it is necessary to input information of hours worked for hourly-paid employees; for those earning a salary this information is fixed, but overtime hours will need to be input. The program automatically calculates each employee's gross pay, tax deductions, National Insurance Contributions, and pension contributions.

For each pay period, e.g. week or month, the program can be used to print out pay slips, together with either a cheque or a bank giro credit. Where employees are paid in cash, a notes and coin analysis is printed which shows the quantities of each bank note and coin required to make up employees' pay packets. Where employees are paid by BACS (automatic transfer by bank computer to the employees' bank account) the payroll package will work out all the necessary details.

Printouts and reports include:

* payslips
* cheques, bank giro credits
* notes and coin analysis
* end-of-year summaries of income tax, National Insurance Contributions, and pension deductions
* list of employees, analysed by department

'Hands-on' Experience

Different computers and programs all operate in a different way, although the general approach is similar. There is nothing like 'hands-on' experience with accounting programs as a good learning technique.

You will need to refer to the instruction manual that is supplied with the computer, and also to the specific manual for the accounting program you wish to use. Some of the manuals for accounting programs are very good and include a number of sample transactions to work through: if you decide to follow one of these always try to bear in mind the overall objective of what you are doing, rather than getting too involved in the minor detail of entering a list of names and addresses.

The following is a *general* list of instructions to help you get started but, for specific details, refer to the manuals:

• Switch on the power supply and ensure that the printer (if fitted) has sufficient stationery.

• Insert the program disc that you wish to use into the disc drive (probably drive 1 or A). Get the computer to read the information from this disc and transfer it to its memory. To do this you might need to type in RUN, LOAD ... (name of program), and press the RETURN key. As the program loads the disc drive will operate and a red light on the disc drive will come on.

• Enter the password (to prevent unauthorised access), and the 'main menu' should be displayed.

• From the menu select the kind of processing you wish to do. It may be necessary to set up accounts to work on.

• Insert the disc containing the data files that you wish to work on, e.g. sales ledger, into the disc drive (probably drive 2 or B).

• During processing the program will give various 'prompts' which tell the operator what to do next.

• After processing, any printout required can be undertaken before the program disc and the data file disc (after taking a back-up copy) are removed from the disc drive.

• Switch off. This action will erase everything from the computer's internal memory; however, the work that has been processed will be stored in a magnetic form on the discs and can be read again by the disc drive next time they are needed.

Chapter Summary

❏ Accounting by computer enables an organization to handle the majority of regular routine book-keeping transactions.

❏ Common applications for computerized accounting include stock control, invoicing, sales ledger, purchases ledger, general ledger and payroll.

❏ Don't just read about computers in accounting, get some 'hands on' experience now!

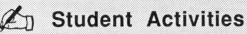

Student Activities

1. List the main types of accounting packages available for use in a microcomputer. Indicate the accounting functions undertaken by each package and state the management reports available from each.

2. Set up the following accounts using a *sales ledger* program in a suitable micro-computer: A. Brown, C. Dennis, E. French and G. Harrison. (Information such as account number, address, credit limit, etc. can be entered as required.) The following transactions are then to be entered:

   5 Feb.   Sold goods to A. Brown £125, invoice no. 2891
   10 Feb. Sold goods to C. Dennis £100, invoice no. 2892
   12 Feb. Sold goods to E. French £80, invoice no. 2893
   15 Feb. Sold goods to G. Harrison £110, invoice no. 2894
   16 Feb. Sold goods to A. Brown £130, invoice no. 2895
   20 Feb. Sold goods to G. Harrison £75, invoice no. 2896
   21 Feb. Sold goods to E. French £65, invoice no. 2897
   23 Feb. Sold goods to A. Brown £55, invoice no. 2898
   26 Feb. Sold goods to C. Dennis £45, invoice no. 2899
   28 Feb. Sold goods to E. French £85, invoice no. 2900

   After entering the transactions, obtain a print-out of the balance of each account, together with a total of sales for the month.

3. Set up the following accounts using a *purchases ledger* program in a suitable micro-computer: M. Nicholls, O. Peters and Q. Radlett. (As before, details can be entered as required). The following transactions are then to be entered:

   8 Apr.   Bought goods from M. Nicholls £55, invoice no. 6789
   12 Apr. Bought goods from O. Peters £125, invoice no. 1245
   15 Apr. Bought goods from Q. Radlett £65, invoice no. A365
   20 Apr. Bought goods from M. Nicholls £110, invoice no. 6810
   22 Apr. Bought goods from Q. Radlett £45, invoice no. A372
   23 Apr. Bought goods from O. Peters £180, invoice no. 1261
   27 Apr. Bought goods from M. Nicholls £85, invoice no. 6831

   After entering the transactions, obtain a print-out of the balance of each account, together with a total of purchases for the month.

4. Using a *payroll* program in a suitable micro-computer, you are to enter the details of the following three employees of your organization at the start of the tax year:

Employee number	Name	Hourly Rate of Pay	Tax Code
B21	Mrs. Jean Box	£3.00	260L
J18	Ms. Janet Jones	£2.75	270L
W15	Mr. T. Waring	£3.50	430H

   During Week 1 each employee worked for 35 hours.

   You are to print out a pay list for Week 1, and produce a pay slip for each employee in Week 1.

Assignment Seven

Wyvern Wholesalers: a Case for Computer Accounting

GENERAL OBJECTIVES COVERED
C

SKILLS DEVELOPED
Information gathering, identifying and tackling problems, communicating.

SITUATION
Wyvern Wholesalers is a wholesaler of toys, games and stationery items. The business was set up four years ago by Andy Carr and has expanded each year since then. It is located at Unit 7, The Business Park, Wyvern, Worcestershire, WR3 2BX.

The business buys goods direct from the manufacturers and is currently dealing with about sixty suppliers. Andy's policy is to buy large quantities of popular items from each supplier at the keenest possible prices. He is then able to pass on the savings to his customers, who number about 400 toy and stationery shops located mainly in the West Midlands.

Since first setting up the business Andy has relied on a manual book-keeping and stock control system. He has also exercised a good deal of personal control over purchases, stock re-ordering, and sales. However, keeping such records has never been his strongest point and errors have been made. For example, he still has a stock of 250 skateboards and is waiting for them to become popular once again. Despite such occasional errors of judgement, the business has expanded rapidly and has now reached the point where he must relinquish some of the routine day-to-day activities in favour of developing the business over the next five years.

He currently employs a full-time book-keeper together with three warehouse staff, a sales representative, and a general clerk. The latter person keeps the business 'ticking over' when Andy is out of the office.

Knowing that you are following a business studies course, Andy asks you to investigate his business systems with a view to introducing computers and replacing the existing handwritten systems. His particular concerns are:

(a)   Although he decides which lines are to be stocked, he hasn't got a suitable system to tell him when to re-order. At present it relies on him going round the warehouse once a week and seeing which stock is running low. Sometimes stock has run out and, as a result, sales have been lost and, most importantly, he has been unable to supply valued customers.

(b)   Sales invoices are prepared once a week by the book-keeper and statements of account are sent out at irregular intervals, when the book-keeper can find the time. This has led to some customers taking a long time to pay. In addition, because things are not properly controlled, a few customers purchasing goods have been given greater credit than he would have wished.

(c)   Payments to suppliers are made when statements are received. This has led to problems in the past because sometimes statements have been mislaid and one supplier reached the point of refusing to deliver more goods to him until payment was made. At that time there was plenty of money in the business bank account, but Andy hadn't realised how much was owing and how far back the debt went.

(d)   When he first set up in business Andy didn't employ any staff; as the business has expanded he has taken on people and, if expansion continues, more will be taken on in the future. When he took on his first employee, Andy handled the pay, tax and National Insurance calculations. He is now finding this task more and more onerous and would like to pass this on to his general clerk. However, as the business takes on more staff, these calculations will take more time.

(e)   With the expansion of his business, he is now borrowing heavily from the bank. The manager of the local branch is more than willing to offer overdraft facilities but must have regular information, on a monthly basis, of sales, purchases, debtors, creditors, and stocks. It takes Andy a long time to extract this information from the manual book-keeping system and, even when he has assembled the figures, he is not sure that they are entirely accurate.

STUDENT TASKS

1.   Using computer and office equipment magazines, you are to find out details and prices of a computer system that would be suitable for Andy's business. Remember that the business is still relatively small and the amount of money spent on the system should be justified in terms of gains by his business both now and in the next few years.

       Tasks 2-5 are to be presented in the form of a report to Andy Carr.

2.   List the hardware required, together with current prices, and add a note addressed to Andy explaining in non-technical language the function of each piece of equipment.

3.   Take each of the concerns that he has expressed above and suggest a suitable software package that would help his business to solve the problem. In particular you should point out the benefits to the business and its customers or suppliers; also point out the information that he, as owner of the business, will get from computerising his systems.

4.   Point out any other computer applications that could be used in his business. Suggest suitable software and indicate the benefits to the business.

5.   Explain to Andy how you would implement the computer systems and any procedures you would adopt during the first months of using the new system. (For example, it is important to keep the existing manual system in operation for the first few months as a 'back-up' to the computer system.)

Chapter Thirteen
Basic Financial Statements

For most business organizations the basic financial statements that are produced at the end of each year's trading comprise:

- Trading Account
- Profit and Loss Account
- Balance Sheet

Each of these can be produced more often than once a year in order to give information to the owner(s) on how the business is progressing. However, it is customary to produce annual, or 'final' accounts for the benefit of the tax authorities, bank manager, and other interested parties. Limited companies also have a legal responsibility to report to their shareholders each year (see Chapter 20). The financial statements of public sector organizations, and non-trading organizations (such as clubs and societies) are considered separately in Chapters 25 and 26 respectively.

Trading Account

The main activity of a trading organization is to buy goods at one price and then to sell the same goods at a higher price. The difference between the two prices represents a profit known as *gross profit*.

Instead of calculating the gross profit on each item bought and sold, the accounting system stores up the totals of all transactions during the year in two separate accounts called *purchases account* and *sales account*. Remember that purchases account and sales account only record the buying and selling of the goods in which the business trades: the purchase of an item for use in the business is capital expenditure and is recorded in the Balance Sheet (see later in this Chapter).

At the end of the business' financial year, which can end at any date - it does not have to be a calendar year - the totals of purchases and sales accounts are used to form the basis of a *trading account*. However, it is also necessary to take account of the stock of goods for resale which is held by most businesses at the beginning of the financial year, and at the year-end.

A trading account is illustrated on the next page, combined, as it normally is, with a profit and loss account.

Profit and Loss Account

In this account are listed the various running expenses (or *revenue expenditure*) of the business. The total of running expenses is deducted from gross profit to give *net profit* for the year.

The layout of the trading account and profit and loss account usually combines the two in the following form, which are the accounts of John Smith who keeps a stationery shop:

TRADING AND PROFIT AND LOSS ACCOUNTS OF JOHN SMITH FOR THE YEAR ENDED 31 DECEMBER 19-1

	£	£
Sales		155 000
Opening stock (1 January 19-1)	12 500	
Purchases	105 000	
	117 500	
Less Closing stock (31 December 19-1)	10 500	
Cost of Goods Sold		107 000
Gross Profit		48 000
Less:		
Salaries	23 500	
Heating and lighting	6 200	
Rent and rates	5 800	
Sundry expenses	500	
		36 000
Net Profit		12 000

- The trading account forms the first half of the account, as far as gross profit, while the profit and loss account is the second half of the account.

- Stock is valued by the business, and often verified by the auditor, at the end of each financial year. This figure forms the closing stock for that year and, also, the opening stock for the following financial year. Techniques of stock valuation are discussed in Chapter 17.

- The figure for *cost of goods sold* represents the cost to the business of the goods which have been sold in this financial year. Cost of goods sold is opening stock, plus purchases, minus closing stock.

- The various running expenses shown in the profit and loss section can be listed to suit the needs of a particular business: the headings used here are for illustrative purposes only.

- Net profit belongs to the owner(s) of the business.

Balance Sheet

A balance sheet is a different type of financial statement from the trading account and the profit and loss account. These two accounts show two types of profit - gross profit and net profit respectively - *for the financial year* (or such other time period as may be chosen by the business). A balance sheet, on the other hand, shows the state of the business *at one moment in time*. It lists the *assets* (amounts owned by the business) and the *liabilities* (amounts owed by the business) at a particular date. For example:

BALANCE SHEET OF JOHN SMITH AS AT 31 DECEMBER 19-1

	£	£
Fixed Assets		
Premises		100 000
Machinery		20 000
		120 000
Current Assets		
Stock	10 500	
Debtors	15 500	
Bank	450	
Cash	50	
	26 500	
Less Current Liabilities		
Creditors	16 500	
Working Capital*		10 000
NET ASSETS		130 000
FINANCED BY		
Capital		
Opening capital		75 000
Add net profit		12 000
		87 000
Less drawings		7 000
		80 000
Long-Term Liabilities		
Loan from bank		50 000
		130 000

* Working capital (see Chapter 18) = current assets, less current liabilities.

There are a number of points to note in connection with a balance sheet:

Fixed assets and current assets
The assets are divided between those which are *fixed* and those which are *current*.

Fixed assets comprise the long-term items owned by a business which are not bought with the intention of early resale, e.g. premises, machinery, motor vehicles, office equipment, fixtures and fittings, etc. When a business buys new fixed assets, such expenditure is called *capital expenditure,* in contrast to *revenue expenditure* which is the running cost of the business charged to profit and loss account.

Current assets comprise short-term assets which change regularly, e.g. stocks, debtors (amounts owed to the business by customers), bank balances and cash. Each one of these items will alter as the business trades, e.g. stocks will be sold, or more will be bought; debtors will make payment to the business, or sales on credit will be made; the cash and bank balances will alter with the flow of money paid into the bank account, or as withdrawals are made.

By tradition, assets are listed starting with the most permanent, i.e. premises, and working through to the most liquid, i.e. nearest to cash: either cash itself, or the balance at the bank.

Current liabilities
These are liabilities which are due for repayment *within twelve months* of the date of the balance sheet, e.g. creditors (amounts owed by the business to suppliers), and bank overdraft (which is technically repayable on demand, unlike a bank loan which is negotiated for a particular time period).

Net assets

This shows the net amount of assets used by the business, i.e. fixed and current assets, less current liabilities. The net assets are financed by the owner(s) of the business, in the form of capital, and by means of loans, such as bank loans. The total of the net assets therefore equals the total of the 'Financed by' section, i.e. the balance sheet 'balances'.

Capital

Capital is the owner(s) investment, and is a liability of a business, i.e. it is what the business owes the owner. It is important to realise that the assets and liabilities of a business are treated separately from the *personal* assets and liabilities of the owner(s) of the business. For example, if a group of people decided to set up in business they would each agree to put in a certain amount of capital to start the business. As individuals they regard their capital as an investment, i.e. an asset which may, at some time, be repaid to them. From the point of view of the business, the capital is a liability, because it is owed back to the owner(s). In practice, it is unlikely to be repaid, for then the business would cease to operate.

To the owner(s)' capital is added net profit for the year, while *drawings*, the amount withdrawn by the owner(s) during the year, is deducted. (Note: drawings must *not* be included amongst the expenses in the profit and loss account.) This calculation leaves a closing capital at the balance sheet date which is added to the other long-term liabilities of the business.

Long-term liabilities

Such liabilities are where repayment is due *in more than one year* from the date of the balance sheet; they are often described as 'bank loan', 'medium-term loan' or 'long-term loan'.

The Trial Balance

In a subject such as Finance we are not concerned with the detail of recording day-to-day transactions in the accounting records: this is the task of the book-keeper. Instead we are concerned with using the figures produced by the book-keeper to prepare financial statements which can then be of benefit to the management of the business. The book-keeper's role is to record day-to-day transactions by means of handwritten or computer systems. Every so often, the book-keeper will prove the accuracy of the work by extracting a trial balance of all the accounts in the books. For example, John Smith's book-keeper will extract the following:

TRIAL BALANCE OF JOHN SMITH AS AT 31 DECEMBER 19-1

	Debit £	Credit £
Stock at 1 January 19-1	12 500	
Purchases	105 000	
Sales		155 000
Salaries	23 500	
Heating and lighting	6 200	
Rent and rates	5 800	
Sundry expenses	500	
Premises	100 000	
Machinery	20 000	
Debtors	15 500	
Bank	450	
Cash	50	
Capital		75 000
Drawings	7 000	
Loan from bank		50 000
Creditors		16 500
	296 500	296 500

Note: Stock at 31 December 19-1 was valued at £10 500.

The trial balance will be produced more often than once a year in order to 'prove' the arithmetical accuracy of the transactions recorded by the book-keeper. It will also be produced at the end of a financial year (as is the above trial balance) in order that the year-end financial statements can be prepared.

What the trial balance tells us is the balance of each accounting record kept by the business, and lists the balances into accounts with debit balances, and accounts with credit balances.

Debit balances

These comprise *assets* of the business, and *expenses* representing totals of purchases made or the cost of benefits received for the year to date. Thus the debit (left-hand) column indicates that this business has made purchases of goods at a cost of £105 000 during the year. While salaries is an expense it has been spent on a benefit: the business has gained the use of workers' time at a cost of £23 500. The balances for premises, machinery, stock, debtors, cash and bank indicate, in money terms, an asset of the business. The debtors' figure includes the individual balances of all the firm's debtors, i.e. those customers who owe money to the firm.

Credit balances

These comprise *liabilities* of the business, and *income* amounts, including the total of sales for the year to date. For example, the sales figure shows the total amount of goods that has been sold by the business during the year. The figures for capital, loan from the bank and the creditors shows the amount of the liability at the trial balance date. The creditors figure includes all the individual balances of the business' creditors, i.e. those suppliers to whom the business owes money.

Preparation of Financial Statements from a Trial Balance

Starting from a trial balance extracted by the book-keeper at the end of the financial year, and with a note of the year-end stock valuation, we can prepare the trading and profit and loss accounts, and the balance sheet. It is a case of picking out the information needed for each of these final accounts. You should note the following points very carefully:

- Each item from the trial balance appears in the final accounts *once only* . It is a good idea, at first, to note in which final account each item appears and then to 'tick' each figure as you use it.

- The year-end (closing) stock figure is not listed in the trial balance, but is shown as a note to the trial balance. The figure for closing stock appears *twice* in the final accounts: firstly in the trading account, and secondly in the balance sheet (as a current asset).

Vertical and Horizontal Presentations of Final Accounts

So far we have used the *vertical presentation* for setting out the final accounts of a business, i.e. we started at the top of the page and worked downwards in a narrative style. An alternative method is the *horizontal presentation*, where each of the financial statements has a definite left and right-hand side. The set of final accounts presented earlier would appear, in horizontal style, as shown on the next page.

TRADING ACCOUNT OF JOHN SMITH
FOR THE YEAR ENDED 31 DECEMBER 19-1

	£		£
Opening stock (1 January 19-1)	12 500	Sales	155 000
Purchases	105 000		
	117 500		
Less Closing stock			
(31 December 19-1)	10 500		
Cost of Goods Sold	107 000		
Gross Profit	48 000		
	155 000		155 000

PROFIT AND LOSS ACCOUNT OF JOHN SMITH
FOR THE YEAR ENDED 31 DECEMBER 19-1

	£		£
Salaries	23 500	Gross profit	48 000
Heating and lighting	6 200		
Rent and rates	5 800		
Sundry expenses	500		
	36 000		
Net profit	12 000		
	48 000		48 000

BALANCE SHEET OF JOHN SMITH AS AT 31 DECEMBER 19-1

	£	£		£
Fixed Assets			**Capital**	
Premises		100 000	Opening capital	75 000
Machinery		20 000	Add net profit	12 000
		120 000		87 000
			Less drawings	7 000
Current Assets				80 000
Stock	10 500		**Long-term Liabilities**	
Debtors	15 500		Loan from bank	50 000
Bank	450			
Cash	50		**Current Liabilities**	
		26 500	Creditors	16 500
		146 500		146 500

In your study of Finance you will see both forms of presentation from time to time in the accounts of different businesses and organizations. It should be noted, however, that the vertical format is more common, and will be used as the standard format in this book. As you will readily appreciate, both use the same information and, after a while, you are soon able to 'read' either version.

Chapter Summary

❑ The year-end financial statements of a business comprise:
  • *trading account,* which shows gross profit
  • *profit and loss account,* which shows net profit
  • *balance sheet,* which shows the assets and liabilities of the business at the year-end

❑ The starting-point for the preparation of 'final accounts' is the book-keeper's trial balance

❑ Each item from the trial balance is entered into the 'final accounts' once only

❑ The trial balance is divided between debit balances (representing assets and expenses), and credit balances (representing liabilities, owner's capital and income)

There is more material to cover in connection with year-end accounts, and the next few Chapters (numbers 14 to 17) give further detail. The final accounts can also be analysed and interpreted (see Chapter 18) to give the user of the accounts information about the financial state of the business. In addition, the more specialist final accounts of partnerships and limited companies are covered in Chapters 19 and 20 respectively.

✍ Student Activities

You are training as a Chartered Accountant and, as part of your work, you are required to draft the final accounts of a number of clients. During the month you deal with six businesses.

1.   Prepare a trading and profit and loss account for 'Speedoprint' for the year ended 31 December 19-8 from the following information:

	£
Opening stock	10 500
Closing stock	9 000
Purchases	52 500
Sales	75 250
Selling expenses	4 750
Administration expenses	7 850
Sundry expenses	1 750

2.   Your next client is Parisien Perfumerie. Prepare a balance sheet as at 31 December 19-8 from the following information, using headings for fixed assets, current assets, current liabilities, capital and long-term liabilities:

	£
Capital at start of year	25 000
Premises	31 000
Stock at end of year	5 450
Net profit for year	6 430
Creditors	3 280
Cash	70
Vehicles	4 850
Debtors	4 655
Office equipment	2 200
Medium term loan from bank	19 500
Bank balance	2 110
Drawings for year	3 875

3. The following trial balance has been extracted by the book-keeper of John Adams at 31 December 19-8:

	£	£
Stock at 1 January 19-8	14 350	
Purchases	114 472	
Sales		259 688
Rates	13 718	
Heating and lighting	12 540	
Wages and salaries	42 614	
Motor vehicle expenses	5 817	
Advertising	6 341	
Premises	75 000	
Office equipment	33 000	
Motor vehicles	21 500	
Debtors	23 854	
Bank	1 235	
Cash	125	
Capital at 1 January 19-8		62 500
Drawings	12 358	
Loan from bank		35 000
Creditors		19 736
	376 924	376 924

Stock at 31 December 19-8 was valued at £16 280.

You are to prepare the trading and profit and loss accounts of John Adams for the year ended 31 December 19-8, together with his balance sheet at that date.

4. The following trial balance has been extracted by the book-keeper of Clare Lewis at 31 December 19-8:

	£	£
Debtors	18 600	
Creditors		13 350
Bank overdraft		4 610
Capital at 1 January 19-8		25 250
Sales		144 810
Purchases	96 318	
Stock at 1 January 19-8	16 010	
Salaries	18 465	
Heating and lighting	1 820	
Rent and rates	5 647	
Motor vehicles	9 820	
Office equipment	5 500	
Sundry expenses	845	
Motor vehicle expenses	1 684	
Drawings	13 311	
	188 020	188 020

Stock at 31 December 19-8 was valued at £13 735.

You are to prepare the trading and profit and loss accounts of Clare Lewis for the year ended 31 December 19-8, together with her balance sheet at that date.

5. The trial balance of Alan Harris, who runs a bookshop, has been prepared by his book-keeper at 31 December 19-8, as follows:

	£	£
Capital		25 000
Premises	35 000	
Fixtures and fittings	1 000	
Motor vehicle	2 500	
Purchases	50 000	
Sales		85 500
Vehicle expenses	850	
Stock at 1 January 19-8	5 000	
General expenses	800	
Rates	1 200	
Debtors	1 350	
Creditors		7 550
Assistants' wages	9 550	
Bank	2 100	
Cash	600	
Drawings	8 100	
	118 050	118 050

Stock at 31 December 19-8 was valued at £8 100.

You are to prepare the trading and profit and loss accounts of Alan Harris for the year ended 31 December 19-8, together with his balance sheet at that date.

6. Your last client is 'The Village Stores'. The trial balance at 31 December 19-8 is as follows:

	£	£
Premises	45 000	
Shop fittings	5 000	
Stock at 1 January 19-8	4 350	
Debtors	870	
Creditors		2 860
Motor vehicle	3 500	
Rates	1 750	
Heating and lighting	840	
Telephone	260	
General expenses	795	
Repairs	220	
Purchases	33 850	
Sales		41 730
Bank overdraft		2 840
Cash	65	
Loan from bank		25 000
Drawings	5 930	
Capital		30 000
	102 430	102 430

Stock at 31 December 19-8 was valued at £5 120

You are to prepare the trading and profit and loss accounts of The Village Stores for the year ended 31 December 19-8, together with a balance sheet at that date.

Chapter Fourteen
Accruals and Prepayments

In the last Chapter, we prepared the basic financial statements - trading and profit and loss accounts, and balance sheet - from the trial balance. It often happens that a number of adjustments need to be made to the trial balance figures so that the financial statements show a more accurate view of the state of the business. This and the next two chapters, are concerned with a number of such adjustments. This chapter is concerned with the accrual and prepayment of expenses and also deals with returned goods, and discount allowed and received.

To illustrate the effect of adjustments on the final accounts we shall, throughout this and the next two chapters, be referring to the following set of accounts of Heather Lewis, who owns an antiques shop:

TRADING AND PROFIT AND LOSS ACCOUNTS OF HEATHER LEWIS
FOR THE YEAR ENDED 31 DECEMBER 19-5

	£	£
Sales		60 000
Opening stock	5 000	
Purchases	40 000	
	45 000	
Less Closing stock	6 000	
Cost of Goods sold		39 000
Gross Profit		21 000
Less:		
Rent and rates	4 000	
Salaries	10 000	
Heating and lighting	1 000	
Sundry expenses	1 000	
		16 000
Net Profit		5 000

BALANCE SHEET OF HEATHER LEWIS AS AT 31 DECEMBER 19-5

	£	£
Fixed Assets		
Fixtures and fittings		2 000
Delivery van		4 000
		6 000
Current Assets		
Stock	6 000	
Debtors	2 000	
Bank	500	
	8 500	
Less Current Liabilities		
Creditors	3 000	
Working Capital		5 500
NET ASSETS		11 500
FINANCED BY		
Capital		
Opening capital		10 000
Add net profit		5 000
		15 000
Less drawings		3 500
		11 500

Accrual of Expenses

In the profit and loss accounts that have been prepared so far we have taken the trial balance figure for each expense and listed it in the profit and loss account. The book-keeper records the expenses as they take place and this means that, when an expense has been paid, it will be entered in the accounting system.

For example, the trial balance of Heather Lewis would have shown a debit balance of £1 000 for heating and lighting. However, Heather tells us that, on 1 January 19-6, i.e. on the first day of her new financial year, she received an electricity bill for £250 covering the period of the last quarter of 19-5. An adjustment needs to be made in her final accounts for 19-5 to record this *accrued expense*.

Accruals of expenses are money amounts which are due but unpaid at the financial year-end.

Accrued amounts must be:

• added to the expense from the trial balance before showing it in the profit and loss account

• added to current liabilities in the year-end balance sheet

In the above example, therefore, the total cost of £1 250 for heating and lighting will be shown in profit and loss account, while £250 will be shown as a separate current liability 'heating and lighting accrued £250' in the year-end balance sheet.

The reason for dealing with accruals in this way is to ensure that the profit and loss account records the cost that has been *incurred* for the year, instead of only the amount that has been *paid*. The year-end balance sheet shows a liability for the amount that is due, but unpaid.

Prepayment of Expenses

A prepayment is a money amount which is paid in advance.

A prepayment, therefore, is the opposite of an accrual: with a prepayment of expenses, some part of the expense has been paid in advance.

For example, Heather Lewis tells you that the figure for rent and rates amounting to £4 000 includes the rent on the shop for January 19-6, amounting to £200. An adjustment must, therefore, be made in her final accounts for 19-5 to take note of this *prepaid expense*. The amount of the prepayment will be:

• deducted from the expense before showing it in profit and loss account
• added to current assets in the year-end balance sheet

In the above example, therefore, the cost of rent and rates will be shown in the profit and loss account as £3 800, while £200 will be shown as a separate current asset (coming after debtors, but before bank and cash balances) 'rent prepaid £200' in the year-end balance sheet.

Case Problem: Accruals and Prepayments - Heather Lewis

Situation

We must now show the effect of the two adjustments in the final accounts of Heather Lewis. We are taking note of the following items at 31 December 19-5:

• heating and lighting expenses accrued of £250
• rent prepaid £200

Solution

TRADING AND PROFIT AND LOSS ACCOUNTS OF HEATHER LEWIS FOR THE YEAR ENDED 31 DECEMBER 19-5

	£	£
Sales		60 000
Opening stock	5 000	
Purchases	40 000	
	45 000	
Less Closing stock	6 000	
Cost of Goods sold		39 000
Gross Profit		21 000
Less:		
Rent and rates £4 000 - £200	3 800	
Salaries	10 000	
Heating and lighting £1 000 + £250	1 250	
Sundry expenses	1 000	
		16 050
Net Profit		4 950

Note: the figures on the shaded background are shown here *for illustrative purposes only;* they would not normally appear in the final accounts.

BALANCE SHEET OF HEATHER LEWIS AS AT 31 DECEMBER 19-5

	£	£	£
Fixed Assets			
Fixtures and fittings			2 000
Delivery van			4 000
			6 000
Current Assets			
Stock		6 000	
Debtors		2 000	
Rent prepaid		200	
Bank		500	
		8 700	
Less: Current Liabilities			
Creditors	3 000		
Heating and lighting accrued	250		
		3 250	
Working Capital			5 450
NET ASSETS			11 450
FINANCED BY			
Capital			
Opening capital			10 000
Add net profit			4 950
			14 950
Less drawings			3 500
			11 450

Notes:

- The effect of taking note of accruals and prepayments is to alter the net profit. Thus:

Net profit (before adjustments)	£5 000
Add rent prepaid	£200
	£5 200
Less heating and lighting accrued	£250
Net profit (after adjustments)	£4 950

- A third money column has been used in the balance sheet to list the two current liabilities; the amounts are sub-totalled in the middle column when the sub-total can be deducted from the current assets.

Income and Expenditure Accounting

The reason for making adjustments for accruals and prepayments is to ensure that the profit and loss account shows the correct amount of the expense for the financial year, i.e. what should have been paid, instead of what has actually been paid. By recording what should have been paid we are adopting the principle of *income and expenditure accounting:* the expenses due for the year are related to the income that is due. If we simply used the trial balance figures, which show the payment amounts, we would be following the principle of *receipts and payments accounting,* i.e. comparing money coming in, with money going out.

The principle of income and expenditure accounting is applied in the same way to purchases and sales figures, although no adjustment is needed because of the way in which these two are handled in the accounting records. For purchases of goods for resale, the amount is normally entered in the accounts when the supplier's invoice is received, although the agreement to buy will be contained in the legal contract which exists between buyer and seller. Thus, from an accounting viewpoint, it is receipt of the supplier's invoice that causes an accounting entry to be made; the subsequent payment is handled as a different accounting transaction. Therefore a business could have bought goods, not paid for any of them, but will have a purchases figure to enter into the trading account - however, the creditors will soon be wanting their payment.

Sales are recorded when the invoice for the goods is sent, rather than when payment is made; thus applying the principle of income and expenditure accounting. Likewise, a business could have made a large amount of sales, which will be entered in the trading account, but may not yet have received any payments.

Case Problem: Accruals and Prepayments

Situation
How would you deal with each of the following situations in the profit and loss account, and balance sheet of a business at the financial year-end of 31 December 19-1?

- Rental payable on a photocopier is £100 per month; at the end of December eleven payments have been made, while the payment due in December is made during the first few days of January 19-2.

- Property insurance paid amounting to £500 covers the period from 1 January 19-1 to 31 March 19-2.

- The trial balance shows heating and lighting costs to be £725; in early January 19-2 a gas bill is received for £145 covering the quarter ended 31 December 19-1.

Solution

- Photocopier rental is recorded in the profit and loss account as £1 200; in the balance sheet, show a current liability of accrued expense for £100.

- Insurance is recorded in the profit and loss account as £400; a prepayment of £100 is shown as a current asset in the balance sheet.

- Heating and lighting in the profit and loss account £870; a current liability of £145 for the accrued expense.

Returns Inwards and Returns Outwards

We must now consider the aspect of returned goods (see also Chapter 8) which affects the trading account. A trial balance may include amounts for returns inwards and returns outwards, as well as figures for purchases and sales.

Returns inwards (also known as sales returns) represent goods which have been sold by the business and then, for whatever reason, have been returned. The logical step is to deduct these items from the sales figure. This is done in the trading account when it is prepared. For accounting purposes during the year returns inwards are recorded as and when they occur:

- as a deduction from the account of the relevant debtor in the sales ledger, i.e. the debtor now owes a smaller amount

- separately, in a returns inwards account, in the general ledger; the total of the account will appear in the debit column of the trial balance

Returns outwards (or purchases returns) occur when a business returns unsatisfactory purchases to the supplier. Here the logical step is to deduct the figure from purchases in the trading account. For accounting purposes they are recorded when they occur:

- as a deduction from the account of the creditor (in the purchases ledger) from whom the business has bought the goods, i.e. a smaller amount is now owing to the creditor

- separately in a returns outwards account in the general ledger, appearing in the credit column of the trial balance

At the end of a business' financial year, the total amount of each returns account for the year must be deducted from the purchases or sales account (as appropriate) in the trading account.

Case Problem: Returns Inwards and Returns Outwards

Situation

Bill Bowen's business has the following figures in the trial balance at 31 December 19-7:

TRIAL BALANCE (EXTRACT) OF BILL BOWEN
AS AT 31 DECEMBER 19-7

	DEBIT	CREDIT
	£	£
Stock at 1 January 19-7	7 500	
Purchases	65 000	
Sales		113 000
Returns inwards	500	
Returns outwards		1 000
etc.		

At 31 December 19-7 the closing stock is valued at £10 000.
Prepare the trading account for the year ended 31 December 19-7.

Solution

TRADING ACCOUNT OF BILL BOWEN
FOR THE YEAR ENDED 31 DECEMBER 19-7

	£	£	£
Sales			113 000
Less Returns in			500
			112 500
Opening stock (1 January 19-7)		7 500	
Purchases	65 000		
Less Returns out	1 000		
		64 000	
		71 500	
Less Closing stock (31 December 19-7)		10 000	
Cost of Goods sold			61 500
Gross Profit			51 000

Note that returns in is deducted from sales giving a figure of £112 500 for net sales; similarly returns out is deducted from purchases to give a figure of £64 000 for net purchases.

Discount Allowed and Discount Received

A final topic to cover in this Chapter is how cash discounts (*not* trade discount) *allowed* and *received* appear in the trial balance and in the financial statements. As you will remember from Chapter 7, 'Commercial Documents', a cash discount is often offered by a supplier to encourage prompt settlement by the buyer. The distinction between discounts allowed and received is:

- **discount allowed** - the amount of cash discount given by an organization to encourage its debtors to pay promptly

- **discount received** - the amount of cash discount taken by an organization when it settles with its creditors promptly

Many organizations, therefore, will be both allowing *and* receiving cash discount. In the book-keeping system, the two must be kept separately in their respective accounts. Sometimes a cash book, as we have seen in Chapter 9, can be modified to include an additional column on each side to record cash discount. At the end of every month the total of each column is transferred either to discount allowed account (the total of the column on the *receipts* side of the cash book, i.e. we have allowed discount), or to discount received account (the total from the payments side, i.e. we have received discount). Whatever method is used, the trial balance will have a figure for each account, with discount allowed on the *debit* side (as an expense), and discount received on the *credit* side (as income). At the end of a financial year the total of these two accounts are entered in the profit and loss account, with discount allowed shown as an *expense,* and discount received as *income* which is added to the gross profit.

Case Problem: Discount Allowed and Discount Received

Situation

Bill Bowen's business (see previous Case Problem) has the following figures in the trial balance at 31 December 19-7:

TRIAL BALANCE (EXTRACT) OF BILL BOWEN
AS AT 31 DECEMBER 19-7

	DEBIT	CREDIT
	£	£
Discount allowed	1 250	
Discount received		1 000
Expenses (various)	32 500	
etc.		

Prepare the profit and loss account for the year ended 31 December 19-7, starting with the gross profit (see previous Case Problem) of £51 000.

Solution

**PROFIT AND LOSS ACCOUNT OF BILL BOWEN
FOR THE YEAR ENDED 31 DECEMBER 19-7**

	£	£
Gross Profit (see previous Case Problem)		51 000
Add discount received		1 000
		52 000
Less:		
Discount allowed	1 250	
Expenses (various)	32 500	
		33 750
Net Profit		18 250

Chapter Summary

❏ Financial statements should be prepared on the income and expenditure basis rather than the receipts and payments basis.

❏ An adjustment must be made at the end of a financial year in respect of accruals and prepayments of expense items.

❏ The balance sheet, too, must record accruals and prepayments of expenses as current liabilities and current assets respectively.

❏ The total of returns outwards for the year is deducted from purchases in the trading account to give net purchases for the year; similarly the total of returns inwards is deducted from sales to give net sales.

❏ Discount allowed is shown as an expense in profit and loss account, while discount received is a source of additional income, added to gross profit.

Accruals and prepayments are just one of the adjustments made at the end of a financial year in order to present the financial statements more accurately. The next Chapter continues the theme by considering depreciation of fixed assets.

Student Activities

1. Explain how the following would be dealt with in the profit and loss account, and balance sheet of a business with a financial year-end of 31 December 19-2.

    (a) Wages and salaries paid to 31 December 19-2 amount to £55 640. However, at that date, £1 120 is owing: this amount is paid on 4 January 19-3.

    (b) Rates totalling £3 565 have been paid to cover the period 1 January 19-2 to 31 March 19-3.

    (c) A computer is rented at a cost of £150 per month. The rental for January 19-2 was paid in December 19-1 and is included in the total payments during 19-1 which amount to £1 950.

2. You work for Don Smith who runs a wholesale stationery business. The book-keeper has extracted the following trial balance at 31 December 19-4:

	£	£
Debtors	24 325	
Creditors		19 684
Capital		30 000
Bank		1 083
Rent and rates	10 862	
Electricity	2 054	
Telephone	1 695	
Salaries	55 891	
Motor vehicles	22 250	
Office equipment	7 500	
Motor vehicle expenses	10 855	
Drawings	15 275	
Discount allowed	478	
Discount received		591
Purchases	138 960	
Sales		257 258
Stock at 1 January 19-4	18 471	
	308 616	308 616

You are to prepare the trading and profit and loss accounts of Don Smith for the year ended 31 December 19-4, together with his balance sheet at that date, taking into account the following:

- Stock at 31 December 19-4 was valued at £14 075
- At 31 December 19-4 rates are prepaid £250
- At 31 December 19-4 electricity owing £110
- At 31 December 19-4 salaries are owing £365

3. The following trial balance has been extracted by the book-keeper of John Barclay at 30 June 19-6:

	£	£
Sales		864 321
Purchases	600 128	
Returns inwards	2 746	
Returns outwards		3 894
Office expenses	33 947	
Salaries	122 611	
Motor vehicle expenses	36 894	
Discounts allowed	3 187	
Discounts received		4 951
Debtors and creditors	74 328	63 416
Stock at 1 July 19-5	63 084	
Motor vehicles	83 500	
Office equipment	23 250	
Land and buildings	100 000	
Bank loan		75 000
Bank	1 197	
Capital		155 000
Drawings	21 710	
	1 166 582	1 166 582

Notes at 30 June 19-6:
- Stock was valued at £66 941
- Motor vehicle expenses owing £1 250
- Office expenses prepaid £346

You are to prepare the trading and profit and loss accounts of John Barclay for the year ended 30 June 19-6, together with his balance sheet at that date.

4.   You work as book-keeper to Cindy Hayward who runs a delicatessen shop. You have produced the
following trial balance at the end of the financial year on 30 June 19-5:

	£	£
Capital		20 932
Purchases	148 500	
Sales		210 900
Repairs to buildings	848	
Delivery van	5 000	
Van expenses	1 540	
Land and buildings	85 000	
Loan from bank		50 000
Bank balance	540	
Shop fittings	2 560	
Wages and salaries	30 280	
Discounts allowed	135	
Discounts received		1 319
Rates and insurance	2 690	
Debtors	3 175	
Creditors		8 295
Heating and lighting	3 164	
General expenses	2 170	
Returns in	855	
Returns out		1 221
Stock at 1 July 19-4	6 210	
	292 667	292 667

Notes at 30 June 19-5:
• Stock was valued at £7 515
• Rates prepaid £255
• Wages owing £560
• Van expenses owing £85

You are to prepare the trading and profit and loss accounts of Cindy Hayward for the year ended 30
June 19-5, together with her balance sheet at that date.

Assignment Eight

Using the Trial Balance: Southtown Supplies

GENERAL OBJECTIVES COVERED
D, E.

SKILLS DEVELOPED
Numeracy, information processing.

SITUATION
You work in the accounts department of Southtown Supplies, a wholesaling business. At 31 December 19-3, the end of the financial year, the book-keeper extracts the following list of balances:

	£
Stock at 1 January 19-3	70 000
Purchases	280 000
Sales	420 000
Returns inwards	6 000
Returns outwards	4 500
Discount received	750
Discount allowed	500
Heating and lighting	13 750
Salaries	35 600
Post and packing	1 400
Premises	120 000
Fixtures and fittings	45 000
Debtors	55 000
Creditors	47 000
Bank	5 000
Capital	195 000
Drawings	35 000

STUDENT TASKS

1. From the list of balances above, prepare a trial balance at 31 December 19-3.

2. Using the trial balance and taking into account the following points, prepare appropriate financial statements for the year ended 31 December 19-3, including a year-end balance sheet:

   • Closing stock is valued at £60 000
   • Heating and lighting owing at the year-end is £350
   • Salaries prepaid at the year-end amount to £400

3. A junior clerk sees the financial statements you have prepared and comments that he doesn't understand them. After all, as he points out, you have prepared a trial balance and then arranged the figures in a different way and called them 'financial statements'. Write your explanation of why separate financial statements have been prepared and the purpose served by each.

4. Your supervisor asks you to compile a list of names and addresses of people and organizations who will be interested in the financial statements once they have been audited. Annotate the list with brief reasons as to why the person or organization concerned will want to see the results.

Chapter Fifteen
Depreciation of Fixed Assets

Fixed assets, for example machinery and vehicles, reduce in value as time goes by, largely as a result of wear and tear. While we are concerned in this Chapter with depreciation of fixed assets owned by businesses, the same principles apply to items that are owned by other types of organizations, and also by individuals. You may be thinking of buying a car in the next year or so, and people will be quick to tell you that you are spending your money on a 'depreciating asset'.

Depreciation represents the estimate of the amount of the fall in value of fixed assets.

In finance we need to adjust the profit and loss account by showing the year's depreciation of fixed assets as an expense: in this way net profit is reduced. At the same time the value of the fixed assets shown in the balance sheet must be reduced to reflect the amount that they have depreciated. The reason for making these adjustments for depreciation is because the business has had the use of the assets during the year. Compare this with a business that chooses to rent a machine, instead of buying. Here rental payments to the hire company would be recorded in profit and loss account. On the same basis, a business that buys a machine must include the estimated fall in value in profit and loss account, so that a more accurate profit figure is shown. In the balance sheet, fixed assets are reduced in value to indicate their approximate 'true' value.

You might be wondering if buildings need to be depreciated - such assets would seem to rise in value rather than fall. However, buildings do 'wear out' over time and need to be knocked down and replaced; it is only the land that doesn't need depreciating (except for quarries and mines). Land and buildings are sometimes increased in value from time-to-time, i.e. a revaluation takes place, and this is recorded in the accounts.

Methods of Calculating Depreciation

There are several different ways in which we can allow for the fall in value of fixed assets. All of these are *estimates,* and it is only when the asset is sold will we know the accuracy of the estimate (see also later in this Chapter).

The two main methods of calculating depreciation are:

- straight-line method
- reducing balance method

Straight-Line Method

A fixed percentage is written off the *original cost* of the asset as the depreciation amount each year. For example, a machine costs £2 000 and it is decided to depreciate it at twenty per cent each year by the straight-line method. The depreciation amount for *each year* is:

£2 000 x 20% = £400 per year

The depreciation percentage will be decided by an individual business on the basis of how long it considers the asset will last. Different classes of fixed assets are often depreciated at different rates, i.e. motor vehicles will be depreciated at a different rate to office equipment, and so on.

An alternative method of calculating straight-line depreciation (taking into account the asset's estimated value on resale) is:

cost of asset - estimated residual sale proceeds
      number of years' expected use of asset

For example, a computer system is purchased for £2 000 and will be sold after three years' use for an estimated amount of £500. The straight-line depreciation amount is:

£2 000 - £500 = £500 per year
   3 years

Reducing Balance Method

With this method, each year a fixed percentage is written off the *reduced balance,* i.e. after deducting the previous years' depreciation amount from the cost of the asset. For example, a car is purchased for £8 000 and it is decided to depreciate it by twenty-five per cent each year by the reducing balance method. The depreciation amounts for the first three years of ownership are:

Original cost	£8 000
Year 1 depreciation: 25% of £8 000	£2 000
Value at end of year 1	£6 000
Year 2 depreciation: 25% of £6 000	£1 500
Value at end of year 2	£4 500
Year 3 depreciation: 25% of £4 500	£1 125
Value at end of year 3	£3 375
	and so on

Case Problem: Comparison of Straight-line and Reducing Balance Methods

Situation

You work as a clerk for West-Mid Micros, a company selling micro computers throughout the West Midlands. The company accountant asks you to investigate and compare straight-line and reducing balance methods of depreciating the company's office furniture and fittings. These have recently been purchased at a cost of £5 500 and are expected to be replaced in five years' time; it is expected that they will have a resale value at the end of this time of approximately £500. The company accountant, in particular, would like you to suggest appropriate rates (to the nearest 5 per cent) for each depreciation method, and to make comparisons between the two.

Solution

Furniture and fittings costing £5 500, to be depreciated to approximately £500 (expected sale value) in five years' time.

	Straight-line £1 000 per year	Reducing balance 40%
Original cost	£5 500	£5 500
Year 1 depreciation	£1 000	£2 200
Value at end of year 1	£4 500	£3 300
Year 2 depreciation	£1 000	£1 320
Value at end of year 2	£3 500	£1 980
Year 3 depreciation	£1 000	£792
Value at end of year 3	£2 500	£1 188
Year 4 depreciation	£1 000	£475
Value at end of year 4	£1 500	£713
Year 5 depreciation	£1 000	£285
Value at end of year 5	£500	£428

The year-by-year depreciation amounts from the case problem are shown on the following bar chart:

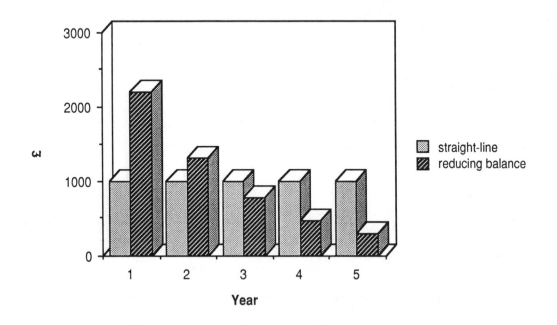

Depreciation amounts using the Straight Line and Reducing Balance Methods

For comparisons between the two methods of depreciation, see the next section.

Comparisons of Depreciation Methods

Straight-line

- Same money amount each year

- Lower depreciation percentage
- Best for use with fixed assets likely to be kept for the whole of their expected lives, e.g. machinery, office equipment, fixtures and fittings

Reducing balance

- Different money amounts each year: more than straight-line in early years, less in later years
- Higher depreciation percentage required
- Best for use with fixed assets which depreciate more in early years and which are not to be kept for whole of expected lives, e.g. vehicles

Depreciation in Financial Statements

- **Profit and Loss Account:** the depreciation amount calculated for each class of asset, is listed amongst the other expenses as a **provision for depreciation** for that particular asset.

- **Balance Sheet:** each class of asset is shown at cost, and total **depreciation to date** (i.e. this year's depreciation, plus depreciation from previous years, if any) is deducted from each class of asset.

Case Problem: Heather Lewis

Situation

We will now look back at the financial statements of Heather Lewis referred to in the previous Chapter. The financial statements of Heather, which were adjusted for accruals and prepayments, are shown on pages 129 and 130. Heather tells you that the fixed assets, being fixtures and fittings, and delivery van, will need replacing in a few year's time. After discussions, it is decided to depreciate fixtures and fittings by 20 per cent each year, using the straight-line method, and the delivery van by 30 per cent each year using the reducing balance method.

Solution

The depreciation amounts for this year will be:

fixtures and fittings	£2 000 x 20%	=	£400
delivery van	£4 000 x 30%	=	£1 200

These amounts will be shown as expenses in her profit and loss account, and will be deducted from the cost price of the appropriate fixed asset in the balance sheet. Thus her year-end financial statements will appear as shown on the next page (the trading account is not affected by depreciation adjustments and therefore it is not shown).

TRADING AND PROFIT AND LOSS ACCOUNTS OF HEATHER LEWIS FOR THE YEAR ENDED 31 DECEMBER 19-5   (EXTRACT)

	£	£
Gross Profit		21 000
Less:		
Rent and rates	3 800	
Salaries	10 000	
Heating and lighting	1 250	
Sundry expenses	1 000	
Provision for depreciation -		
fixtures and fittings	400	
delivery van	1 200	
		17 650
Net Profit		3 350

BALANCE SHEET OF HEATHER LEWIS AS AT 31 DECEMBER 19-5

	£ cost	£ depreciation to date	£ net
Fixed Assets			
Fixtures and fittings	2 000	400	1 600
Delivery van	4 000	1 200	2 800
	6 000	1 600	4 400
Current Assets			
Stock		6 000	
Debtors		2 000	
Rent prepaid		200	
Bank		500	
		8 700	
Less Current Liabilities			
Creditors	3 000		
Heating and lighting accrued	250		
		3 250	
Working Capital			5 450
NET ASSETS			9 850
FINANCED BY			
Capital			
Opening capital			10 000
Add net profit			3 350
			13 500
Less drawings			3 500
			9 850

Notes:

• As this is the first year that she has made a provision for depreciation, the amount shown in the balance sheet is the same as that shown in the profit and loss account; next year, however, things will be different. For example, for fixtures and fittings, the amount shown in the profit and loss account will still be £400, i.e. 20 per cent of cost, but the balance sheet will show:

	£ cost	£ depreciation to date	£ net
Fixtures and fittings	2 000	800	1200

- The effect of creating a provision for depreciation has been to reduce the net profit by £1 600 to £3 350. In fact, you will see that Heather has now drawn more out of the business than the net profit for the year.

Case Problem: Depreciation and the Trial Balance

Situation

Usually the trial balance will distinguish between the cost of an asset and the depreciation already charged for that particular class of asset. For example:

TRIAL BALANCE (EXTRACT) OF JAMES WILSON AS AT 30 JUNE 19-2

	Debit £	Credit £
Fixed assets at cost:		
Buildings	100 000	
Vehicles	30 000	
Machinery	25 000	
Provision for depreciation:		
Buildings		10 000
Vehicles		12 000
Machinery		10 000

In the profit and loss account for the year ended 30 June 19-2, depreciation is calculated as:

Buildings £2 000
Vehicles £6 000
Machinery £5 000

Show the profit and loss account for the year assuming that gross profit is £76 000 and that other expenses for the year total £52 000. Show the fixed asset section of the balance sheet of James Wilson as at 30 June 19-2.

Solution

TRADING AND PROFIT AND LOSS ACCOUNTS (EXTRACT) OF JAMES WILSON FOR THE YEAR ENDED 30 JUNE 19-2

	£	£
Gross Profit		76 000
Less:		
Expenses	52 000	
Provision for depreciation -		
buildings	2 000	
vehicles	6 000	
machinery	5 000	
		65 000
Net Profit		11 000

BALANCE SHEET (EXTRACT) OF JAMES WILSON
AS AT 30 JUNE 19-2

	£ cost	£ depreciation to date	£ net
Fixed Assets			
Buildings	100 000	12 000	88 000
Vehicles	30 000	18 000	12 000
Machinery	25 000	15 000	10 000
	155 000	45 000	110 000

Here, the middle column depreciation amounts are calculated by adding the trial balance provision for depreciation (previous years) to the profit and loss depreciation for the year.

Depreciation: a non-cash Expense

It is very important to realise that, from a finance viewpoint, depreciation is a non-cash expense. Unlike the other expenses that we have come across in the profit and loss account, no cheque is written out to pay for depreciation. While rent and rates, salaries and telephone all have to be paid for by cheque (or in cash), depreciation causes no outflow of money. You will be able to understand this on a personal level by considering any fixed assets that you own, e.g. car, cycle, home computer, etc.; such assets are depreciating, but there is no immediate effect on your bank or cash balance. However, when the asset comes to be sold, you will receive rather less than was originally paid for it. Nevertheless, it is correct, in the financial statements of a business, to show in the profit and loss account an allowance for depreciation, because the business has had the use of the asset and needs to record a fall in value to present a true picture of its financial state.

Often in business we need to know how much cash, or *funds,* has been generated from the trading activities during the year. ('Trading activities' in this context means the main activities of the business). The calculation is:

FUNDS GENERATED FROM TRADING = NET PROFIT + DEPRECIATION

For example, refer to the business of James Wilson above. Funds generated from the trading activities for the year ended 30 June 19-2 are:

£11 000 + £2 000 + £6 000 + £5 000 = £24 000.

Thus, as a result of the year's trading, the bank account has benefited by £24 000. However, it is likely that most of this increase will have been used up in a number of ways, e.g. to buy more fixed assets, for owner's drawings, to buy more stock, to allow debtors longer to pay, or to reduce the time the business takes to pay its creditors. So, it is highly unlikely that the year-end balance of the bank account will have increased by anything like the funds generated from trading.

Sale of Fixed Assets

When a fixed asset is sold it is necessary to make a comparison between

(1) the original cost of the asset, and

(2) sale proceeds + depreciation provided over the life of the asset.

If *(1) is greater than (2)* there has been an *underprovision of depreciation* on the particular asset. The amount necessary to bring the total up to the original cost of the asset is shown as an expense in profit and loss account as 'underprovision of depreciation'. For example, a machine originally cost £5 000; it is depreciated for four years at ten per cent straight-line depreciation, and is then sold for £2 500. The comparison is:

(1) £5 000
(2) £2 500 + £2 000 (i.e. £500 x 4 years) = £4 500.

An extra £500 must, therefore, be *deducted* from profit and loss account, along with the other expenses, for underprovision of depreciation (often described more simply as 'loss on sale').

The effect of this is that net profit for the year will be reduced by £500. The estimate of depreciation over the years for this machine was slightly understated, but this is no reflection on the financial management of the business.

If *(2) is greater than (1)* there has been an *overprovision of depreciation,* and the excess amount must be added to gross profit in the profit and loss account in the year of sale. For example, a car was purchased for £10 000; depreciation to date totals £6 000 and the car has been sold for £5 000. The comparison is:

(1) £10 000
(2) £5 000 + £6 000 = £11 000.

The £1 000, which represents an overprovision of depreciation (or 'profit on sale'), is added to gross profit and any other income amounts.

Small adjustments for under or overprovision of depreciation are needed because it is impossible, at the start of an asset's life, to predict exactly what it will sell for in a number of years' time.

Chapter Summary

❏ Depreciation is an estimate, in money terms, of the fall in value of fixed assets.

❏ Two common methods of calculating depreciation are the straight-line method and the reducing balance method.

❏ The depreciation amount for each class of fixed asset is included amongst the expenses in profit and loss account, while the value of the asset, as shown in the balance sheet, is reduced by the same amount.

❏ Depreciation is a non-cash expense.

❏ Net profit is reduced by the amount of depreciation charged.

❏ When an asset is sold it is necessary to make an adjustment in respect of any underprovision or overprovision of depreciation during the life of the asset.

In the next Chapter we look at another expense to be shown in profit and loss account: bad debts, and provision for bad debts.

✍ Student Activities

1. A friend of yours has recently started in business; knowing that you are studying Finance, she seeks your assistance. She has just bought a machine at a cost of £1 000 and asks you to advise on depreciation methods. The machine is expected to last for five years after which it will be valueless. She tells you that, if there is a choice of depreciation methods, she would like to use the one "that gives the larger net profit in the early years because the business could make good use of the extra cash". Advise your friend.

2. On 1 January 19-1, Martin Jackson bought a car for £6 000. In his financial statements, which have a year-end of 31 December, he has been depreciating it at 25 per cent per annum using the reducing balance method. On 31 December 19-3 he sells the car for £2 750.

    You are to show:

    (a) The depreciation amounts that would have been shown in his profit and loss accounts for 19-1, 19-2 and 19-3.

    (b) How the asset would have been shown in his balance sheets at 31 December 19-1 and 19-2.

    (c) How the profit or loss on sale will be shown in his profit and loss account for the year ended 31 December 19-3.

3. The following trial balance has been extracted by the book-keeper of Hazel Harris at 31 December 19-4:

	£	£
Bank loan		75 000
Capital		125 000
Purchases and sales	465 000	614 000
Building repairs	8 480	
Motor vehicles at cost	12 000	
Provision for depreciation on motor vehicles		2 400
Motor expenses	2 680	
Land and buildings at cost	100 000	
Bank overdraft		2 000
Furniture and fittings at cost	25 000	
Provision for depreciation on furniture and fittings		2 500
Wages and salaries	86 060	
Discounts	10 610	8 140
Drawings	24 000	
Rates and insurance	6 070	
Debtors and creditors	52 130	41 850
General expenses	15 860	
Stock at 1 January 19-4	63 000	
	870 890	870 890

Notes at 31 December 19-4:
*   Stock was valued at £88 000
*   Wages and salaries outstanding: £3 180
*   Rates and insurance paid in advance: £450
*   Depreciate motor vehicles at 20 per cent using the straight-line method
*   Depreciate furniture and fittings at 10 per cent using the straight-line method

As accountant to Miss Harris, you are to prepare her trading and profit and loss accounts for the year ended 31 December 19-4, together with her balance sheet at that date.

4.   Martin Hough, sole owner of Juicyburger, a fast food shop, operating from leased premises in the town, is suspicious of his accountant, Mr S Harris, whom he claims doesn't really understand the food business. On the telephone he asks Mr Harris why depreciation is charged on a rigid formula, as surely no-one really knows how much his equipment is worth, and in fact he might not get anything for it. Draft a reply to Mr Hough from Mr Harris explaining the importance of depreciation and its application to financial statements, together with its effect on Mr Hough's tax bill.

5.   Cindy Smith owns an engineering supplies business, and the following trial balance has been extracted by her book-keeper at 30 June 19-3:

	£	£
Capital		38 825
Stock at 1 July 19-2	18 050	
Purchases	74 280	
Sales		149 410
Discounts	3 210	1 140
Rent and rates	7 280	
Returns	1 645	875
Cash	820	
Bank		13 300
Debtors and creditors	14 375	10 565
Wages and salaries	43 895	
General expenses	2 515	
Motor vehicles at cost	25 000	
Provision for depreciation on motor vehicles		5 000
Fixtures and fittings at cost	10 000	
Provision for depreciation on fixtures and fittings		3 000
Motor vehicle expenses	6 725	
Drawings	14 320	
	222 115	222 115

Notes at 30 June 19-3:
* Stock was valued at £20 145
* General expenses owing £175
* Rates prepaid £95
* Depreciate motor vehicles at 20 per cent per annum, using the reducing balance method
* Depreciate fixtures and fittings at 10 per cent per annum, using the straight-line method

As accountant to Cindy Smith, you are to prepare her trading and profit and loss accounts for the year ended 30 June 19-3, together with her balance sheet at that date.

Chapter Sixteen
Bad Debts and Provision for Bad Debts

Most businesses selling their goods to other businesses do not receive payment immediately. Instead they often have to allow a period of credit and, until the payment is received, they have a current asset of *debtors*. Unfortunately, it is likely that not all debtors will eventually settle the amount they owe - some debts will become *bad debts*.

Let us consider Heather Lewis' business that has debtors of £2 000. This total will, most probably, be made up of a number of smaller debtors' accounts. At any one time a few of these accounts will be bad, and therefore the amount due is uncollectable: these are *bad debts,* and they need to be written off, i.e. the business will give up trying to collect the debt and will accept the loss. At the same time there are likely to be some debtors' accounts which, although they are not yet bad, may be giving some concern as to their ability to pay: a *provision for bad debts* needs to be made in respect of these. The one thing that Heather, with debtors of £2 000, cannot do is to show this debtors amount as a current asset in the balance sheet: to do so would be to imply to the user of the balance sheet that the full £2 000 is collectable. Instead this *gross* debtors' figure might be reduced in two stages:

• two debtors' accounts with balances totalling £100 are to be written off as bad

• a general provision for bad debts is to be made amounting, in this case, to five per cent of remaining debtors

Thus the debtors figure becomes:

	£
Gross debtors	2 000
Less: bad debts written off	100
	1 900
Less: provision for bad debts,	
*five per cent in this example	95
Net debtors (recorded in balance sheet)	1 805

* The amount of the provision for bad debts will vary from business to business depending on past experience.

Bad Debts

As already noted, bad debts are written off when they become uncollectable. This means that all reasonable efforts to recover the amount owing have been exhausted, i.e. statements and letters have been sent to the debtor requesting payment, and legal action, where appropriate, or the threat of legal action has failed to obtain payment.

In writing off a debtor's account as bad, the business is bearing the cost of the amount due. The debtor's account is closed and the amount (or amounts, where a number of accounts are dealt with in this way) is deducted from profit and loss account as an expense. At the same time, the gross debtors figure is reduced by the amount being written off.

Therefore, for writing off bad debts:

- Deduct the total amount being written off from profit and loss account as an expense, describing the amount as *bad debts written off*.

- If the bad debts figure is not already shown in the trial balance, reduce the debtors figure for the balance sheet: there is no need to show the deduction, just the reduced figure (before making any provision for bad debts - see below).

Provision for Bad Debts

This is different from writing off a bad debt because there is the possibility - not the certainty - of future bad debts. The debtors figure is reduced either by totalling the balances of the accounts that may not pay or, more likely, by applying a percentage to the total figure for debtors. The percentage chosen will be based on past experience and will vary from business to business.

The money amount chosen as a provision for bad debts is deducted as an expense from profit and loss account (described as *provision for bad debts,* and kept separate from bad debts written off). At the same time the amount of the provision must be deducted from the debtors figure in the balance sheet, and the net amount of debtors is included in the current assets of the business.

Therefore, to create a provision for bad debts:

- Deduct the amount of the provision for bad debts as an expense to profit and loss account.

- Deduct the amount of the provision from the debtors figure in the balance sheet, after first writing off bad debts. Show the deduction in the balance sheet (see the example below).

Case Problem: Heather Lewis

Situation
Refer back to the set of financial statements for Heather Lewis shown on page 143. These have already been adjusted for accruals and prepayments, and depreciation. Heather now tells you to make the adjustments referred to earlier in this chapter, i.e. of the total debtors of £2 000, there are two debtors totalling £100 to be written off, and a general provision for bad debts should be made at 5 per cent of debtors to allow for possible future bad debts.

How will the financial statements be affected by these adjustments?

Solution

Gross debtors	£2 000
Less bad debts written off	£100
	£1 900
Less provision for bad debts at 5 per cent	£95
Net debtors	£1 805

Her year-end financial statements will appear as shown on the next page (the trading account is not affected by bad debts written off and provision for bad debts, and therefore it is not shown).

TRADING AND PROFIT AND LOSS ACCOUNTS (EXTRACT)
OF HEATHER LEWIS FOR THE YEAR ENDED 31 DECEMBER 19-5

	£	£
Gross Profit		21 000
Less:		
Rent and rates	3 800	
Salaries	10 000	
Heating and lighting	1 250	
Sundry expenses	1 000	
Provision for depreciation -		
fixtures and fittings	400	
delivery van	1 200	
Bad debts written off	100	
Provision for bad debts	95	
		17 845
Net Profit		3 155

BALANCE SHEET OF HEATHER LEWIS AS AT 31 DECEMBER 19-5

	£ cost	£ depreciation to date	£ net
Fixed Assets			
Fixtures and fittings	2 000	400	1 600
Delivery van	4 000	1 200	2 800
	6 000	1 600	4 400
Current Assets			
Stock		6 000	
Debtors	1 900		
Less provision for bad debts	95		
		1 805	
Rent prepaid		200	
Bank		500	
		8 505	
Less Current Liabilities			
Creditors	3 000		
Heating and lighting accrued	250		
		3 250	
Working Capital			5 255
NET ASSETS			9 655
FINANCED BY			
Capital			
Opening capital			10 000
Add net profit			3 155
			13 155
Less drawings			3 500
			9 655

Notes:

- This is now a much more accurate set of financial statements than those prepared on the first occasion (on pages 127 and 128). This is because adjustments have been made for accruals and prepayments, depreciation, bad debts written off, and provision for bad debts.

- Net profit has been reduced because two further costs in connection with bad debts written off and provision for bad debts have been deducted from profit and loss account.

Increases/decreases in Provision for Bad Debts

Having once created a provision for bad debts, the amount of the provision must be reviewed at the end of each subsequent financial year. The level of debtors is likely to be different at the end of each year as the business expands or contracts; if provision for bad debts is a fixed percentage of debtors, the amount of the provision will also need altering. A more radical change will be if the business decides to increase or decrease the *blanket* percentage of debtors it estimates may go bad, e.g. an increase from five per cent to ten per cent. Whatever the cause, the amount required as provision for bad debts will alter and it is *the amount of the change* that must be entered in profit and loss account; the *new total* is recorded in the balance sheet.

Case Problem: Provision for Bad Debts

Situation one

At 31 December 19-5, the balance sheet of Heather Lewis shows debtors of £1 900, and a 5 per cent provision for bad debts of £95. Let us assume that, twelve months later, debtors are £3 000 (after bad debts have been written off). Heather decides that the figure of 5 per cent of debtors is to be retained as a provision for bad debts. How will this be recorded in her financial statements for 19-6?

Solution

The provision for bad debts must now be £3 000 x 5% = £150. As the existing provision is £95, only the *difference* of £55 is deducted from profit and loss account as an expense. It is described as an *increase in provision for bad debts*. The new figure of £150 is deducted *in full* from debtors in the balance sheet:

BALANCE SHEET (EXTRACT) OF HEATHER LEWIS
AS AT 31 DECEMBER 19-6

	£	£
Current Assets		
Debtors	3 000	
Less provision for bad debts	150	
		2 850

Situation two

In the above example the provision for bad debts increased by £55 over the previous amount. In the following year, debtors (after allowing for bad debts) have fallen to £2 500. How will this be recorded in her financial statements for 19-7?

Solution

Now the provision for bad debts will need reducing to £125 (5% of £2 500). This is achieved by adding to profit and loss account the difference of £25, described as a *reduction in provision for bad debts*. The figure will be added to gross profit in the profit and loss account and will be recorded in the right hand column below gross profit. The balance sheet will show:

BALANCE SHEET (EXTRACT) OF HEATHER LEWIS
AS AT 31 DECEMBER 19-7

	£	£
Current Assets		
Debtors	2 500	
Less provision for bad debts	125	
		2 375

The above Case Problem shows that to change an existing provision for bad debts it is necessary to:

- Deduct as an expense to profit and loss account the amount of the increase, or add to profit and loss account the amount of the decrease in provision for bad debts. In both cases we are only concerned, in profit and loss account, with the *amount of the change* .

- Deduct the amount of the *total* provision, i.e. existing provision plus increase or less decrease, from debtors in the balance sheet.

Chapter Summary

❏ Bad debts and the creation of a provision (or the increase in an existing provision) have the effect of reducing net profit. They represent costs which businesses that only sell goods for cash avoid. Many businesses, though, have to sell their goods on credit and they should take steps to minimize the possibility of bad debts.

❏ In the balance sheet the net figure for debtors included in current assets should give an indication of the *true* amount the business can expect to collect from its debtors.

❏ In adjusting the profit and loss account and balance sheet to take note of *bad debts written off* and *provision for bad debts* we are presenting more accurate financial statements.

Having looked at some specific methods of adjusting accounts to take note of accruals and prepayments, depreciation, and bad debts, the next Chapter considers the basic framework within which financial statements are prepared.

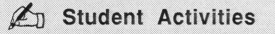 **Student Activities**

1. You are an accounts clerk for Waterston Plant Hire. At 31 December 19-2, the end of its financial year, the business has gross debtors of £20 210. The owner decides to:

   (a) write off, as bad debts, the accounts of:

P. Ross	£55
J. Ball	£105
L. Jones	£50

   (b) make a provision for bad debts of $2\frac{1}{2}$ per cent of debtors (after writing off the above bad debts)

   You are to show how these transactions will be recorded in the financial statements at the end of the financial year.

2. Ross Engineering Ltd has an existing provision for bad debts of £300, based on 5 per cent of debtors. After writing off bad debts, the amounts of debtors at the end of the next two financial years are found to be:

30 June 19-2	£8 000
30 June 19-3	£7 000

The company continues to keep the provision for bad debts equal to 5 per cent of debtors.

As accountant to Ross Engineering Ltd, you are to show how the amount of the provision for bad debts will be adjusted at the end of the financial years ended 30 June 19-2 and 30 June 19-3, and how it will be recorded in the appropriate financial statements.

3. The following trial balance has been extracted by the book-keeper of P Sanders, who runs an import/export business, at 31 December 19-6:

	£	£
Purchases and sales	51 225	81 762
Returns	186	254
Stock at 1 January 19-6	6 031	
Discounts	324	438
Motor expenses	1 086	
Wages and salaries	20 379	
Electricity	876	
Telephone	1 241	
Rent and rates	4 565	
Sundry expenses	732	
Bad debts written off	219	
Debtors and creditors	1 040	972
Bank	3 501	
Cash	21	
Motor vehicles at cost	15 000	
Provision for depreciation on motor vehicles		3 000
Office equipment at cost	10 000	
Provision for depreciation on office equipment		5 000
Capital		33 000
Drawings	8 000	
	124 426	124 426

Notes at 31 December 19-6:

- Stock was valued at £8 210
- Electricity owing £102
- Rent prepaid £251
- Depreciate motor vehicles at 20 per cent and office equipment at 10 per cent per annum, using the straight-line method
- Create a provision for bad debts of 5 per cent of debtors

As accountant to P Sanders, you are to prepare the trading and profit and loss accounts for the year ended 31 December 19-6, together with a balance sheet at that date.

4. The book-keeper of James Jenkins, who owns a patisserie and coffee lounge, has extracted the following trial balance at 30 June 19-2:

	£	£
Capital		32 175
Drawings	19 050	
Purchases and sales	105 240	168 432
Stock at 1 July 19-1	9 427	
Debtors and creditors	3 840	10 786
Returns	975	1 237
Discounts	127	643
Wages and salaries	30 841	
Motor vehicle expenses	1 021	
Rent and rates	8 796	
Heating and lighting	1 840	
Telephone	355	
General expenses	1 752	
Bad debts written off	85	
Motor vehicle at cost	8 000	
Provision for depreciation on motor vehicle		3 500
Shop fittings at cost	6 000	
Provision for depreciation on shop fittings		2 000
Provision for bad debts		150
Cash	155	
Bank	21 419	
	218 923	218 923

Notes at 30 June 19-2:

- Stock was valued at £11 517
- Motor vehicle expenses owing £55
- Rent prepaid £275
- Depreciate the motor vehicle at 25 per cent per annum, using the reducing balance method
- Depreciate shop fittings at 10 per cent per annum, using the straight-line method
- The provision for bad debts is to be equal to 2.5 per cent of debtors

As accountant to James Jenkins, you are to prepare his trading and profit and loss accounts for the year ended 30 June 19-2, together with his balance sheet at that date.

Chapter Seventeen
Accounting Concepts and Stock Valuation

In the preparation of financial statements there are a number of basic rules that are followed. These rules, or *accounting concepts* as they are known, form a framework within which the financial statements of all organizations are constructed. By following the same concepts, broad comparisons can then be made between the financial results of different organizations.

Two Basic Accounting Concepts

There are two concepts so basic that they are followed in all circumstances:

• business entity concept
• money measurement concept

Business Entity Concept
This refers to the fact that financial statements show the activities of one particular entity, i.e. business, local authority, society, etc., and do not include the activities of those who play a part in managing the organization. For example, John Smith lives in a large house and owns a shoe shop. The financial statements of his shoe shop will not include any mention of his house, because the house is his personal asset and has nothing to do with the business entity. His wife, Jane Smith, is the treasurer of a local society which has a bank account with the National Bank, at the same branch of which she maintains her personal bank account. In producing the financial statements of the society (see also Chapter 26), no mention will be made of her own bank balance, only that of the society. The reason is that the two are separate entities.

Money Measurement Concept
This means that, in finance, all items have to be expressed in the common denominator of money, e.g. the balance sheet of a farmer cannot measure his assets as being 50 cows, 200 sheep, etc.; everything must be expressed in money. Only by using money can items be added together to give, for example, a net profit, or a balance sheet total. However, the money measurement concept does mean that a financial statement is only able to record items which can be expressed in terms of money. A business with an efficient management, and good labour relations will appear to have the same value as one that is overstaffed and has poor labour relations. Only in the longer term, with different levels of profit and balance sheet structure, will the differences between the two become apparent.

Another disadvantage of the money measurement concept is the effect of inflation on prices. For example, a business achieved sales of £100 000 this year, and hopes for £105 000 next year. Is this an improvement? The answer is that if inflation is greater than 5 per cent per annum, there has been no improvement at all and, in real terms, sales are reduced; if inflation is below 5 per cent, sales have increased in real terms.

Case Problems: For Discussion

1. Profits last year were £10 000; this year they are £10 250. Has the business improved?

2. Two businesses each have fixed assets at cost of £100 000 in their balance sheets. One business bought the assets three years ago, while the other business bought them last week. What are the problems of comparison?

3. The owner of a business has a firm's car; her husband, a teacher, owns his own car. Which car will be shown on the business balance sheet? Would it make any difference if the husband was also a partner in the business?

4. A district nurse uses her own car for visiting patients and is reimbursed for petrol and other running expenses so incurred by the Area Health Authority. Is the car an asset of the A.H.A.?

Further Accounting Concepts

The two concepts we have just considered are so basic that they are fundamental to all financial statements. Four further accounting concepts should also be applied:

- going concern concept
- accruals concept
- consistency concept
- prudence concept

Going Concern Concept

This presumes that the business to which the financial statements relate will continue to trade in the foreseeable future. The trading and profit and loss accounts and balance sheet are prepared on the basis that there is no intention to reduce significantly the size of the business or to liquidate the business. If the business was not a going concern, assets would have very different values, and the balance sheet would be affected considerably. For example, a large, purpose-built factory has considerable value to a going concern business but, if the factory had to be sold, it is likely to have a limited use for other industries, and therefore will have a lower market value. The latter case is the opposite of the going concern concept and is known as the gone concern concept.

Accruals Concept

This means that expenses and revenues must be matched so that they concern the same goods and the same time period. We have already put this concept into practice in Chapter 14, where expenses and revenues were adjusted to take note of prepayments and accruals. The trading and profit and loss accounts should always show the amounts of the expense that should have been incurred, i.e. the expenditure for the year, whether or not it has been paid. This is the principle of income and expenditure accounting, rather than using receipts and payments as and when they fall due.

Consistency Concept

This requires that, when a business adopts particular accounting methods, it should continue to use such methods consistently. For example, a business that decides to make a provision for depreciation on machinery at ten per cent per annum, using the straight-line method, should continue to use that percentage and method for future financial statements. Of course, having once chosen a particular method, a business is entitled to make changes provided there are good reasons for so doing, and a note to the year-end accounts would explain what has happened. By applying the consistency concept, direct comparison between the financial statements of different years can be made.

Prudence Concept

This concept, also known as conservatism in accounting, requires that financial statements should always, where there is any doubt, report a conservative figure for profit or the valuation of assets. To this end, profits are not to be anticipated and should only be recognized when it is reasonably certain that they will be realized; at the same time all known liabilities should be provided for. A good example of the prudence concept is where a provision is made for bad debts (see Chapter 16) - the debtors have not yet gone bad, but it is expected, from experience, that a certain percentage will eventually need to be written off as bad debts. The valuation of stock (see below) also follows the prudence concept. 'Anticipate no profit, but anticipate all losses' is a summary of the concept which, in its application, prevents an over-optimistic presentation of a business through the financial statements.

Valuation of Stock

As stated above, the prudence concept is applied in valuing the closing stock of a business.

The most common stock valuation is *at the lower of cost and net realizable value*.

This valuation method is taken from Statement of Standard Accounting Practice (SSAP) No. 9. SSAPs are approved by the main professional accountancy bodies as a means of obtaining uniformity and objectivity in accounting.

In valuing stock we are concerned with comparing:

- cost
- net realizable value (which is generally the selling price)

We use the lower of these two amounts to place a valuation on stock.

For example, a shop bought some swimwear at the beginning of the summer for £15 each. The goods were priced at £30 in the shop and most were sold. In the autumn the shop holds a sale and prices them at £12.50 each. The stock valuation of the unsold items is now £12.50, i.e. the net realizable value, which is lower than the cost of £15.

To find the cost price of stock is not easy when quantities of a particular stock item are continually being bought in - perhaps at different prices - and then sold.

Case Problem: Stock Valuation

Situation

A garage has the following purchases and sales of a particular make of tyre:

	PURCHASES	SALES	BALANCE
January	100 @ £10 per tyre		100 tyres
February		70 tyres	30 tyres
March	100 @ £11 per tyre	50 tyres	80 tyres
April		60 tyres	20 tyres
May	200 @ £12 per tyre	100 tyres	120 tyres
June		50 tyres	70 tyres

The current selling price of each tyre is £20.
What valuation would you place on the seventy tyres remaining at the end of June?

Solution

To answer this we need to know the cost price, but is the cost of the remaining tyres £10, £11 or £12 per tyre? The answer depends on which *method* the firm adopts in its stock records. There are two main methods that might be used to calculate cost:

- **FIFO (first in, first out)** - the *first* stocks received are considered to be the *first* stocks used

- **LIFO (last in, first out)** - the *last* stocks received are considered to be the *first* stocks used

Using these two methods the closing stock of seventy tyres would be valued at:

• **FIFO**	70 units at £12 per tyre	= £840
• **LIFO**	*20 units at £10 per tyre	= £200
	50 units at £12 per tyre	= £600
	70	£800

(* As the stock level fell to twenty tyres at the end of April, only this number can be valued at the original £10 per tyre; also, all the purchases at £11 per tyre have been sold by the end of April, so none will feature in the closing stock.)

Depending on the method of stock valuation adopted, a different *cost* price can be calculated. (There are other methods in use in addition to FIFO and LIFO). The net realizable value (selling price) needs to be compared with cost to give the appropriate valuation at the lower figure, i.e. the prudence concept, mentioned earlier, is applied. In this Case Problem, the stock will be valued at cost, because the selling price is above cost.

You should note that LIFO and FIFO (and other methods) are only ways of calculating cost: they are not necessarily the order in which the physical stock is handled, although perishable goods should be physically moved on the FIFO basis.

Advantages and Disadvantages of FIFO and LIFO

FIFO (first in, first out)

Advantages:
- realistic, i.e. it assumes that goods are issued in order of receipt
- it is easy to calculate
- stock valuation comprises actual prices at which items have been bought
- the closing stock valuation is close to the most recent prices

Disadvantages:
- prices at which goods are issued are not necessarily the latest prices
- in times of rising prices, profits will be higher than with other methods

LIFO (last in, first out)

Advantages:
- goods are issued at the latest prices
- it is easy to calculate
- in times of rising prices, it gives a more conservative stock valuation than FIFO

Disadvantages:
- illogical, i.e. it assumes goods are issued in reverse order from that in which they are received
- the closing stock valuation is not usually at most recent prices
- when stocks are being run down, issues will 'dip into' old stock at out-of-date prices

Chapter Summary

❑ The two basic accounting concepts of business entity and money measurement always apply to the preparation of financial statements.

❑ In order to improve the usefulness of financial statements the four concepts of going concern, accruals, consistency and prudence should also be applied.

❑ Stock is normally valued on the basis of *lower of cost and net realizable value.*

❑ For particular items of stock which are constantly being bought and sold, the techniques of FIFO (first in, first out) and LIFO (last in, first out) are often used to ascertain the *cost.*

 Student Activities

1.   A discussion is taking place between Wendy Adams, a sole trader, who owns a furniture shop, and her husband, John, who solely owns an engineering business. The following points are made:

   (a)   John says that, having depreciated his firm's machinery last year on the reducing balance method, for this year he intends to use the straight-line method. By doing this he says that he will deduct less depreciation from profit and loss account, so his net profit will be higher and his bank manager will be impressed. He says he might revert back to reducing balance method next year.

   (b)   At the end of her financial year, Wendy comments that the stock of her shop had cost £10 000. She says that, as she normally adds 50 per cent to cost price to give the selling price, she intends to put a value of £15 000 for stock in the trading account and balance sheet.

   (c)   John's car is owned by his business but he keeps referring to it as *my car.* Wendy reminds him that it does not belong to him, but to the firm. He replies that of course it belongs to him and, furthermore, if the firm went bankrupt, he would be able to keep the car.

   (d)   On the last day of her financial year, Wendy sold a large order of furniture, totalling £3 000, to a local hotel. The furniture was invoiced and delivered from stock that day, before year-end stocktaking commenced. The payment was received early in the new financial year and Wendy now asks John if she will be able to put this sale through the accounts for the new year, instead of the old, but without altering the figures for purchases and closing stock for the old year.

   (e)   John says that his accountant talks of preparing his accounts on a going concern basis. John asks Wendy if she knows of any other basis that can be used, and which it is usual to follow.

   You are to take each of the points and state the correct accounting treatment, referring to appropriate accounting concepts.

2. Tradeparts Ltd. is a company which imports electrical parts for cars and sells in bulk to garage groups and car accessory shops. The stock record card for December 19-6 for a particular type of starter motor shows the following:

Opening stock	1 December	40 units @ £33 each
Receipts	4 December	50 units @ £36 each
	12 December	80 units @ £40 each
Sales	8 December	70 units
	21 December	50 units

As clerk in the accounts department of Tradeparts Ltd., you are to calculate the value of the closing stock at 31 December 19-6 using:

(a) first in, first out (FIFO) method
(b) last in, first out (LIFO) method

If the selling price for each unit at 31 December 19-6 is found to be (firstly) £60, or (secondly) £30, would your closing stock valuations alter?

3. XY Ltd. is a wholesaling business which trades in two items of stock, 'X' and 'Y'. At the end of six months' trading, the stock record cards show the following:

X				Y		
19-1	Receipts (Units)	Sales (Units)		19-1	Receipts (Units)	Sales (Units)
Jan	100 @ £4.00			Jan	200 @ £10.00	
Feb		80		Feb	100 @ £8.50	
Mar	140 @ £6.00			Mar		240
Apr	100 @ £3.80			Apr	100 @ £11.50	
May		140		May	140 @ £10.00	
Jun	80 @ £5.00			Jun		100

As an accounts clerk, working for XY Ltd., you are to:

•   Using (a) the first in, first out (FIFO), and (b) the last in, first out (LIFO) methods, calculate the cost price of the closing stock for X and Y held on 30 June 19-1.

•   Prepare two trading accounts, each for the six months ended 30 June 19-1, for item X, assuming that the selling price has been £10 per unit. One trading account will use for FIFO stock valuation for the closing stock, the other will use the LIFO stock valuation (in both cases there was no opening stock).

•   Prepare two trading accounts, on the same basis, for stock item Y, assuming that the selling price has been £20 per unit.

•   Write a memorandum to the managing director of XY Ltd. in response to his request that you are to implement the stock valuation method *that gives the larger profit*.

Assignment Nine

Year-end Accounts: T. Blake

GENERAL OBJECTIVES COVERED
D, E.

SKILLS DEVELOPED
Numeracy, communicating, information processing.

SITUATION
You are a junior clerk at Tickit & Runne, (address: Victoria Chambers, Ransome Walk, Rowcester, RW1 2EJ) a firm of chartered accountants. The firm has a wide range of clients for whom it prepares year-end accounts and provides financial advice. The following year-end trial balance has been received from the book-keeper of T. Blake, a retailer:

TRIAL BALANCE AS AT 31 DECEMBER 19-1

	£	£
Debtors and creditors	34 600	20 900
Delivery van at cost	7 000	
Provision for depreciation on delivery van		1 400
Fixtures and fittings at cost	12 800	
Provision for depreciation on fixtures and fittings		2 560
Purchases and sales	94 500	166 100
Returns inwards and returns outwards	7 600	4 100
Salaries	29 600	
Bank	7 500	
Cash	700	
Bad debts written off	1 900	
Rates and insurance	2 700	
Electricity	3 960	
Premises	60 000	
Drawings	18 200	
Sundry expenses	1 200	
Stock at 1 January 19-1	19 800	
Capital at 1 January 19-1		107 000
	302 060	302 060

Subsequent discussions with the book-keeper reveal that at 31 December 19-1:

*   The closing stocks had the following values:
    selling price   £31 750
    cost price   £20 500

*   £250 of the rates for next year has been paid in advance

*   £150 was owing for electricity

*   The delivery van is being depreciated at 20 per cent per annum using the reducing balance method

*   Fixtures and fittings are being depreciated using the straight-line method at 10 per cent per annum

*   Past experience shows that 2 per cent of debtors are likely to become bad debts; you agree to create a provision to allow for this

STUDENT TASKS

1. Using the information above, prepare financial statements for T. Blake covering the year to 31 December 19-1.

2. Draft an accompanying letter for signature by one of the partners of Ticket & Runne, Chartered Accountants, explaining the adjustments you have made to the trial balance figures, giving the reasons for so doing.

3. How would you respond if, on receipt of the financial statements you have prepared, T. Blake says, "this is all very well, but the financial statements ought to include an allowance for my loyal workforce and the excellent products we sell."

    Draft a further letter for signature by the same partner, explaining this apparent omission.

Chapter Eighteen
Interpretation of Financial Statements

The ability to interpret financial statements is an important aspect of finance. Questions which can be answered from a basic financial interpretation include:

Did the organization perform better this year than last?
Is organization A better than organization B?
How efficiently is the organization managing the resources it uses?

Interpretation is carried out by calculating a number of accounting ratios and percentages, and then using the results to draw relevant conclusions. A number of the more important ratios, and percentages are considered below; however, it is not always possible to apply all the calculations to every set of financial statements, although they can all be used on the accounts of trading organizations such as sole-traders, partnerships (see Chapter 19), and limited companies (see Chapter 20). It is important to note that interpretation consists of far more than simply calculating a series of ratios and percentages; appropriate conclusions need to be drawn and presented in the form of a written or verbal report.

To help in the task of interpretation, we will consider the calculations under three headings:

- Profitability - the amount of profit the organization makes
- Liquidity - the availability of cash, or near cash, in an organization
- Activity - the control of stocks, debtors and creditors

The method of calculating the various ratios and percentages is given below, together with some points to consider when making a report. Later on in the Chapter, a simple set of financial statements will be analysed.

Profitability

Gross Profit Percentage

$\dfrac{\text{Gross profit for year}}{\text{Sales for year}} \times \dfrac{100}{1} = \text{Gross profit/sales percentage}$

This expresses, as a percentage, the gross profit in relation to sales. For example, a gross profit percentage of 20 per cent means that for every £100 of sales made, the gross profit is £20.

The gross profit percentage should be similar from year-to-year for the same organization. It will vary between organizations in different areas of business, e.g. the gross profit percentage on jewellery is considerably higher than that on basic items of food. A significant change from one year to the next, particularly a fall in the percentage, needs further investigation.

Net Profit Percentage

$$\frac{\text{Net profit for year}}{\text{Sales for year}} \times \frac{100}{1} = \text{Net profit/sales percentage}$$

As with gross profit percentage, the net profit percentage should be similar from year-to-year for the same business, and should also be comparable with other firms in the same line of business. Ideally the net profit percentage should show a slight increase, which indicates that the profit and loss account costs are being kept under control. Any significant fall should be investigated to see if it has been caused by an increase in one particular expense, e.g. wages and salaries, advertising, etc.

A large expense item can always be expressed as a percentage of sales, e.g.

$$\frac{\text{Specified expense}}{\text{Sales for year}} \times \frac{100}{1} = \text{Expense/sales percentage}$$

For example, the relationship between advertising and sales might be found to be 10 per cent in one year, but 20 per cent the next year. This would indicate that an increase in advertising had failed to produce a proportionate increase in sales.

Note that some expenses are fixed costs, while others vary as sales increase or decrease (see Chapter 21).

Return on Capital Employed

$$\frac{\text{Net profit for year}}{\text{Capital employed at start of year}} \times \frac{100}{1} = \text{Percentage return on capital employed}$$

This expresses the net profit of the business in relation to the owner's capital. For this calculation, the capital at the start of the year should, ideally, be used but, if this is not known, the year-end figure can be used. The percentage return is best thought of in relation to other investments, e.g. a building society might offer a return of eight per cent, or a bank might offer five per cent on a deposit account. A person running a business is investing a sum of money in that business, and the net profit is the return that is achieved on that investment. However, it should be noted that the risks in running a business are considerably greater than depositing the money with a building society or bank, and an additional return to compensate for the extra risk is needed.

The calculation of return on capital employed can be varied to consider not only the owner's capital, but also to include any long-term loans, because they are a part of the semi-permanent capital of the organization.

Liquidity

Working Capital Ratio/Current Ratio

$$\frac{\text{Current assets}}{\text{Current liabilities}} = \text{Working capital ratio (also known as the } current\ ratio)$$

Using figures from the balance sheet, this ratio measures the relationship between current assets and current liabilities. Working capital (calculated as *current assets minus current liabilities*) is needed by all organizations in order to finance day-to-day trading activities. Sufficient working capital enables an organization to hold adequate stocks, allow a measure of credit to its customers (debtors), and to pay its suppliers (creditors) as payments fall due.

Although there is no ideal working capital ratio, an often accepted ratio is about 2:1, i.e. £2 of current assets to every £1 of current liabilities. However, an organization in the retail trade may be able to work with a lower ratio, e.g. 1.5:1 or even less, because it deals mainly in sales for cash and so does not have a large figure for debtors. A working capital ratio can be *too* high: if it is above 3:1 an investigation of the make-up of current assets is needed: e.g. the organization may have too much stock, too many debtors, or too much cash at the bank, or even too few creditors.

Liquid Capital Ratio

$\dfrac{\text{(Current assets - stock)}}{\text{Current liabilities}}$ = Liquid capital ratio (also known as the *acid test*)

This ratio uses the current assets and current liabilities from the balance sheet, but stock is omitted. This is because stock is the most illiquid current asset: it has to be sold, turned into debtors, and then the cash has to be collected from the debtors. Also, some of the stock included in the balance sheet figure may be unsaleable or obsolete.

The balance between liquid assets, that is debtors and cash/bank, and current liabilities should, ideally, be about 1:1, i.e. £1 of liquid assets to each £1 of current liabilities. At this ratio an organization is expected to be able to pay its current liabilities from its liquid assets, a figure below 1:1, e.g. 0.75:1, indicates that the organization would have difficulty in meeting pressing demands from creditors. However, as with the working capital ratio, certain types of organization are able to operate with a lower liquid ratio than others.

With both the working capital and the liquid capital ratios, trends from one year to the next need to be considered, or comparisons made with similar organizations.

Activity

Stock Turnover

$\dfrac{\text{Cost of goods sold}}{\text{Average stock}}$ = Stock Turnover

This calculation uses information from the trading account: cost of goods sold is the figure before gross profit is ascertained; average stock is usually found by taking the simple average of the opening and closing stocks, i.e. (opening stock + closing stock) ÷ 2.

Stock turnover is the number of times that the average stock is turned over during the financial year. For example, a market trader selling fresh flowers who finishes each day when sold out will have a stock turnover of about 300 times per year (assuming no Sunday trading). By contrast a furniture shop may have a stock turnover of perhaps four times a year.

The period of time for which stocks are held can be calculated by dividing the stock turnover figure into 12 months, 52 weeks, or 365 days. For example, a stock turnover of six times a year means that two months' stock is held on average.

An organization which is improving in efficiency will have a higher stock turnover when one compares one year with the next, or with the stock turnover of similar organizations.

Debtors' Collection Period

$\dfrac{\text{Debtors}}{\text{Credit sales for year}}$ x 52 weeks = Debt collection time (in weeks)

This calculation shows how long, on average, debtors take to pay for goods sold to them by the organization. If the answer is needed in months, or in days, then it will, clearly, be necessary to multiply by 12 or 365 respectively. The figure of *credit sales for the year* may not be disclosed in the trading account, in which case the sales figure should be used. Some organizations make the majority of their sales on credit but others, such as shops, will have a considerably lower proportion of credit sales.

The debt collection time can be compared with that for the previous year, or with that of a similar organization. In Britain, most debtors should make payment within about four weeks; however, sales made abroad will take longer for the proceeds to be received. A comparison from year-to-year of the collection period is a measure of the organization's efficiency at collecting the money that is due to it.

Creditors Payment Period

$$\frac{\text{Creditors}}{\text{Credit Purchases}} \times 52 \text{ weeks} = \text{Creditors' payment time (in weeks)}$$

This calculation is the 'other side of the coin' to that of debtors: here we are measuring the speed it takes to pay creditors. While creditors can be a useful temporary source of finance, delaying payment too long may cause problems.

Conclusion

In any assessment of ratios and percentages, an overall conclusion should be drawn, often from the point of view of interested parties, e.g. bank manager, trade unions, the owner of the business, creditors, etc., as will be seen in the following Case Problem.

Case Problem: Financial Statements of J. Brown

Situation

The accounts of J. Brown have been submitted to you for analysis.

TRADING AND PROFIT AND LOSS ACCOUNTS
FOR THE YEAR ENDED 31 DECEMBER 19-1

	£	£
Sales		150 000
Opening stock	10 000	
Purchases	66 000	
	76 000	
Less Closing stock	16 000	
Cost of Goods sold		60 000
Gross Profit		90 000
Less:		
Wages and salaries	60 000	
Advertising	15 000	
Sundry expenses	5 000	
		80 000
Net Profit		10 000

BALANCE SHEET AS AT 31 DECEMBER 19-1

	£	£	£
Fixed Assets			
Premises			70 000
Machinery			30 000
			100 000
Current Assets			
Stock		16 000	
Debtors		12 500	
		28 500	
Less Current Liabilities			
Creditors	11 000		
Bank overdraft	24 500		
		35 500	
Working Capital			(7 000)
NET ASSETS			93 000
FINANCED BY			
Capital			
Opening capital			90 000
Add net profit			10 000
			100 000
Less drawings			7 000
			93 000

Solution

Calculations

PROFITABILITY

Gross profit/sales percentage $= \dfrac{£90\,000}{£150\,000} \times \dfrac{100}{1} \qquad = 60\%$

Net profit/sales percentage $= \dfrac{£10\,000}{£150\,000} \times \dfrac{100}{1} \qquad = 6.7\%$

Wages and salaries/sales $= \dfrac{£60\,000}{£150\,000} \times \dfrac{100}{1} \qquad = 40\%$

Advertising/sales $= \dfrac{£15\,000}{£150\,000} \times \dfrac{100}{1} \qquad = 10\%$

Return on capital employed $= \dfrac{£10\,000}{£90\,000} \times \dfrac{100}{1} \qquad = 11.1\%$

LIQUIDITY

Working capital ratio $= \dfrac{£28\,500}{£35\,500} \qquad = 0.8{:}1$

Liquid capital ratio $= \dfrac{£12\,500}{£35\,500} \qquad = 0.35{:}1$

ACTIVITY

Stock turnover $= \dfrac{£60\,000}{£13\,000} \qquad = 4.6$ times per year, or 11.3 weeks

Debt collection time $\qquad = \dfrac{£12\ 500}{£150\ 000} \times 52 \qquad = 4.3$ weeks

Creditors' payment time $\qquad = \dfrac{£11\ 000}{£66\ 000} \times 52 \qquad = 8.7$ weeks

Comments
PROFITABILITY
This business has a product with a high gross profit percentage of 60% (comparisons with the previous year/similar firms need to be made). Unfortunately the high gross profit percentage is not fully reflected in the fairly low net profit percentage. Wages form 40% of the selling cost and an investigation should be made by the owner of the business to see if savings can be made here; similarly the advertising percentage appears to be quite high. Nevertheless, the business has provided a satisfactory return on the owner's capital.

LIQUIDITY
Both the working capital and the liquid capital are extremely low. The problems here seem to stem from the high bank overdraft, and the reasons for this need investigating.

ACTIVITY
The stock turnover is 4.6 times per year, and comparisons need to be made to see if this is satisfactory for the type of business. The debt collection time is satisfactory, indicating good control procedures. However, the creditors' payment time is twice as long. It may be that the bank refuses to pay any more cheques and this has resulted in the lengthy period of credit being taken: these are very real danger signals to the owner of the business and, of course, to the bank.

Conclusion
This appears to be a profitable business, although there may be scope for cutting down somewhat on the profit and loss account expenses of wages and salaries, and advertising. The business offers a reasonable return on capital. However, the business needs additional capital in order to reduce the bank overdraft and to pay any pressing creditors: this would help to restore the working capital and liquid ratios to more acceptable levels. It might be that the owner of the business should consider taking on a partner (see Chapter 19), provided that any potential partner brings in sufficient cash.

Problems in Interpretation

It is important to appreciate a number of problems that make interpretation of financial statements that much more difficult. Some of these are:

* In order to be able to make true comparisons, financial statements of the same business need to be prepared on a consistent basis (see Chapter 17). This problem is highlighted even more when the financial statements of one organization are compared with those of another: different accounting policies may have been followed, e.g. in respect of depreciation, and valuation of stock.

* Most financial statements are prepared on an historical cost basis, i.e. assets and liabilities are recorded at their original cost. Only recently have attempts been made to tackle the effects of inflation on financial statements.

* The financial statements record what has gone on in the past and are not a certain guide to what will happen in the future. Therefore decisions made on the basis of last year's financial statements may be invalid on the basis of changed circumstances - for example, consider the international price fluctuations of a barrel of oil and the effect this has on companies (and not just oil companies), or the effect of exchange rate fluctuations on companies which trade abroad.

• The balance sheet shows the assets and liabilities at one particular date, but may not be representative of the year as a whole - it may have been *window-dressed* for the financial year-end.

• The financial statements can only measure what can be recorded in money terms, i.e. in accordance with the money measurement concept (see Chapter 17).

Chapter Summary

❑ Accounting ratios and percentages can be used to measure the profitability, liquidity and activity of an organization.

❑ Comparisons need to be made between previous financial statements, or those of similar organizations.

❑ A number of limitations should be borne in mind when drawing conclusions from ratios.

Student Activities

1. You are working as a trainee accountant and come across, in your firm's files, the following information relating to two businesses, A and B.

	BUSINESS A		BUSINESS B	
	£000s	£000s	£000s	£000s
PROFIT AND LOSS ACCOUNT EXTRACTS				
Sales		3 057		1 628
Cost of goods sold		2 647		911
Gross Profit		410		717
Expenses		366		648
Net Profit		44		69
SUMMARISED BALANCE SHEETS				
Fixed Assets		344		555
Current Assets				
Stock	242		237	
Debtors	6		269	
Bank/cash	3		1	
	251		507	
Less Current Liabilities	195		212	
Working Capital		56		295
NET ASSETS		400		850
FINANCED BY				
Capital		400		850

One business operates a chain of grocery supermarkets; the other is a heavy engineering company.

As a training exercise your boss asks you to:

- Calculate the following accounting ratios for both businesses:

  (a) gross profit percentage
  (b) net profit percentage
  (c) stock turnover (use balance sheet figure as *average* stock)
  (d) working capital (current) ratio
  (e) liquid capital ratio
  (f) debtors' collection period
  (g) return on capital employed

- Indicate which company you believe to be the grocery supermarket chain and which the heavy engineering business. Briefly explain the reasons for your choice based on the ratios calculated and the accounting information.

Present your findings in the form of a memorandum. Your boss is Gareth Davies, Senior Partner in Davies, Davies and Lloyd.

2. You are the trainee who features in Activity 1, and are later presented with the following summarized information concerning J.D. Rowles:

J.D. ROWLES
TRADING AND PROFIT AND LOSS ACCOUNTS (EXTRACTS)
FOR THE YEAR ENDED 30 APRIL 19-4 AND 30 APRIL 19-5

	19-4	19-5
	£	£
Sales (all on credit)	120 000	200 000
Cost of Goods Sold	80 000	150 000
Gross Profit	40 000	50 000
Expenses	10 000	15 000
Net Profit	30 000	35 000

BALANCE SHEET (EXTRACTS) AS AT 30 APRIL 19-4 AND 30 APRIL 19-5

	19-4 £	19-4 £	19-4 £	19-5 £	19-5 £	19-5 £
Fixed Assets			15 000			12 000
Current Assets						
Stock		7 000			18 000	
Debtors		12 000			36 000	
Bank		1 000			-	
		20 000			54 000	
Less Current Liabilities						
Creditors	6 000			15 000		
Bank overdraft	-			10 000		
		6 000			25 000	
Working Capital			14 000			29 000
NET ASSETS			29 000			41 000
FINANCED BY						
Capital						
Opening capital			22 000			29 000
Add net profit			30 000			35 000
			52 000			64 000
Less drawings			23 000			23 000
			29 000			41 000

Notes:
- there were no purchases or disposals of fixed assets during the year
- during 19-4 and 19-5 Rowles reduced his selling prices in order to stimulate sales
- it may be assumed that price levels were stable

You are to use accounting ratios to analyse and assess the profitability, liquidity and activity of J.D. Rowles of 7 Sabrina Avenue, Weatherbury, Dorset. Present your findings in a letter to Mr Rowles, who is shortly to visit his bank manager to discuss the recent year's figures.

3. Caxton Printers is an old family concern with a well established business in your town. It undertakes all types of commercial printing, and also has a retail outlet which carried a wide range of stationery lines. Recently a new manager has been appointed and has boosted sales and profitability, much to the suspicion of the older members of staff who do not like his brash salesmanship. You, as the trainee who features in Activity 1, have just received the latest set of accounts, which are summarised below.

Using accounting ratios and other measures of performance, assess the strength of the business, paying particular attention to:

- profitability
- liquidity
- activity

EXTRACTS FROM THE ACCOUNTS OF CAXTON PRINTERS
FOR THE YEAR ENDED 31 DECEMBER 19-8

TRADING AND PROFIT AND LOSS ACCOUNT EXTRACT

	19-8 £	previous year £
Sales	840 000	500 000
Cost of Goods Sold	425 000	375 000
Net Profit	75 500	50 000

BALANCE SHEET EXTRACT

	cost £	depreciation to date £	net £	previous year £
Fixed Assets				
Premises	175 000	-	175 000	115 000
Fixtures and Fittings	50 000	10 000	40 000	45 000
	225 000	10 000	215 000	160 000
Current Assets				
Stock	70 000			40 000
Debtors	100 000			70 000
Cash	15 500			5 000
			185 500	115 000
Less Current Liabilities				
Creditors	75 000			50 000
Bank	50 000			25 000
			125 000	75 000
Working Capital			60 500	40 000
NET ASSETS			275 500	200 000
FINANCED BY				
Capital			275 500	200 000

Chapter Nineteen
Financial Statements: Partnerships

In Chapter 13 we considered the basic financial statements of business organizations. These statements consist of trading account, profit and loss account, and balance sheet. They are produced usually at the end of each financial year and report the gross profit and net profit for the year, together with the assets and liabilities at the year-end. Until now we have considered only the financial statements of a sole trader, i.e. one person in business; in this chapter we will see how they are presented where two or more people own a business in the form of a partnership, an entity which we have already considered in outline in Chapter 6.

Definition of a Partnership

The Partnership Act of 1890 defines a partnership as:

the relation which subsists between persons carrying on a business in common with a view of profit.

Accounting Requirements of the Partnership Act, 1890

The Partnership Act states the following accounting rules:

* profits and losses are to be shared equally between the partners
* no partner is entitled to a salary
* partners are not entitled to receive interest on their capital
* interest is not to be charged on partners' drawings (the amount they have taken out of the business)
* when a partner contributes more capital than agreed, he or she is entitled to receive interest at five per cent per annum on the excess

These rules *must* be followed unless the partners agree amongst themselves, by means of a *partnership agreement,* to follow different accounting rules. In particular, a partnership agreement will often cover the following:

* division of profits or losses between partners
* whether interest is to be paid on capital, and at what rate
* whether interest is to be charged on partners' drawings, and at what rate

Financial Statements of a Partnership

A partnership prepares the same type of financial statements as a sole-trader business:

- trading and profit and loss accounts
- balance sheet

One main difference is that, immediately after the profit and loss account, follows an *appropriation section* (see below). This shows how the net profit from profit and loss account is divided between the partners. A second difference is that the capital section of the balance sheet needs to be presented in such a way as to show the capital account of each partner separately. Partners usually have a current account (not to be confused with a bank current account), and this must also be stated on the balance sheet (see below).

Apart from these differences, the other financial statements are presented in *exactly* the same way as for a sole trader.

Appropriation of Profits

As mentioned above, the appropriation section (often described as the appropriation account) follows the profit and loss account and shows how net profit has been divided amongst the partners.

For example, Able, Baker and Cox are partners sharing profits and losses equally; their profit and loss account for the current year shows a net profit of £30 000. The appropriation of profits appears as:

	£
Net Profit	30 000
Appropriation of Profits	
Able	10 000
Baker	10 000
Cox	10 000
	30 000

The appropriation of profits above is very simple. A more complex appropriation would show a salary paid to a partner (*not* to be shown in profit and loss account), interest allowed on partners' capital, and interest charged on partners' drawings.

An example for the partnership of Davis and Eady is as follows:

	£	£
Net Profit		25 000
Add interest charged on partners' drawings:		
Davis	1 000	
Eady	1 500	
		2 500
		27 500
Appropriation of Profits		
Salary: Eady		9 000
Interest allowed on partners' capitals:		
Davis	2 500	
Eady	1 000	
		3 500
Share of remaining profits:		
Davis (60%)	9 000	
Eady (40%)	6 000	
		15 000
		27 500

Note that all of the available profit, after allowing for any salary, and interest charged and allowed, is shared amongst the partners, in the ratio in which they share profits and losses.

Case Problem: Partnership Fox and Gun

Situation

Fox and Gun are in partnership with capitals of £20 000 and £15 000 respectively. The partnership agreement states that:

- Gun is to be paid a salary of £8 000 each year
- interest is allowed on partners' capital accounts at eight per cent per year
- interest is to be charged on drawings at five per cent
- remaining profits are to be shared by Fox and Gun in the ratio of 3:2 respectively

For the financial year which ended on 31 March 19-5, the profit and loss account shows a net profit of £21 000. During the year Fox made drawings of £9 000, Gun made drawings of £12 000. Show how the profits will be appropriated.

Solution

	£	£
Net Profit		21 000
Add interest charged on partners' drawings:		
Fox	450	
Gun	<u>600</u>	
		<u>1 050</u>
		22 050
Appropriation of Profits		
Salary: Gun		8 000
Interest allowed on partners' capitals:		
Fox	1 600	
Gun	<u>1 200</u>	
		2 800
Share of remaining profits:		
Fox (60%)	6 750	
Gun (40%)	<u>4 500</u>	
		<u>11 250</u>
		22 050

Capital Accounts and Current Accounts

Most partnerships keep a capital account and a current account for each partner. The capital account is *fixed,* and only alters if a permanent increase or decrease in capital contributed by the partner takes place. The current account is *fluctuating* and it is to this account that:

- share of profits is added
- salary (if any) is added
- interest allowed on partners' capital is added
- drawings are deducted
- interest charged on partners' drawings is deducted

Thus, the current account is treated as a *working* account, while capital account remains fixed, except for capital introduced or withdrawn.

The balance sheet must show the year-end balances on each partner's capital and current account. However, it is usual to show the transactions that have taken place on each account in summary form, in the same way that, in a sole-trader's balance sheet, net profit is added, and drawings are deducted.

The following is an example layout for the capital and current accounts of the partnership of Fox and Gun (see above) as they will be shown in the balance sheet (the other sections of the balance sheet are not shown; the opening balances on partners' current accounts are Fox £1 000, Gun £200.

BALANCE SHEET (EXTRACT) OF FOX AND GUN AS AT 31 MARCH 19-5

	£	£	£
Capital Accounts			
Fox		20 000	
Gun		15 000	
			35 000

	FOX	GUN	
Current Accounts			
Opening balance	1 000	200	
Add: salary	-	8 000	
interest on capital	1 600	1 200	
share of profit	6 750	4 500	
	9 350	13 900	
Less: drawings	9 000	12 000	
interest on drawings	450	600	
	(100)	1 300	
			1 200
			36 200

Notes:
- Fox has drawn more out of the current account than the balance of his account; accordingly, at the end of the year, Fox has a negative (debit) balance on the account with the partnership. By contrast, Gun has a positive (credit) balance of £1 300 on current account.

- The other sections of the balance sheet, i.e. fixed assets, current assets, and current liabilities are presented in the same way as for a sole-trader.

Chapter Summary

❑ A partnership is formed when two or more (usually up to a maximum of twenty) people set up in business.

❑ The Partnership Act, 1890, states certain accounting rules, principally that profits and losses must be shared equally.

❑ Many partnerships *over-ride* the accounting rules of the Act by creating a partnership agreement.

❑ In partnership accounting, an appropriation section follows profit and loss account to show the division of profits or losses between partners.

❑ The usual way to account for partners' capital is to maintain a fixed capital account for each partner. This is complemented by a fluctuating current account which is used as a *working* account for share of profits, drawings, etc.

The next Chapter continues the theme of more specialist financial statements by looking at the year-end accounts of limited companies.

✍ Student Activities

You are a trainee accountant working in the local office of Anderson, Kerr, Price and Co., an international firm of Chartered Accountants. You have reached the point in your training when you are dealing with partnership accounts and today you have to work on the year-end accounts of four clients.

1. Box and Cox are in partnership running an electrical shop. On 30 June 19-5 their capital accounts, which have not changed during the previous 12 months, are: Box £15 000; Cox £10 000.

    Their deed of partnership provides that:

    • Cox is to receive a salary of £5 000 p.a. for managing the business
    • each partner is to be credited with interest on capital at 8 per cent per annum
    • profits or losses are to be shared equally
    • interest is charged on drawings at 5 per cent on the total amount drawn in each year

    On 1 July 19-4 Box's current account showed a negative (debit) balance of £120 and Cox's a positive (credit) balance of £150. During the year ended 30 June 19-5, their drawings were: Box £3 500 and Cox £6 500. Profits for the year ended 30 June 19-5 were £12 000 before appropriation.

    You are to show the appropriation of profits for the year ended 30 June 19-5, together with the partners' capital and current accounts as they would appear in the balance sheet at 30 June 19-5.

    Write a letter to the partners (The Electric Shop, Green Street, Barchester) enclosing the figures produced and explaining what they show. You know that each partner owns a large house and, yesterday, on the telephone, Box expressed his concern to you that these assets should not, under any circumstances, feature in the partnership accounts: give appropriate advice to Box and Cox in your letter.

2. Clark and Pearce are in partnership selling business computer systems. They share profits and losses: Clark two-thirds, Pearce one-third. After the completion of the trading account their book-keeper has extracted the following trial balance at 30 June 19-5:

	£	£
Gross Profit		55 000
Salaries	10 400	
Electricity	420	
Rent and rates	10 000	
Discount allowed	140	
Stationery	410	
*Stock at 30 June 19-5	21 570	
Debtors and creditors	19 000	6 950
Bad debts written off	200	
Provision for bad debts		780
Office equipment	52 000	
Fixtures and fittings	13 400	
Clark: Capital account		60 000
Current account		430
Drawings	10 600	
Pearce: Capital account		30 000
Current account		300
Drawings	5 700	
Bank	9 620	
	153 460	153 460

* Closing stock is included in the trial balance here because the trading account for the year has already been prepared.

Notes at 30 June 19-5:

- Office equipment is to be depreciated by 20 per cent, using the straight-line method
- Provide for interest on partners' capitals at 5% per annum
- Increase the provision for bad debts to £900
- Rates paid in advance: £600
- Electricity owing £180

You are to prepare the profit and loss account (including appropriation section) of Clark and Pearce for the year ended 30 June 19-5, together with a balance sheet at that date.

3. Booth and Webster are partners in a wholesale stationery business. They share profits and losses in the ratio of 3:2. The following trial balance was extracted by their book-keeper at 30 June 19-5:

		£	£
Current accounts:	Booth		200
	Webster		100
Capital accounts:	Booth		27 800
	Webster		13 900
Drawings:	Booth	6 800	
	Webster	4 400	
Furniture and fittings at cost		1 700	
Provision for depreciation on furniture and fittings			340
Stock at 1 July 19-4		21 000	
Debtors and creditors		16 328	12 750
Purchases and sales		152 000	206 000
Freehold property at cost		68 500	
Wages and salaries		25 454	
Rates		300	
General expenses		9 832	
Bank		2 408	
Discounts		4 154	1 630
Rents received			156
Bank loan			50 000
		312 876	312 876

Notes at 30 June 19-5:
- Stock is valued at £23 500
- Wages and salaries outstanding: £304
- Rates paid in advance: £60
- Rent received includes £12 for July 19-5
- Depreciation on furniture and fittings to be provided at 10% per annum on cost
- Interest on capital is to be allowed at 5% per annum
- No interest is charged on drawings

You are to prepare the trading and profit and loss accounts (including appropriation account) of Booth and Webster for the year ended 30 June 19-5, together with a balance sheet at that date.

4.   Anne Adams and Jenny Beeson are partners in an electrical supplies shop called 'A & B Electrics'. They share profits and losses equally. The following trial balance was extracted by their book-keeper at 30 June 19-5:

		£	£
Capital accounts:	A. Adams		30 000
	J. Beeson		20 000
Current accounts:	A. Adams		780
	J. Beeson		920
Drawings:	A. Adams	16 000	
	J. Beeson	10 000	
Stock at 1 July 19-4		26 550	
Purchases and sales		185 290	250 140
Returns		1 360	850
Rent and rates		8 420	
Wages and salaries		16 290	
Motor vehicle expenses		2 470	
General expenses		6 210	
Motor vehicles at cost		12 000	
Fixtures and fittings at cost		4 000	
Provision for depreciation: motor vehicles			3 000
fixtures and fittings			800
Debtors and creditors		6 850	12 360
Bank		22 009	
Cash		1 376	
Bad debts written off		175	
Provision for bad debts			150
		319 000	319 000

Notes at 30 June 19-5:
- Stock is valued at £27 750
- Rates paid in advance £250
- Wages and salaries owing £320
- Provision for bad debts to be equal to 2 per cent debtors
- Depreciation on fixtures and fittings to be provided at 10% per annum on cost using the straight-line method
- Depreciation on motor vehicles to be provided at 25% per annum using the reducing balance method
- Interest on capital is to be allowed at 8% per annum
- Interest on drawings is to be charged at 5% per annum

You are to prepare the trading and profit and loss accounts (including appropriation account) of A & B Electrics for the year ended 30 June 19-5, together with a balance sheet at that date.

Chapter Twenty
Financial Statements: Limited Companies

In Chapter 6 we considered the different types of business entity - the sole trader, the partnership, the limited company - and examined the liability of the owner(s) in each case. The limited company is often chosen as the business entity for a number of reasons, which include:

- Liability of members (i.e. the shareholders, and directors who are shareholders) is *strictly limited* and their personal assets, unless pledged as security to a lender, are not available to the company's creditors.

- An expanding sole trader or partnership aiming to raise more finance by way of capital, may do so by incorporating into a company, enabling it to issue shares to the owner(s), family, business associates, and Venture Capital Companies. This small or medium-sized company is often referred to as a 'private company'.

- A larger company (with share capital over £50 000) may become a 'public limited company' (plc), and may raise finance from the public by means of a listing on the Stock Exchange, or a related market, although not all plcs do so.

Our study of Finance requires us to examine the year-end financial statements of limited companies. These statements broadly follow the layout of those prepared for sole-traders and partnerships. The Companies Act 1985 (amended by the Companies Act 1989), however, stipulates that certain annual financial statements must be filed with the Registrar of Companies and copies are sent to shareholders. Such 'published accounts', as they are known, will not be discussed in this chapter: it may be that you will study these in detail as part of later accounting courses. Nevertheless, you should take the opportunity of obtaining a set of such 'published accounts' (see Student Activity 3). In this Chapter we will concentrate on the basic form of company year-end financial statements. Before we examine these statements in detail we will first look at the principal way a company raises finance: shares. There are different types of shares which appear in the company balance sheet as a capital item.

Types of Shares Issued by Limited Companies

One clause contained in the Memorandum of Association (the document setting out the powers and objects of a company) states the share capital of that company and its division into shares of a fixed amount. This is known as the *authorized share capital,* i.e. the share capital that the company is allowed to issue. The authorized share capital may not be the same as the amount that the company has actually issued - this is known as the *issued share capital*. The latter can never exceed the former: if a company which has issued the full extent of its authorized share capital wishes to make an increase, it must first pass the appropriate resolution at a general meeting of the shareholders.

The authorized and issued share capital is divided into a number of classes or types of share, the principal of which are ordinary shares and preference shares. Each share has a nominal or face value which is entered in the accounts. Shares may be issued with nominal values of 5p, 10p, 25p, 50p or

£1, or indeed for any amount. Thus a company with an authorized share capital of £100 000 might state in its Memorandum of Association that this is divided up into:

100 000 ordinary shares of 50p each	£50 000
50 000 seven per cent preference shares of £1 each	£50 000
	£100 000

The nominal value of a share often bears little relationship to its true value. It is easy to find out the value of shares in a public limited company - if they are quoted on the Stock Exchange, the price may well be listed in the *Financial Times*. Shareholders receive *dividends* on their shares, being a distribution of a part of the company's earnings for a year or half-year. The dividend paid half-way through a financial year is known as an *interim dividend,* while that paid at the end of a year is a *final dividend*.

Ordinary (equity) shares

These are the most commonly issued class of share. They take a share of the profits available for distribution after allowance has been made for all expenses of the business, including loan interest, taxation, and after preference dividends (if any). When a company makes large profits, it will have the ability to pay higher dividends to the ordinary shareholders; when profits are low or losses are made, the ordinary shareholders may receive a smaller or even no dividend. Companies rarely pay out all of their profits in the form of dividends; most retain some profits as reserves. These can always be used to enable a dividend to be paid in a year when the company makes little or no profit, always assuming that the company has sufficient cash in the bank to make the payment. Ordinary shareholders, in the event of the company ceasing to trade or 'winding up', will be the last to receive any repayment of their investment: other creditors will have to be paid off first.

Preference shares

Such shares usually carry a fixed rate of dividend - ten per cent for example - which, as their name suggests, is paid in preference to the ordinary shareholders; but it is only paid if the company makes profits. In the event of winding up the company, the 'preference' will also extend to repayment of capital before the ordinary shareholders.

Preference shares may be non-cumulative or cumulative. If insufficient profits are made during a certain year to pay the preference dividend and the shares are designated as non-cumulative, then there is no provision for 'catching up' with missed dividends in future years. This contrasts with cumulative preference shares: if the dividend on these is not paid in one year, it accumulates and will be paid in the future. In this way missing dividends will always be paid provided that the company makes sufficient profits in the future. All preference shares are cumulative unless otherwise stated.

Loans and Debentures

In addition to money provided by shareholders, who are the owners of the company, further funds can be obtained by borrowing in the form of loans or debentures, for example, from a bank. The term 'debenture' usually refers to a formal certificate issued by a company acknowledging that a sum of money is owing to a specified person. Both loans and debentures usually carry a fixed rate of interest that must be paid, just like other business expenses, whether a company makes profits or not. As loan and debenture interest is a business expense, this is deducted from the profit and loss account along with all other expenses. In the event of the winding-up of the company, loan and debenture-holders would be repaid before any shareholders. Often debentures are secured, being backed by assets of the company pledged as security. In the event of winding up, the assets would be sold and used to repay the debenture-holders first. Unsecured debentures - sometimes known as *naked* debentures - do not have this backing.

Limited Companies: Trading and Profit and Loss Accounts

A limited company uses the same type of year-end financial statements as a sole trader or partnership. However there are two items commonly found in the profit and loss account of a limited company that are not found in those of other business entities:

- **Directors' remuneration** i.e. amounts paid to directors. As directors are employed by the company, their *pay* appears amongst the expenses of the company.

- **Debenture interest** as already noted, when debentures are issued by companies, the interest is shown as an expense in the profit and loss account.

In a similar way to a partnership, a limited company follows the profit and loss account with an *appropriation section* (often described as an appropriation account) to show how the net profit has been divided amongst the owners of the business - the shareholders. Here is an example of a simple appropriation account:

	£
Net Profit for year	100 000
Less corporation tax	20 000
Profit after taxation	80 000
Less proposed ordinary dividend	50 000
Retained profit for year	30 000
Add balance of retained profits at beginning of year	35 000
Balance of retained profits at end of year	65 000

Notes:

- The company has recorded a net profit of £100 000 in its profit and loss account - this is brought into the appropriation section.

- Corporation tax, the tax that a company has to pay on its profits, is shown in the appropriation account.

- The company proposes to distribute £50 000 to the ordinary shareholders as a dividend. This will be paid in the early part of the next financial year.

- Added to net profit is a balance of £35 000. This represents profits of the company from previous years that are undistributed, i.e.they have not been paid to the shareholders in the form of dividends. Unlike a sole trader or partnership, where all profits are added to owner's capital, a company will rarely distribute all its profits. You will note that this appropriation account shows a balance of retained profits at the year-end of £65 000. Such retained profits form a *revenue reserve* of the company. It is usual for a company to keep back some part of its profits in the form of reserves, to help the company build for the future.

- It should be noted that reserves are *not* a cash fund to be used whenever the company needs money, but are in fact represented by assets shown on the balance sheet. These assets may, or may not be realisable. The reserves recognise the fact that the assets belong to the shareholders (via the company).

- Besides the balance of retained profits - sometimes described as profit and loss account balance - companies often have several different revenue reserve accounts, e.g. general reserve or, for a specific purpose, reserve for the replacement of machinery. Transfers to or from these revenue reserve accounts are made in the appropriation section of the profit and loss account.

A more comprehensive appropriation account is shown on the next page.

APPROPRIATION ACCOUNT OF ORION LTD
FOR THE YEAR ENDED 31 DECEMBER 19-4

	£	£
Net Profit for year before taxation		43 000
Less corporation tax		15 000
Profit for year after taxation		28 000
Less: interim dividends paid		
ordinary shares	5 000	
preference shares	2 000	
final dividends proposed		
ordinary shares	10 000	
preference shares	2 000	
		19 000
		9 000
Less transfer to general reserve		5 000
Retained profit for year		4 000
Add balance of retained profits at beginning of year		16 000
Balance of retained profits at end of year		20 000

Limited Companies: Balance Sheet

Balance sheets of limited companies follow the same layout as those of sole traders and partnerships but the capital section is more complex because of the different classes of shares that may be issued, and the various reserves. Fig. 20.1 shows the balance sheet of Orion Ltd. as an example.

A word of explanation about some of the items appearing in company balance sheets is appropriate at this point.

Fixed assets
Like other balance sheets, this section comprises those items that do not change daily and are likely to be retained for use in the business for some time to come. It is usual for fixed assets, with the possible exception of freehold land, to be depreciated over a period of time or with use. The headings used for fixed assets in a balance sheet should read: *cost, depreciation to date* and *net* (see fig. 20.1).

Current assets
The usual current assets will be included, i.e. stocks, debtors, balance at bank, and cash in hand.

Current liabilities
As with the balance sheets of sole traders and partnerships, this section contains those liabilities that are normally due to be paid within twelve months from the date of the balance sheet, e.g. creditors, bank overdraft. For limited companies, this section also contains the amount of proposed dividends and the amount of corporation tax to be paid within the next twelve months. Both of these amounts are also included in the appropriation account.

Authorized share capital
As already explained, this is the share capital of the company and its division into shares of a fixed amount as authorized by the company's Memorandum of Association. It is included on the balance sheet 'for information', but is not added into the balance sheet total, as it may not be the same amount as the issued share capital.

BALANCE SHEET OF ORION LTD AS AT 31 DECEMBER 19-4

Fixed Assets	Cost	Dep'n to date	Net
	£	£	£
Freehold land and buildings	180 000	20 000	160 000
Machinery	280 000	110 000	170 000
Fixtures and fittings	100 000	25 000	75 000
	560 000	155 000	405 000

Current Assets

Stock		50 000	
Debtors		38 000	
Bank		22 000	
Cash		2 000	
		112 000	

Less Current Liabilities

Creditors	30 000		
Proposed dividends	12 000		
Corporation tax	15 000		
		57 000	
Working Capital			55 000
NET ASSETS			460 000

FINANCED BY:
Authorized Share Capital

100 000 10% preference shares of £1 each		100 000
600 000 ordinary shares of £1 each		600 000
		700 000

Issued Share Capital

40 000 10% preference shares of £1 each, fully paid		40 000
300 000 ordinary shares of £1 each, fully paid		300 000
		340 000

Revenue Reserves

General reserve (including transfer of £5 000)	40 000	
Profit and loss account	20 000	
		60 000
		400 000

Long Term Liabilities

12% debentures		60 000
		460 000

Fig. 20.1   An example of a limited company balance sheet

Issued share capital

Here are detailed the classes and number of shares that have been isued. As stated earlier the issued share capital cannot exceed the amount authorized. In the balance sheet of Orion Ltd., the shares are described as being *fully paid,* meaning that the company has received the full amount of the value of each share from the shareholders. Sometimes shares will be *partly paid*, e.g. ordinary shares of £1, but 75p paid. This means that the company can make a *call* on the shareholders to pay the additional 25p to make the shares fully paid. Companies often issue partly paid shares and then make calls at certain times: for example, a company that is issuing shares to raise the finance for a new factory may wish to receive the proceeds of issue at different stages of the building and equipment of the factory. For the purpose of entering the amount of issued share capital in the balance sheet, always multiply the number of shares by the amount paid on them, e.g. 100 000 ordinary shares of £1 each, 75p paid = £75 000.

Revenue reserves

The reserves from profits are the amounts which the directors of the company have retained in the business. There is no reason why such reserves should not be drawn on in the future to pay a dividend, provided that the company has the cash to pay a dividend. (In addition to revenue reserves, some companies have *capital reserves* which cannot be used for the payment of dividends. An example of a capital reserve is a revaluation reserve which occurs when a fixed asset, most probably property, has been revalued in the balance sheet: the amount of the revaluation is placed in a revaluation reserve).

Long-term liabilities

These are generally considered to be liabilities that are due to be repaid more than twelve months from the date of the balance sheet, e.g. loans and debentures.

Chapter Summary

❏ A limited company, unlike a sole trader or a partnership, has a separate legal entity from its owners and is regulated by the Companies Act 1985 (as amended by the Companies Act 1989).

❏ The main types of shares issued by companies are ordinary shares and preference shares.

❏ Borrowings in the form of loans and debentures are a further source of finance.

❏ The year-end accounts of a company include an appropriation section, which follows the profit and loss account.

❏ The balance sheet of a limited company is similar to that of sole traders and partnerships but the capital and reserves section reflects the ownership of the company by its shareholders: the authorized and issued share capitals are listed, together with reserves.

✍ Student Activities

1. (a) Broadheath Ltd., a music publishing company, has an authorized share capital of £500 000 divided into 100 000 8 per cent preference shares of £1 each and 400 000 ordinary shares of £1 each. All the preference shares are issued and fully paid; 200 000 ordinary shares are issued and fully paid.

   On 31 December 19-2 the company's reserves were £60 000; current liabilities £35 000; current assets £125 500; fixed assets (at cost) £350 000 and provisions for depreciation on fixed assets £80 500.

   Prepare a summarised balance sheet as at 31 December 19-2 to display this information.

   (b) Explain to a potential shareholder the difference between ordinary shares and preference shares.

2. Rupert Ltd., a company selling cars, has retained profits of £5 000 on 1 January 19-7. The net profit for 19-7 amounts to £10 000. It is decided to create a general reserve of £2 000, and dividends are proposed as follows:

   6% preference share dividend, the company having issued £20 000 of preference share capital

   10% ordinary share dividend on issued share capital of £30 000

   As accountant to Rupert Ltd., show the appropriation section of the profit and loss account for the year ended 31 December 19-7. Explain to one of the directors, Sid Smith, who does not understand finance, what you have done in the appropriation account. In particular, he wants to know why the transfer to general reserve has been made: as he comments, "it seems to me as though we have got another bank account and, surely, it would be better to pay off our existing overdraft with this money".

3. Choose a public limited company that is of interest to you. Write to the company secretary asking for a copy of the latest report and accounts (many companies advertise the availability of their report and accounts in the financial press).

   To illustrate the statutory accounts, the company may well use bar and pie charts to describe its progress to users of the accounts (you may also be sent a copy of the employees' report).

   Study the report and accounts from the viewpoint of a potential investor: calculate the accounting ratios, described in Chapter 18, over the past two years, and assess the progress of the company.

4. You are a trainee accountant working for Rossiter and Rossiter, a local firm of Chartered Accountants. The senior partner, Mrs Rossiter, hands you the following trial balance at 31 December 19-2, of Sidbury Trading Co. Ltd., a local stationery supplies firm:

	£	£
Share capital		240 000
Freehold land and buildings at cost	142 000	
Motor vans at cost	55 000	
Provision for depreciation on motor vans		
at 1 January 19-2		21 800
Purchases and sales	189 273	297 462
Rent and rates	4 000	
General expenses	9 741	
Wages and salaries	34 689	
Bad debts written off	948	
Provision for doubtful debts at 1 January 19-2		1 076
Directors' salaries	25 000	
Debtors and creditors	26 482	16 974
Retained profit at 1 January 19-2		18 397
Stock at 1 January 19-2	42 618	
Bank	65 958	
	595 709	595 709

You are given the following additional information:

*   The authorized share capital is 300 000 ordinary shares of £1 each; all the shares which have been issued are fully paid
*   Wages and salaries outstanding at 31 December 19-2 amounted to £354
*   The provision for doubtful debts is to be increased by £124
*   Stock at 31 December 19-2 is valued at £47 288
*   Rent and rates amounting to £400 were paid in advance at 31 December 19-2
*   It is proposed to pay a dividend of £8 000 for 19-2
*   Depreciation on motor vans is to be charged at the rate of 20 per cent per annum on cost

You are to:

*   Prepare appropriate final accounts for the year 19-2, together with a balance sheet at 31 December 19-2.

*   Mrs Rossiter is to meet the directors tomorrow and asks you to prepare a memorandum addressed to her on your impressions of the financial state of this business from the accounts and balance sheet you have just prepared (use accounting ratios as appropriate).

5.   Another client of Rossiter and Rossiter, Chartered Accountants, is Playfair Ltd., a wholesaler of children's toys. The company has an authorized share capital of 50 000 ordinary shares of £1 each and 10 000 8% preference shares of £1 each. At 31 December 19-2, the following trial balance was extracted:

	£	£
Ordinary share capital		50 000
8% preference share capital		8 000
Plant and machinery at cost	34 000	
Motor vehicles at cost	16 000	
Debtors and creditors	34 980	17 870
Bank	14 505	
10% debentures		9 000
Stock (1 January 19-2)	25 200	
General expenses	11 020	
Purchases and sales	164 764	233 384
Bad debts written off	2 400	
Debenture interest	900	
Discounts	325	640
Salaries	24 210	
Insurance	300	
Provision for depreciation:		
plant and machinery		16 000
motor vehicles		7 200
Directors' fees	17 000	
Interim preference dividend paid	320	
Profit and loss account (1 January 19-2)		3 300
Provision for bad debts (1 January 19-2)		530
	345 924	345 924

Additional information:

• Stock at 31 December 19-2 is valued at £28 247
• Depreciation on plant and machinery is to be provided for at the rate of 10 per cent per annum calculated on cost
• Depreciation on motor vehicles is to be provided for at the rate of 20 per cent per annum using the reducing balance method
• Insurance prepaid at 31 December 19-2 amounted to £60
• General expenses owing at 31 December 19-2 amounted to £110
• The provision for bad debts is to be increased to £750
• The directors propose to pay an ordinary dividend of 6 per cent to the ordinary shareholders and to pay the remaining dividend due to the preference shareholders
• £2 000 is to be transferred to General Reserve

You are to prepare appropriate final accounts for the year ended 31 December 19-2, together with a balance sheet at that date.

Assignment Ten

Limited Company Accounts: Severn DIY Limited

GENERAL OBJECTIVES COVERED
E, G, H.

SKILLS DEVELOPED
Learning and studying, communicating, numeracy, information gathering, identifying and tackling problems, working with others.

SITUATION
Severn DIY Ltd. operates a chain of do-it-yourself shops throughout Gloucestershire and the County of Hereford and Worcester. The company employs some 25 full-time staff, together with a number working part-time. The three directors, who originally founded the company and continue to work in it full-time, believe they have an enlightened attitude to employee involvement in the business. They have encouraged the development of a 'works' committee which meets at regular intervals to review progress. In recent weeks some bad feeling has been shown at these meetings because the employees' representatives have been seeking a substantial pay rise, something which the company claims they cannot afford.

The company has an authorized share capital of 500 000 ordinary shares of £1 each. At 30 April 19-6 the following trial balance was extracted:

	£	£
Ordinary share capital		500 000
Property	350 000	
Fixtures and fittings at cost	90 000	
Motor vehicles at cost	60 000	
Debtors and creditors	349 800	178 700
Bank overdraft		18 350
10% Debentures		90 000
Stock (1 May 19-5)	252 000	
General expenses	110 200	
Purchases and sales	1 652 140	2 333 840
Bad debts written off	24 000	
Debenture interest	4 500	
Discounts	3 250	6 400
Salaries	242 100	
Insurance	3 000	
Provision for depreciation:		
fixtures and fittings		27 000
motor vehicles		21 600
Directors' fees	73 200	
Profit and loss account (1 May 19-5)		33 000
Provision for bad debts (1 May 19-5)		5 300
	3 214 190	3 214 190

Additional information provided by the Accounts Department:

- Stock at 30 April 19-6 is valued at £282 470
- Depreciation of fixtures and fittings is to be provided for at the rate of 10 per cent per annum calculated on cost
- Depreciation on motor vehicles is to be provided for at the rate of 20 per cent per annum using the reducing balance method
- Insurance prepaid at 30 April 19-6 amounted to £600
- General expenses owing at 30 April 19-6 amounted to £1 100
- The provision for bad debts is to be increased to £7 500
- The company will pay the debenture interest of £4 500 due for the year ended 30 April 19-6 on 11 May 19-6
- The directors propose to pay an ordinary dividend of 6 per cent to the ordinary shareholders

STUDENT TASKS

1.   As a clerk in the accounts department you are asked to prepare the trading and profit and loss accounts for the year ended 30 April 19-6, together with a balance sheet at the year-end. These financial statements are then circulated to the directors and the members of the works committee.

2.   A confrontation between the management and the works committee is due to take place shortly. From the point of view of:
either the management ofSevern DIY Ltd.
or the employee representatives,
the class as a whole should prepare a case to support the contrasting viewpoints concerning the disputed pay increase. Reference should be made to the latest financial statements. Accounting ratios and/or diagrammatic presentations could be used in support.

Note to teachers: Task 2

It is suggested that the class should meet as a whole for a debate between management and works committee. This may best be handled as follows:

- divide class into two groups (management and works committee) to discuss issues

- a deputation from each group to meet in front of the whole class for staged meeting

- the class then votes on issues as disinterested parties

Chapter Twenty One
Management Accounting

Management accounting is defined by the accountancy profession as:

the presentation of accounting information in such a way as to assist management in the formation of policies and in the day-to-day planning and control of an undertaking.

It is concerned, therefore, with providing the management of an organization with recommendations, based on accounting information, in order to help in making day-to-day decisions and in longer-term planning. This is different from much of what has been studied so far in Finance, which has been concerned with financial transactions and statements that have *already taken place*. Management accounting uses information from past transactions as an aid to making decisions for the future. For example, a business manufacturing two products, A and B, might decide, using last year's financial transactions as a guide, to concentrate on making only product A for the next six months. At the end of the six months' period the results will be analysed to see how closely what happened in practice followed what was predicted to happen; and so the monitoring process will go on.

Management accounting needs certain basic information from which to work. It needs to know accurate costs of individual products or services, together with the total costs of running the organization: such information is found from the costing records. Nowadays the use of costing information to make decisions is assuming increasing importance as businesses seek to maximise profits and public sector organizations are required to provide the best services at lowest cost. To this end, many organizations have specialist costing sections and employ cost clerks. Here the information required is gathered together so that it is available to help in the decision-making process of management accounting.

Case Problem: S & T Manufacturing Co.

Situation
The following information is given for S & T Manufacturing Co., a two-product (S and T) company, for the year 19-1:

			£	£
Sales:	S			100 000
	T			200 000
				300 000
Less:	Cost of materials:	S	50 000	
		T	95 000	
	Labour costs:	S	40 000	
		T	50 000	
*Cost of overheads:		S	20 000	
		T	30 000	285 000
Profit				15 000

* Overheads include factory rent, depreciation of machinery, and other factory costs.

Try presenting this information in a way which will be of more use to the management of this business. What conclusions do you draw for this business?

Solution

The information is best presented in a way which analyses the profit of each product:

	S £	T £	Total £
Cost of materials	50 000	95 000	145 000
Labour costs	40 000	50 000	90 000
Cost of overheads	20 000	30 000	50 000
Cost of Goods Sold	110 000	175 000	285 000
Sales	100 000	200 000	300 000
Less Cost of Goods Sold	110 000	175 000	285 000
Profit/(Loss)	(10 000)	25 000	15 000

On the basis of this information, product S should be discontinued. However, this may be a simplistic solution, and other factors will have to be considered, e.g. sales of product T may be linked to sales of product S; the overheads of T may increase if S is discontinued.

Elements of Cost

For a manufacturing business, there are three main elements of cost:

- **raw materials,** i.e. those materials that go to make up the finished product

- **direct labour,** i.e. the cost of the workforce engaged in production (note that the wages of those who supervise the production workers are an overhead, not a direct cost, and are often described as 'indirect labour')

- **factory overheads,** i.e. all other costs of manufacture, e.g. wages of supervisors, rent of factory, depreciation of factory machinery, heating and lighting of factory

The total of these three costs gives a manufacturing cost and it would be usual to present the costs, at the end of a financial year, in the form of a manufacturing account.

Manufacturing Account

The layout of a manufacturing and trading accounts (with sample figures) follows on the next page:

MANUFACTURING AND TRADING ACCOUNTS OF ACE MANUFACTURING FOR THE YEAR ENDED 31 DECEMBER 19-2

	£	£
Opening stock of raw materials		5 000
Purchase of raw materials		50 000
		55 000
Less closing stock of raw materials		6 000
Cost of Raw Materials used		49 000
Direct labour		26 000
Prime Cost		75 000
Factory overheads:		
Rent of factory	5 000	
Indirect labour	18 000	
Depreciation of factory machinery	10 000	
Factory light and heat	4 000	
		37 000
		112 000
Add opening stock of work-in-progress		4 000
		116 000
Less closing stock of work-in-progress		3 000
Manufacturing Cost of Goods Completed		113 000
Sales		195 000
Opening stock of finished goods	8 000	
Manufacturing cost of goods completed	113 000	
	121 000	
Less closing stock of finished goods	7 000	
Cost of Goods sold		114 000
Gross Profit		81 000

Points to note:

- The total of raw materials and direct labour is known as *prime cost,* i.e. the basic cost of the product before factory overheads are added.

- *Manufacturing cost* is simply the total of the costs for the accounting period.

- A manufacturing account forms one part of the year-end financial statements for a manufacturing business, and precedes the trading account. The latter is prepared in the usual way except that manufacturing cost takes the place of purchases; also, for the trading account, the opening and closing stocks are the *finished goods* held by a business.

- Manufacturing businesses usually hold stocks of goods in three different forms:
    raw materials
    work-in-progress
    finished goods

The first two appear in the manufacturing account, while finished goods is in the trading account. The *closing stock* valuation of all three form the year-end balance sheet stocks.

Organizations have many different costs: for example, the costs shown in a manufacturing account usually include raw materials, labour - direct and indirect, factory rent, depreciation of factory machinery, etc. What would be the effect on such costs if production was, for example, doubled? Would total manufacturing costs also double? The answer is that they would not: total costs would increase, with certain costs increasing proportionately to the increase in production, while others will remain unchanged. This is because certain costs are *variable* with changes in the level of production, while others are *fixed* and are not affected, in the short-term at least, with production changes.

Fixed and Variable Costs

The two main variable costs for a manufacturing business are raw materials and direct labour. With both of these, as production increases so more of each will be needed in direct proportion to the increase. In practice such increases may not be quite so direct, e.g. the purchase of raw materials in larger quantities may enable the manufacturer to obtain discounts in bulk. Also, we usually regard direct labour as varying with production: where payment is made on a piecework basis, i.e. each production worker is paid a certain amount for each unit made, this will be true; however, piecework is not common nowadays - most production workers are paid a basic wage, plus a production bonus which varies with overall output. Despite this, there is a close relationship between goods produced and the costs of direct labour.

All costs for any organization can, therefore, be categorized as *fixed* or *variable*. Fixed costs remain constant despite other changes; variable costs alter with changed circumstances, such as increases in production or sales. However, these 'rules' are only true within certain, restricted limits; for example, a rapidly expanding business must eventually reach the point at which more premises are needed, and then rent, and other costs, will increase. In the short term, though, it is correct to classify costs between those that are fixed and those that are variable.

Break-even Point

A knowledge of fixed and variable costs is important when calculating the *break-even point* of an organization.

Break-even is the point at which neither a profit nor a loss is made.

Case Problem: Break-even

Situation
A business manufactures soft toys, and is able to sell all that can be produced. The variable costs (materials and direct labour) for producing each toy are £10 and the selling price is £20 each. The fixed costs of running the business are £5 000 *per month*. How many toys need to be produced and sold each month for the business to break-even?

Solution

This problem can be solved by calculation, by constructing a table, or by means of a graph.

❏ Calculation

Selling price per unit	£20
Less variable costs per unit	£10
Contribution per unit	£10

Each toy sold gives a *contribution* (selling price, less variable costs) of £10. This contributes towards the fixed costs and, in order to break-even, the business must have sufficient £10 lots to meet the fixed costs. Thus, with fixed costs of £5 000 per month, this business must sell £5 000 ÷ £10 = 500 toys each month. The break-even formula is:

$$\frac{\text{Total fixed costs (£)}}{\text{Contribution per unit (£)}} = \text{Break-even point (number of units)}$$

❑ Table

Units of production	Variable costs	Fixed cost	Total cost	Revenue	Profit/(loss)
	£	£	£	£	£
100	1 000	5 000	6 000	2 000	(4 000)
200	2 000	5 000	7 000	4 000	(3 000)
300	3 000	5 000	8 000	6 000	(2 000)
400	4 000	5 000	9 000	8 000	(1 000)
500	5 000	5 000	10 000	10 000	nil
600	6 000	5 000	11 000	12 000	1 000
700	7 000	5 000	12 000	14 000	2 000

❑ Graph

A graphical presentation uses money amounts as the common denominator between fixed costs, variable costs, and sales revenue. The graph appears as follows:

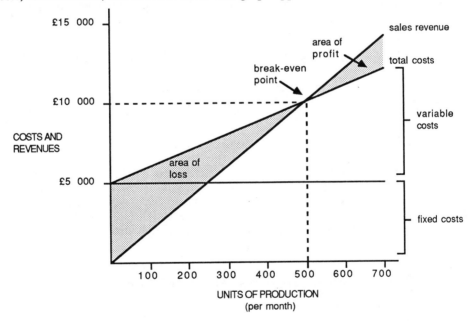

Notes:

- With a break-even graph, it is usual for the vertical axis (the 'y' axis) to show money amounts; the horizontal axis ('x') shows units of production/sales.

- The fixed costs are unchanged at all levels of production, in this case they are £5 000.

- The variable costs commence, on the 'y' axis, *from the fixed costs amount,* not from 'zero'. This is because the cost of producing zero units is the fixed cost.

- The fixed costs *and* the variable costs form a *total costs line.*

- The point at which the total costs and sales revenue lines cross is the break-even point.

Hints for Drawing a Break-even Graph

• In an accountant's break-even chart *all lines are straight*. This means that only two points need be plotted for each line; for example, with sales, choose a number that is fairly near to the maximum expected, multiply by selling price per unit, and this is the point to be marked on the graph. As the sales line always passes through zero, you now have two points along which to draw a straight line.

• When drawing a break-even graph it is often difficult to know what total value to show on each axis, i.e. how many units, and/or how much in costs and revenues? As a guide, look for a maximum production or sales level that will not be exceeded: this will give the 'x' axis. Multiply the maximum sales, if known, by the unit selling price to give the maximum sales revenue for the 'y' axis. If the figure for maximum sales is not known, it is recommended that the break-even point

• A common error is to start the variable costs from the zero point instead of the fixed costs line.

Interpreting a Break-even Graph

In interpreting a break-even graph, it is all too easy to concentrate solely on the break-even point. However, the graph gives much more than this: it also shows the profit or loss at any level of production/sales contained within the graph. To find this, simple measure the gap between sales revenue and total costs at a chosen number of units, and read the money amounts off on the 'y' axis (above break-even point it is a profit; below, it is a loss). From the graph in the Case Problem above, read off the profit or loss at:

1. 700 units,   2. 650 units,   3. 200 units,   4. 400 units   (answers below).

Break-even analysis, whether by calculation, by table, or by graph, is not used solely by a manufacturer: all organizations can use the concept. For example, a youth club might wish to know how many raffle tickets it needs to sell to meet the costs of prizes and of printing tickets; a shop will wish to know the sales it has to make each week to meet costs; a local authority will wish to know the ticket sales that have to be made at a sports centre to meet costs.

Once the break-even point for an organization has been reached, the *additional* contributions form the profit. For example, if the business considered above was selling 750 toys each month, it would have a total contribution of 750 x £10 = £7 500; of this the first £5 000 would be used to meet fixed costs, and the remaining £2 500 represents the profit (we can also read this off from the break-even graph in the Case Problem). This can be shown by means of a financial statement as follows:

MONTHLY PROFIT STATEMENT

	£
Sales (750 toys at £20 each)	15 000
Less variable costs (750 toys at £10 each)	7 500
Contribution (to fixed costs and profit)	7 500
Less monthly fixed costs	5 000
Profit for month	2 500

Answers: 1. £2 000 profit,   2. £1 500 profit,   3. £3 000 loss,   4. £1 000 loss

Absorption Costing and Marginal Costing

A knowledge of the nature of fixed costs and variable costs can be of great help in making financial decisions. Consider the following information about a manufacturer of bicycles:

MONTHLY MANUFACTURING COSTS FOR PRODUCING 100 BICYCLES

	£
Direct materials (£20 per bicycle)	2 000
Direct labour (£25 per bicycle)	2 500
Prime cost	4 500
Factory overheads	3 500
Total cost of producing 100 bicycles	8 000

What is the cost of producing one bicycle? The answer here is £80, i.e. total cost divided by the number manufactured. Therefore, if each bicycle sells for £100, the manufacturer makes a profit of £20 and, for the month, the profit will be £2 000 (£20 x 100).

Let us now assume that the manufacturer has received an order from a major retail store for 100 bicycles per month; the retailer is seeking a 'keen' price for such a large order and offers £75 per bicycle as a maximum. Such an order will be in addition to current production, and the manufacturer will be able to undertake the work within the existing factory. What advice would you give to the manufacturer, bearing in mind that the total cost, on the figures above, per bicycle is £80? On the face of it the new order is losing the manufacturer £5 per unit ... or is it? Reworking the cost statement, we find the following:

MONTHLY MANUFACTURING COST FOR PRODUCING 200 BICYCLES

	£
Direct materials (£20 x 200 bicycles)	4 000
Direct labour (£25 x 200 bicycles)	5 000
Prime cost	9 000
Factory overheads	3 500
Total cost for producing 200 bicycles	12 500
The sales revenue will be:	
100 bicycles at £100 each	10 000
100 bicycles at £75 each	7 500
	17 500

The profit has increased from £2 000 to £5 000 (£17 500 - £12 500) despite selling to the retail store at 'below cost'. Why is this?

You will probably be able to see that the factory cost of £80, originally calculated, includes the fixed factory overheads. To compute cost on this basis is known as *absorption costing*. Once the fixed factory overheads have been met, each extra unit of production adds only the variable costs to the total costs. Thus, one extra bicycle adds £45 (raw materials and direct labour) to total costs. The extra cost of making one more unit is known as a *marginal cost*. Using the marginal costing technique, a business that has already covered its fixed costs is able to offer special prices to large customers. Provided the special price is above marginal cost, then profits will increase. Note that such increased profits will be reduced by extra administration, distribution, and other costs which have not, in this example, been taken into account. Clearly these profit and loss account costs will have a bearing on the final decision taken. Also, in practice, an increase in production quantities may cause certain 'fixed' costs to increase, e.g. additional factory premises might be needed, etc. Therefore:

absorption cost is total cost divided by the number of units produced

marginal cost is the cost of producing one extra unit and will, generally, comprise the variable costs of production

Chapter Summary

❏ Management accounting helps with decision-making in a business by looking at what has gone on in the past and using the information to estimate future costs.

❏ For a manufacturing business, the three main elements of cost are raw materials, direct labour, and factory overheads. The three costs are shown in a manufacturing account which precedes a trading account in the year-end financial statements.

❏ Most manufacturing costs are either fixed or variable, and the relationship between the two can be used to calculate, tabulate, or show by means of a graph, the break-even point.

❏ Absorption and marginal costing help a business with decision-making when faced with orders at 'special prices'.

Another aspect of management accounting is to assist in making decisions about buying new machinery, and this is considered in the next Chapter, 'Project Appraisal'.

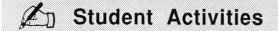 **Student Activities**

1. Which of the following costs are variable, and which are fixed?

   • Raw materials
   • Factory rent
   • Depreciation on factory machinery
   • Direct labour, e.g. production workers paid on a piecework basis
   • Indirect labour, e.g. supervisors' salaries
   • Commission paid to sales staff

   Taking the costs in turn, explain to Louise Smith, who is about to set up a furniture manufacturing business, why you have classified each as either fixed or variable. Answer her comment, "What difference does it make anyway, they are all costs that have to be paid".

2. D. Bradman, a manufacturer of cricket bats, has the following *monthly* costs:

	£
Material cost	8 per bat
Labour cost	12 per bat
Selling price	35 per bat
Fixed expenses	12 000

   You are to:
   • Draw up a table showing costs, revenue and profit or loss for production of bats in multiples of 100 up to 1 200.
   • Draw a graph showing the break-even point.
   • Prove your answer by calculation.
   • Read off the graph the profit or loss if (a) 200 bats, and (b) 1 200 bats are sold each month: prove the answer by calculation.

Sales are currently 1 000 bats each month. Supermail, a mail-order company has approached the manufacturer with a view to buying:
either 200 bats each month at a price of £25 each,
or 500 bats each month at a price of £18 each.

You are to evaluate this order by means of financial statements and advise the manufacturer which order, if either, should be accepted. For both orders the extra production can be carried out within the existing factory.

3. Bert Peters is the owner of a petrol filling station which has the following *weekly* costs:

Cost of fuel (including tax) from oil company	40p per litre
Selling price	45p per litre
Fixed expenses	£750

You are the accountant of the business and are asked to:

- Draw a schedule showing costs, revenue and profit or loss for sale of petrol in multiples of 1 000 litres up to 20 000 litres.
- Draw a graph showing the break-even point.
- Prove your answer by calculation.
- Read off the graph the profit or loss if (a) 12 000 litres, and (b) 18 000 litres are sold each week: prove the answer by calculation.

Sales are currently 20 000 litres each week and the filling station is open from 7 a.m. until 11 p.m. The owner is considering changing the hours to 8 a.m. until 10 p.m. He has estimated that, by doing this, fixed expenses can be reduced to £650 per week, but sales will fall to 18 500 litres.

You are the accountant of the business and are asked to evaluate this proposal by means of financial statements and advise the owner of the decision he should take.

4. From the following figures relating to Crown Heath Woodcrafts you, as the accountant, are to prepare manufacturing and trading accounts for the year-ended 31 December 19-8 to show clearly:

- cost of raw materials used
- prime cost
- manufacturing cost
- cost of goods sold
- gross profit

	£
Stocks at 1 January 19-8	
Raw materials	10 500
Finished goods	4 300
Stocks at 31 December 19-8	
Raw materials	10 200
Finished goods	3 200
Expenditure during year:	
Purchases of raw materials	27 200
Factory wages - direct	12 600
Factory wages - indirect	3 900
Factory rent and rates	1 200
Factory power	2 000
Depreciation of factory machinery	900
Repairs to factory buildings	300
Sundry factory expenses	900
Sales during year	60 400

5.   The following figures relate to the accounts of Barbara Francis, who operates a furniture manufacturing business, for the year ended 31 December 19-3:

	£
Stocks of raw materials, 1 January 19-3	31 860
Stocks of raw materials, 31 December 19-3	44 790
Stocks of finished goods, 1 January 19-3	42 640
Stocks of finished goods, 31 December 19-3	96 510
Purchases of raw materials	237 660
Sale of finished goods	796 950
Rent and rates	32 920
Manufacturing wages	234 630
Manufacturing power	7 650
Manufacturing heat and light	2 370
Manufacturing expenses and maintenance	8 190
Salaries	138 700
Advertising	22 170
Office expenses	7 860
Depreciation of plant and machinery	7 450

Three-quarters of the rent and rates are to be treated as a manufacturing charge.

As Miss Francis' accountant, you are to prepare manufacturing, trading and profit and loss accounts for the year-ended 31 December 19-3, to show clearly:

• the cost of raw materials used,
• prime cost,
• cost of factory overheads,
• manufacturing cost of goods completed,
• cost of goods sold,
• gross profit for the year,
• net profit for the year.

Explain, by memorandum, to Miss Francis why you have presented the accounts in such a form, and what they show.

Chapter Twenty Two
Project Appraisal

You will already know from your other studies in this and other areas that all resources are limited in supply. As a result there is a need to use resources in such a way as to obtain the maximum benefits from them. To do this it is necessary to choose between various alternatives available; for example, on a personal level, we have to make decisions such as:

Should I save my spare cash in a bank or in a building society?
Should I save up for a car, or should I buy on hire purchase?
Which make of car, within my price range, should I buy?
Should I rent a house or should I buy, taking out a mortgage?

While these decisions are personal choices, the management of businesses of all sizes is constantly faced with making choices, as are local authorities and central government.

The management of any business is constantly having to make decisions on *what* to produce, *where* to produce, *how* to produce, and *how much* to produce. Similar considerations must be the concern of organizations providing services. For each major choice to be made, some method of appraisal has to be applied to ensure that, whatever decisions are taken, they are the right ones. This means that it is necessary to look at all the alternatives available and to choose the one that is going to give the most benefit to the organization. For example, a business may have to decide whether to replace its existing machinery with new, more up-to-date machinery. If it decides on new machinery, it then has to choose between different makes of machine and different models, each having a different cost and each capable of affecting output in a different way. At the same time a decision has to be made whether to pay cash outright, to buy on hire purchase, or to lease.

Case Problem: A New Machine

Situation
An organization needs a new machine and has to make the choice between Machine Y and Machine Z. The initial cost and the net cash flow (income, less running expenses but *not* depreciation) to the business have been ascertained for each machine as follows:

	MACHINE Y	MACHINE Z
Initial cost	£20 000	£28 000
Net cash flow:		
Year 1	£8 000	£10 000
Year 2	£12 000	£10 000
Year 3	£5 000	£8 000
Year 4	£4 000	£9 000
Year 5	£2 000	£9 000

Only one machine is needed and, at the end of five years, the machine will have no value and will be scrapped. To finance the project, the organization can borrow money at 10 per cent per annum. Which machine should be chosen?

Solution

Three techniques are in common usage to appraise a project such as this:
- payback
- accounting rate of return
- discounted cash flow

Each of these techniques will be considered in this Chapter in order to help the organization to make its decision.

Payback

This technique, as its name implies, sees how long it takes for the initial outlay to be repaid by the net cash flow coming in. Thus Machine Y costs £20 000 and it is expected that the net cash flow over the first two years will equal the cost. The payback time for Machine Y is, therefore, two years, while that for Machine Z is three years. The faster the payback the better, particularly where high technology or fashion projects are concerned - they may be out-of-date before they reach the end of their useful lives. So, using payback, Machine Y is preferable.

Advantages of payback
- it is easy to calculate
- it is easy to understand
- it places emphasis on the earlier cash flows, which are more likely to be accurate than later cash flows
- an ideal capital investment appraisal technique for high technology projects

Disadvantages of payback
- all cash flows after the payback period are ignored
- within the payback period it fails to take into account the timing of net cash flows, e.g. Machine Y would still have had a payback of two years even if the cash flows for years one and two had been reversed

Accounting Rate of Return

This method is calculated by:

$$\frac{\text{(Total estimated cash flow* } \div \text{ Estimated life of project)}}{\text{Initial cost}} \times \frac{100}{1}$$

* Scrap value or residual value, if any, at the end of the project would be taken into account.

This method gives a percentage accounting rate of return on the initial cost of the project. For Machine Y it is calculated as follows:

$$\frac{(\text{£31 000} \div 5 \text{ years})}{\text{£20 000}} \times \frac{100}{1} = 31 \text{ per cent}$$

For Machine Z the accounting rate of return is 33 per cent; so, using this method, Machine Z is slightly preferable.

Advantages of accounting rate of return
- it is relatively easy to calculate
- all cash flows are used
- it is easy to understand the results

Disadvantage of accounting rate of return

• the timing of cash flows is completely ignored, i.e. the same result would have been reached if the cash flows for Machine Y had been £1 000, £1 000, £1 000, £1 000 for each of the first four years, and £27 000 in year five

Discounted Cash Flow

Discounted cash flow (DCF) is an investment appraisal technique which recognises that money has a time value. For example, supposing that today a friend asks you to lend her £1 and offers to repay you either tomorrow, or in one year's time, which will you choose? The answer is clear: you would want the money back sooner rather than later because, if you don't intend to spend it, you can always save it in a bank or building society, where it will earn interest. Thus, as you will probably know from your studies, the rate of interest represents the time value of money.

Using £1 as an example, if it is invested with a bank or building society at an interest rate of 10 per cent per year, it will increase as follows:

Original investment	£1.00
Interest at 10% on £1	£0.10
Value at end of first year	£1.10
Interest at 10% on £1.10	£0.11
Value at end of second year	£1.21

As you will appreciate this is the technique of compound interest, with which you will, no doubt, already be familiar. So, with interest rates of 10 per cent per year, we can say that the future value of £1 will be £1.10 at the end of year one, £1.21 at the end of year two, and so on; thus £1 set aside now will gain in value so that, at some time in the future, we will have access to a larger sum of money. However, supposing that we were to *receive* £1 at the end of year one, what is it worth to us now? To find the answer to this, we need to carry out the following calculation:

$$£1 \times \frac{100}{110*} = £0.91$$

* 100 per cent, plus the rate of interest (in this example, 10 per cent).

Therefore, if we had £0.91 now and invested it at 10 per cent per year, we would have £1 at the end of year one. We can say that the *present value* of £1 receivable in one year's time is £0.91. In the same way, £1 receivable in two years' time is £0.83, calculated as follows:

$$£1 \times \frac{100}{110} \times \frac{100}{110} = £0.83$$

We can build up a *table of factors* (for 10 per cent interest rates) as follows:

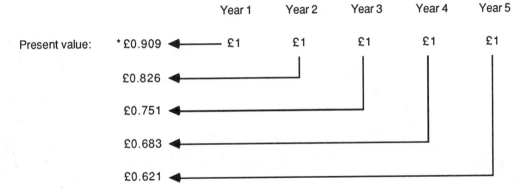

* taken to three decimal places, for greater accuracy.

Using your calculator, check that the table of factors above is correct. Put '1' into your calculator and multiply by 100 ÷ 110 for the first year; multiply the result by 100 ÷ 110 for the second year; and so on. Now produce a five-year table of factors (in the format above) for 15 per cent, and then 20 per cent. As you are doing the exercise, don't forget the basic principle that *money has a time value* and, from this, the further into the future that we expect to receive money, then the lower is its *present value*.

Let us now return to the problem of the organization which has to choose between Machine Y and Machine Z. We will look at this assuming, firstly, a rate of interest or *cost of capital* of 10 per cent. (Cost of capital is the rate of return that an organisation expects on its money, or the rate of interest it has to pay when borrowing money.) For each machine, the expected net cash flows are multiplied by the relevant factor to give the *discounted cash flow;* the difference between total discounted cash flow and the initial cost is the *net present value* of the project. For Machine Y the calculations are:

	Cash Flow		Discount Factor		Discounted Cash Flow
Year 0*					(£20 000)
Year 1	£8 000	x	0.909	=	£7 272
Year 2	£12 000	x	0.826	=	£9 912
Year 3	£5 000	x	0.751	=	£3 755
Year 4	£4 000	x	0.683	=	£2 732
Year 5	£2 000	x	0.621	=	£1 242
			Net Present Value (NPV)	=	£4 913

* Year 0 is the commencement of the project when the initial costs are paid.

Note that the initial cost is shown in brackets because it is a *cost,* whereas the net cash flows are *positive amounts;* net present value is the sum of all cash flows.

For Machine Z the figures are:

	Cash Flow		Discount Factor		Discounted Cash Flow
Year 0					(£28 000)
Year 1	£10 000	x	0.909	=	£9 090
Year 2	£10 000	x	0.826	=	£8 260
Year 3	£8 000	x	0.751	=	£6 008
Year 4	£9 000	x	0.683	=	£6 147
Year 5	£9 000	x	0.621	=	£5 589
			Net Present Value (NPV)	=	£7 094

Here, with a cost of capital of 10 per cent, Machine Z is better, producing a considerably higher net present value than Y. Note that both machines give a positive net present value at 10 per cent: this means that either machine will be of benefit to the organization but Machine Z is preferable; a negative NPV indicates that a project should not go ahead.

Thus, using a discounted cash flow technique, future cash flows are brought to their value now; this means that, the further on in time that cash flows are receivable, the lower is the net present value. As this is often a difficult concept to grasp, to put it another way, future cash flows are all brought back to a common denominator which is *now*.

Advantages of discounted cash flow
- all cash flows are used
- the timing of cash flows is taken into account
- using a table of factors the calculations are easy to make

Disadvantages of discounted cash flow:
- the cost of capital rate is, in practice, difficult to ascertain
- the meaning of net present value is not always clear to users of the information
- the project with the higher net present value does not, in pure financial terms, always represent the better project

Project Appraisal: Conclusion

It is unlikely that an organization will rely on one technique only; instead two or more criteria might be required before a project is given the go-ahead. Supposing, for example, that the organization having to choose between Machines Y and Z applied the following criteria: 'projects must have a payback period not exceeding 2.5 years, *and* must have a positive net present value at a 10 per cent cost of capital'. How do the two machines compare?

	MACHINE Y	MACHINE Z
Payback	2 years	3 years
NPV at 10 per cent	£4 913	£7 094

Under the criteria that the organization has laid down, Machine Y would be chosen. However, Machine Z seems a better project on the net present value basis and is only rejected because it does not meet the payback requirement; also Machine Z has the better accounting rate of return (at 33 per cent, instead of 31 per cent for Machine Y).

Chapter Summary

❑ In project appraisal a number of techniques can be used to help in management decision making.

❑ The techniques include payback, accounting rate of return and discounted cash flow.

❑ Organizations often use a combination of two or more appraisal techniques before making decisions about major projects.

Student Activities

1. Using the discounted cash flow technique, rework the calculations for Machines Y and Z, in the chapter, using the factors for (a) 15 per cent, and (b) 20 per cent per annum, which were calculated earlier.

2. John Smith is considering two major investment projects for his engineering business. Only one project can be chosen and the following information is available:

	Project A	Project B
	£	£
Initial capital outlay	80 000	100 000
Net cash inflows, year: 1	40 000	20 000
2	60 000	30 000
3	10 000	50 000
4	5 000	50 000
5	5 000	50 000

The initial capital outlay will occur immediately and you may assume that the net cash inflows will arise at the end of each year.

Smith's estimated cost of capital over the five year period is 12 per cent per annum.

To assist John Smith make his decision you, as his accountant, Mrs S Harris, are asked to:

• Prepare a table of discounted cash flow factors for a rate of 12 per cent per annum.

• Produce numerical assessments of the two projects based on the following project appraisal techniques:
   (a) Payback
   (b) Net present value (NPV)
   (c) Accounting rate of return

• Comment on the relative merits of the project appraisal techniques, and advise John Smith on which investment project, if either, should be undertaken. Present your advice in the form of a letter to your client, enclosing the calculations you have made for above. His address is Unit 27, Factory Estate, Newtown, Wyvern County.

3. Ken Shah needs some printing equipment for his publishing firm. He has to choose between the following methods of acquisition:

• Purchase of the equipment for cash.
• Purchase under a hire purchase contract, involving an initial deposit and two annual payments.
• Hire of the equipment.

The following information is available:

Cash price of equipment	£10 000
Period of use in Shah's firm	5 years
Scrap value at end of use	£1 000
Initial deposit under hire purchase contract	£4 000
Two annual hire purchase payments due at end of first year and end of second year	£4 000 each
Hire of equipment, five annual hire charge payments due at end of each year	£2 500 each

Shah's estimated cost of capital over the five year period is 10 per cent per annum.

You are his Finance Director and to assist Ken Shah make his decision, you are asked to:

- Prepare a table of discounted cash flow factors for a rate of 10 per cent per annum.
- Produce numerical assessments of the three methods of acquisition using discounted cash flow techniques.
- Advise Ken Shah, in the form of a memorandum, of the best method of acquisition.

4. Hi-Tech Ltd. manufactures sound reproduction equipment. Its research department has discovered a noise reduction method for use with cassette tapes and compact discs. The company has patented the invention, and is faced with a decision on how it might best exploit the invention.

Hi-Tech Ltd. has received two offers from other companies. Sound Systems Ltd. is prepared to buy the patent for £30 000, whereas Wyvern Sound Ltd. seeks exclusive use of the method in exchange for a royalty on the units produced. In the latter case, Hi-Tech Ltd. has estimated that £9 000 per year would be received for seven years; by which time the patent would be valueless.

Two other possibilities are being considered by Hi-Tech Ltd.:

- Production and marketing could be subcontracted to a manufacturer. If this approach is taken, it is estimated that net receipts, after meeting all costs, will be £8 000 per year. These amounts could be maintained for eight years, after which the patent would be valueless.

- Hi-Tech Ltd. could undertake the production itself, and market the product with its other equipment. The company could lease premises, and it is estimated that net receipts after meeting annual outlay costs would amount to £17 000 per year for nine years. However, the company would have to purchase machinery costing £56 000. The machinery would have a scrap value of £6 000 at the end of nine years.

You are a clerk in the company's accounts department and are asked by your boss, Jean Adams, the Finance Director, to prepare a project appraisal report on the choices available to the company. The company uses the discounted cash flow technique and has a cost of capital of 10 per cent per year. You are also told by Miss Adams that the payment from Sound Systems Ltd. would be received immediately if that option is chosen. Similarly, if Hi-Tech Ltd. undertakes production itself, payment for the machinery would be made immediately.

As there is to be a board meeting of the company tomorrow, Miss Adams requests you to submit your report in the form of a memorandum to her, and also asks you to present a short conclusion of your views on the choices available.

Assignment Eleven

Management Accounts: Fitta Fabricators Limited

GENERAL OBJECTIVE COVERED
F.

SKILLS DEVELOPED
Numeracy, information processing, identifying and tackling problems, communicating, information gathering.

SITUATION
You are working in the accounts department of Fitta Fabricators Ltd. The company manufactures a single product, the 'Fitta De Luxe' exercise cycle. Demand for this product increases each year as a result of the growing awareness of the importance of healthy living. The company has, as a result, increased its production capacity and, up until now, little thought has been given to the costing involved in manufacturing the product. However, some figures have recently been collected which show, at current production levels of 5 500 units per year, the following:

Raw material costs	£12 per unit
Direct Labour costs	£10 per unit
Selling price (to retail outlets)	£65 per unit (all units produced can be sold)
Fixed factory costs, and other overheads	£156 950 per year

An enquiry has been received from a company which operates a major mail-order catalogue. The company is considering the inclusion of the 'Fitta De Luxe' in their next catalogue. It is expected that they can sell 1 500 units to new customers who would not have bought the product elsewhere. However, they are seeking a discount, in view of the quantity of the order, and offer a price of £45 per unit. If this order is undertaken, the accountant of Fitta Fabricators Ltd. considers that the variable costs would remain unchanged but that fixed costs would increase by 10 per cent, being the cost of additional factory and warehouse buildings that would have to be rented.

The company is considering the purchase of a new machine to replace an old piece of equipment which bends and shapes the tubular steel of the exercise cycle. The slowness of the old machine often causes production hold-ups and it is expected that the new machine will overcome such problems. There is no doubt that the company should install the new machine, but it can't decide whether to buy outright, buy on hire purchase, or to lease it. The relevant information is:

Outright purchase at a cost of £10 000.
Hire purchase, with a deposit of £3 000 payable immediately and three annual instalments of £3 500 payable at the end of each of the first three years.
Lease, with six annual leasing payments of £2 500 payable at the end of each year.

The machine is expected to last for six years, after which it will be worn out and have a nil scrap value.

The company has an agreed overdraft facility with the bank on which the bank charges interest at 10 per cent. Whichever method of acquisition is chosen, the payment(s) will be made through the bank account.

STUDENT TASKS

Write a memorandum to the accountant of Fitta Fabricators Ltd., your section boss; it should incorporate:

1. A break-even graph on the basis of current production costs; prove your answer by calculation.

2. An explanation of whether or not the proposed contract for the mail-order company should be undertaken. As part of your submission, prepare schedules showing:

   - the expected net profit for a full year at existing production levels

   - the expected net profit for a year if the new contract is taken on

3. An investigation of hire-purchase and leasing as methods of acquiring a fixed asset such as a machine. Obtain leaflets, newspaper articles, etc. and set out the advantages and disadvantages, to a company, of each method.

4. Discounted Cash Flow projections:

   - calculating a table of factors (10 per cent) which can be used to evaluate Fitta Fabricators Ltd.'s project

   - preparing figures to show the net present value under each option (tax is to be ignored) and ranking the choices in preferred order (starting with the best) as indicated by this one project appraisal technique

Chapter Twenty Three
Applying for Finance: The Business Plan

You will recall that when we first discussed business organizations in Chapter 6, we dealt with the type of organization (sole trader, partnership, limited company) and the finance that would be needed to fund its operations. We saw how the business presented its case to the prospective lender in the form of a Business Plan. In this Chapter we will consider more fully the structure and content of a typical Business Plan.

The Business Plan: An Introduction

What is a Business Plan?
A Business Plan is a formal document, often submitted in the form of a ring binder file, which presents the business to a prospective lender or investor. Not all business plans confirm to an identical format, but the following sections will normally be found in any well thought out plan:

- a synopsis of the Plan
- personal details of the borrower
- history and background of the business
- a description of the product or service
- the market for the product or service
- financial considerations and background
- financial requirements
- projected trading and profit and loss account, cash flow forecast, balance sheet

When and why is a Business Plan needed?
A Business Plan is needed either when you are starting up in business, or alternatively when you need to expand an existing business. It could be argued that every business should produce a Business Plan: it is an invaluable exercise in thinking through what you are planning to do; it enables *you,* as well as a prospective lender, to evaluate the proposal.

Professional Advice in Compiling a Business Plan
A Business Plan is clearly a long and complex document. Professional advice in its compilation is highly recommended and available from a number of sources -

The Accountant will be the most valuable source of information. He or she will be able to advise on the structure, assist in the drawing up of the financial projections, and may accompany you on your interviews with prospective lenders. An accountant will charge a fee for his or her services.

The Bank Manager will be pleased to give advice and also to provide free literature. Bank advice is *normally* free of charge, although the customer is well advised to enquire if a consultation fee is to be charged.

The Business Plan: Structure and Contents

Synopsis
An introductory page which the prospective lender can read in a short space of time. It will outline the nature of the business, why it is better than the competition, how much finance will be needed, and for what purpose and period.

The Borrower
Brief personal details of the owner(s) of the business: name, age, qualifications, expertise, contact addresses and telephone numbers.

The Business
This section will give details of the history and background to the business, the length of time it has been trading (if this is the case), the premises it occupies (or will occupy), insurance particulars and the management team. If the business is already trading, full financial details should be enclosed including, if possible, three years' Trading and Profit and Loss Accounts and Balance Sheets.

The Product or Service
This section will include a description, in layman's language, of the product or service. It will include any promotional literature or illustrations that may be available. A positive approach is recommended: the section should state why the product or service is good.

The Market
This section should show that detailed research has been carried out into the relevant market. The following questions should be answered:

- Who are the competitors? Why is your product or service better than the competition?
- What market share is the business aiming at? Is the market expanding?
- How is the product or service to be marketed?
- What is the pricing policy? Is it competitive?
- Are there any orders in the pipeline?
- What are the projected sales figures for the next six and twelve months?

Financial Considerations
The prospective lender will want to know:

- What credit will be given by suppliers?
- What credit will the business give to customers?
- What assets does the business own? What is their value? Are they mortgaged?

Financial Requirements
This should be a summary, based on the Cash Flow Forecast (see below), detailing where applicable:

- the amount the proprietor is contributing
- the short-term requirement and the purpose
- the medium/long-term requirements, and the purpose
- proposals for repayment
- assets available for security purposes (see above)

Financial Projections
The projections will normally include a six or twelve month projected trading and profit and loss account, cash flow forecast, and balance sheet. As we will see, the services of an accountant and a computer spreadsheet are invaluable aids in this section of the Business Plan, which we will explore in the form of a Case Problem.

Case Problem: 'Software Stores'

Situation

Ian Phillips is an expert in computer software. He has worked until recently for a leading British software house which, unfortunately, made him redundant four months ago. He has £2 000 available from his redundancy money to invest as capital, and wishes to set up a computer software retail outlet in a new shopping arcade, which is offering units at preferential rates. He has named his venture 'Software Stores'. His customers will include the general public and also local businesses who need expert guidance on the setting up of business accounting packages. He wishes to raise finance from the bank but is not sure how much he needs. He therefore approaches, on the recommendation of his bank, Jim Stoner, a local accountant, who is known to specialise in small business finance.

Solution

❏ Assembling Financial Information for the Business Plan

Jim Stoner extracts the following information from his client.

Income
- Ian Phillips has capital of £2 000 in the building society to introduce into the business
- expected cash sales from callers at the shop £1 500 per month
- expected credit sales from business software £500 per month on 60 days' credit (i.e. sales in January will be paid for in March)

Expenditure
- initial purchase of stock of £2 000 to be paid for immediately by cheque

- thereafter stock purchases to be £750 each month:
  - (a) in January, February and March paid for immediately by cheque
  - (b) April onwards, £250 to be paid for immediately, £500 on 30 days' credit (i.e. paid for in month following purchase)

  The reason for (a) and (b) is that credit will often only be granted by suppliers *after* the business has shown that it is creditworthy, usually after a few months' trading

- shop fixtures and fittings (fixed assets) £1 250, paid for in February

- equipment purchases (fixed assets) of £490 and £250 in the first two months respectively (paid for when bought)

- monthly payments: rent, rates, insurance £275, services (light, heat, power, telephone) £50, advertising and printing £30 (first month £150), sundries £20

- drawings of £350 per month, National Insurance £4.60 per week

- financial expenses not yet known (bank interest charged quarterly and a £10 set up fee)

- depreciation of fixed assets for the first six months is to be charged (in the profit and loss account) at £500; *as it is a non-cash item it does not appear in the Cash Flow Forecast*

VAT

It is decided that until the sales figure is verified by results, Ian will not register for VAT. If, at the end of the first quarter's trading, the yearly sales look like exceeding the current VAT threshold (see Chapter 11), he will register immediately. For the purposes of the projections, VAT is therefore excluded.

❏ Procedure for applying for finance with a Business Plan

In consultation with his accountant, Ian prepares his Business Plan, leaving the financial projections until last.

He approaches his bank again to arrange a formal interview, as he thinks he will need to borrow. They give him a Cash Flow Forecast to complete, mentioning that if he obtains an overdraft, he might expect to pay 15% p.a. in interest (quarterly) and an arrangement fee of £10 at the outset.

Projections: Six Months Accounts and Cash Flow Forecast

With the help of his accountant he runs the figures through an accounting programme on his computer which prints out a projected Trading and Profit and Loss Account and Cash Flow Forecast for the first six months, and a Balance Sheet as at the end of that period. He transfers the figures to his Business Plan (see accompanying illustrations).

Notes on Completion of the Cash Flow Forecast

* When completing his sales figures, credit sales (60 days) are first received in month three. Sales income (cash flow) for the six month period will be £11 000, but invoiced sales £12 000 (as on Trading Account), giving debtors of £1 000 at the end of June.

* When recording credit purchases (30 days), which commence in the fourth month of trading, his first payment will be in month five. The total on the trading account is the amount invoiced (£5 750), not the total paid (£5 250), giving creditors of £500 at the end of June.

* He estimates his closing stock on 30 June 19-8 will be valued at £1 000.

* Minus figures are recorded in brackets, as on the bottom line where they represent a bank overdraft.

Assessment of the Projections

An examination of the figures (see adjacent pages) shows that:

* his gross profit margin is healthy at 60%
* his liquidity is excellent: current ratio = 6.2:1
* his maximum bank requirement will be an overdraft of £1 356 in month two
* the borrowing will be repaid in month four, and thereafter the bank account is well in credit

He will send a copy of the Business Plan in advance to his bank and then go for an interview with the Bank Manager, possibly with his Accountant accompanying him.

❏ The Response of the Bank Manager

The Bank Manager will see that the borrowing can be repaid quickly, and is pleased to offer an overdraft limit of £1 500 over 6 months, after which time he will review the situation. He may ask for security, in which case the borrower will offer a second mortgage over his house, which is his only major asset. Alternatively he may be able to persuade someone to sign a guarantee.

Cash Flow Forecast completed by Ian Phillips

National Bank plc   Branch   WORCESTER

CASHFLOW FORECAST

for   IAN PHILLIPS T/A SOFTWARE STORES for the period 1 JAN 19-8 To 30 JUN 19-8

	JAN.	FEB.	MAR.	APL.	MAY	JUN.	Total
RECEIPTS							
Sales - cash	1500	1500	1500	1500	1500	1500	9000
Sales - credit	–	–	500	500	500	500	2000
Other receipts (Capital)	2000						2000
TOTAL RECEIPTS (A)	3500	1500	2000	2000	2000	2000	13000
PAYMENTS							
Cash purchases	2000	750	750	250	250	250	4250
Credit purchases	–	–	–	–	500	500	1000
Fixed assets	490	1500					1990
Wages							
Rent & rates ⎱	275	275	275	275	275	275	1650
Insurance ⎰							
Services	50	50	50	50	50	50	300
Bank charges	10		23			18	51
Advertising	150	30	30	30	30	30	300
Sundries	20	20	20	20	20	20	120
Other (N.I.C.)	18	18	23	18	18	23	118
Drawings	350	350	350	350	350	350	2100
TOTAL PAYMENTS (B)	3363	2993	1521	993	1493	1516	11879
Opening bank balance	NIL	137	(1356)	(877)	130	637	
Add total receipts (A)	3500	1500	2000	2000	2000	2000	
Less total payments (B)	3363	2993	1521	993	1493	1516	
Closing bank balance	137	(1356)	(877)	130	637	1121	

Projected six months' Trading and Profit and Loss Account and Balance Sheet produced on Ian Phillips' micro

```
IAN PHILLIPS TRADING AS SOFTWARE STORES
PROJECTED TRADING & PROFIT & LOSS ACCOUNT
6 MONTHS TO 30 JUNE 19-8

                                    £                    £
Sales                                               12,000
Cost of Sales
Purchases                         5,750
Less Closing Stock                1,000
                                                     4.750
Gross Profit                                         7,250

Less Expenses
Rent, rates, insurance            1,650
Light, heat, power, phone           300
Advertising, printing               300
Sundries                            120
National Insurance                  118
Finance costs                        51
Depreciation of fixed assets        500
Total Expenses                                       3,039

Net Profit                                           4,211




IAN PHILLIPS TRADING AS SOFTWARE STORES
PROJECTED BALANCE SHEET AS AT 30 JUNE 19-8

                                    £          £         £
                                    Cost       Dep'n     Net
Fixed Assets
Fixtures, fittings & equipment    1,990        500       1,490

Current Assets
Stock                             1,000
Debtors                           1,000
Bank                              1,121
                                             3,121
Current Liabilities
Creditors                                      500
                                                         2,621
                                                         4,111

Financed by

Capital                                                  2,000
Add Net Profit                                          4,211
                                                         6,211
Less Drawings                                          2,100

                                                        4,111
```

Chapter Summary

❑ The writing of a Business Plan is an invaluable exercise for anyone wishing to start or expand a business.

❑ The Bank and, most particularly, an Accountant, should be consulted when compiling a Business Plan.

❑ A computer accounting package can be a useful tool in projecting figures for a Business Plan.

❑ A Business Plan, when properly presented to a prospective lender of funds, can considerably improve the chances of obtaining finance, and the speed with which the finance may be offered.

This Chapter concludes our study of the documentation, the accounting methods and fund raising of business organizations. We will now turn our attention to non-profit making organizations - the public sector and clubs and associations - before drawing the social and business themes together by looking at the social implications of decision making in business organizations in Chapter 27.

Student Activities

1. Using the Case Problem, Ian Phillips T/A Software Stores, prepare a Business Plan, containing all the main headings referred to in this Chapter, and making use of the projected figures as shown. You will need to supply personal details about Mr. Phillips. Details about the market and the competition can readily be obtained from leading monthly computer magazines. If your College has a Computer Department they may also be able to assist.

2. Using a computer spreadsheet program, input the Cash Flow figures contained in the Case Problem, Ian Phillips T/A Software Stores. What will be the effect on the Cash Flow if you

    • increase sales by 15%?
    • decrease sales by 15%?

    Which of the three sets of figures would you, as Ian Phillips, be most likely to show the bank manager, and why? Experiment with altering other figures, such as drawings, advertising, rent and rates/insurance, and examine the effect on the Cash Flow.

3. You are an accountant, Gareth Davies, of Davies, Davies and Lloyd. A relatively financially unsophisticated client, Basil Noakes of 10 Springfield Avenue, Mellstock, Dorset, is trying to raise money to start a craft studio in his village. He needs approximately £10 000 to finance the venture; he has £5 000. Draft a letter telling him, *in brief,* the main sources of finance and the advantages of his presenting a business plan. Your letter should contain a description of the contents of a business plan.

4.   You are planning to set up in business at the beginning of the year 19-8. Your enterprise is a small bookshop which you call 'Anne's Bookshop'.

You plan to introduce capital of £6 000 in January. You also intend to purchase for cash an initial stock of books costing £5 000, together with fixtures and fittings costing £3 750, also to be paid for in January.

You hope to start trading in January 19-8 and you have estimated sales for the first six months as follows:

January £3 000; February £2 400; March £3 600; April £4 500; May £4 200; June £3 900.
All sales will be for cash. You plan to work to a gross profit margin of one-third of the selling price. Towards the end of each month you will replenish the stock to ensure that, at the month-end, it will be restored to £5 000. Your suppliers for book purchases, excluding the initial cash stock purchase, will allow one month's credit (e.g. purchases made in January will be paid for in February).

You estimate the monthly overheads of the shop will be rent and rates £250, wages £280, heat/light/telephone £95. You plan to withdraw for your own use drawings of £500 per month. Your accountant has advised you to depreciate fixtures and fittings at the rate of 20% per annum (straight line method).

Your accountant also advises you to prepare a cash flow forecast, together with a projected trading and profit and loss account for the six months ending 30 June 19-8, and a projected balance sheet as at that date. These will form part of a Business Plan which you will submit to the bank as part of your application for the finance, which your accountant suspects you will need. Prepare these documents and pass them to your accountant for checking.

5.   You are an accountant in the firm of Price Charterhouse, and have been asked to advise a client, John Carr.

John Carr has been unemployed for 12 months and intends to set up a mail order holiday guide business, to be known as "Medfact". He used to work in a travel agency, and knows the travel business well. He plans to sell an A4 format holiday resort brochure giving invaluable information about all the popular resorts in Spain and Portugal. It will be entitled "Medfact".

John Carr will operate under the Government's Enterprise Allowance Scheme which will pay him £40 a week for the first year of operation. He has £2,500 of his own in a Building Society account, saved when he was in employment.

You have talked through his figures with him and he has produced the following estimates for his first six months' trading (1 January to 30 June 19-8):

•   he will introduce capital on 1 January of £2,500

•   opening stocks of materials will cost £2,000 and be paid for by cash

•   estimated sales for the first six months (based on a peak month of May) are:

January	£1000
February	£1600
March	£1800
April	£2000
May	£4000
June	£2400

- most sales are for cash, but he does expect to sell 25% of his brochures through travel agents, and will have to wait a month for payment from them

- his materials cost 50% of his selling price; stocks of materials will be replaced each month so that the closing stock value will always be £2000; January's stock purchases will therefore be £1000 (sales figure) x 50% = £500

- purchases will be made from his suppliers who allow 1 month's credit (apart from the initial cash purchase of stock)

His costs are:

- advertising £500 per month, £800 in April

- post and packing £200 for January, February and March, £300 for April, May and June

- sundry expenses will be £10 per month except for April when they will be £40

- you should ignore interest costs

Also,

- he wishes to buy office equipment for £1,000 for cash in January; it is expected to last for five years

- drawings from the bank account will be £180 per month (the Enterprise Allowance £40 per week will *not* be passed through the business.)

John Carr suspects that he will have to approach the bank for finance in the early months of operation of the business. You realise that a business plan will have to drawn up, and you therefore advise him accordingly.

You are to

1. Write a letter to Mr Carr (10 Gatwick Avenue, Worcester) explaining what a business plan is, and what Mr Carr will have to do to prepare one.

2. Construct a cash flow forecast for the first six months of operation of the business.

3. Construct the projected trading and profit and loss account for 1 January to 30 June 19-8, and the projected balance sheet as at 30 June 19-8.

4. State in you letter how much Mr Carr may need to borrow from the bank, and what form the borrowing will take.

Assignment Twelve

Presenting the Accounts: the Business Plan

GENERAL OBJECTIVES COVERED
B, E, F, G.

SKILLS DEVELOPED
Communicating, numeracy, information processing.

SITUATION
You are Trevor Cox, a successful dealer in hi-fi equipment in the town of Westford, near Worcester. You have built up a good reputation for your expertise and back-up service; you trade from home, visiting clients and demonstrating equipment in their homes. You do not have a sales outlet in the town because you do not need one.

You have, however, become very conscious recently of the increase in consumer demand for compact disc (CD) systems, and have now decided that a shop in town would enable you to sell CD machines and discs at a considerable profit, while at the same time maintaining your existing home sales service. You know of a small retail shop shortly becoming available in the town centre, and see it as an obvious way of increasing your business and profitability. Your plan is that your brother, Desmond, also an expert in the hi-fi field, will staff the shop for most of the time on a wage-earning basis, while you continue to look after your existing clients.

The financial details of the new project are as follows:

- capital provided by Trevor Cox, £12 500
- cost of fixtures and fittings, to be bought for cash in month one, £5 500. Depreciation to be 20% per year
- initial stock of CD players, 100 @ £200 purchase cost
- initial stock of compact discs, 2 500 @ £6 purchase cost

You expect to sell 30 machines and 400 discs a month. The average selling price of your machines is £325, and of the discs £10. All sales are cash sales. Starting in month one you will need to replace stock sold by buying 30 machines and 400 discs each month. Your estimate of closing stock will therefore be the same as the figure for opening stock. You will have to pay immediately for your initial stock, but can obtain 30 days credit for subsequent purchases (e.g. you will pay in month two for goods bought when you restock at the end of month one).

Monthly running costs of the shop will be: rent £300, services (heating, electricity, telephone, etc.) £95, publicity £48, sundries £35, Desmond's wages £300. You plan to withdraw £500 per month as your own drawings.

You soon realise that you will have to raise finance from the bank in addition to your initial capital of £12 500. You therefore decide to write a business plan in order to convince the bank manager that he will be backing a sound proposition. You decide to prepare your projections on the basis of the shop as a separate trading entity; it will be known as 'CD Systems', of which you will be sole proprietor.

STUDENT TASKS

1.   Prepare a Cash Flow Forecast for the first six months' trading (January - June) of CD Systems, together with a projected trading and profit and loss account for the six months and a balance sheet as at the end of the period. You are to ignore VAT, income tax, National Insurance and finance costs. These projections will form part of your Business Plan. If you wish, you may use a computer spreadsheet to assist you. Do *not* write the whole of the Business Plan.

2.   You have heard that banks often place great emphasis on the importance of accounting ratios. You therefore decide to prepare a schedule to accompany your projections, showing:

   • gross profit percentage
   • net profit percentage
   • current ratio
   • stock turnover rate
   • return on capital employed

   These are calculated on the basis of your projected figures.

3.   Write in full the section of the Business Plan entitled 'Financial Requirements'. You are to state how much you are contributing yourself, how much you hope the bank will provide, for what purpose, and in what form, and how it will be repaid. You expect that the bank will ask for security, and you should note in this section that you own a property, 7 Riverhurst Terrace, Westford, worth £55 000 and subject to a first mortgage of £25 000 from the Westmid Building Society.

4.   At your initial interview with the bank manager, Mr. L. Stirling, he says he is impressed by your presentation and projected figures, but he is sceptical about your estimates for sales receipts. He wonders if you can sustain sales at the level you suggest, and also whether the retail prices of CD equipment and discs may fall. He is particularly worried about the second factor. You are to rework the Cash Flow Forecast *only*, using selling prices 20% lower than those originally projected (purchase prices remain unchanged).

   Write a letter to Mr. Stirling (National Bank, 71 High Street, Worcester), enclosing your new projections, noting any change in the financial requirement and stating why you consider the proposition may still be sound.

5.   By arrangement with a lecturer, or a bank manager invited to your College for the purpose, stage an interview between Mr. Cox and Mr. Stirling. In this interview,

   Mr. Stirling will examine the revised figures closely with Mr. Trevor Cox, and state the bank's position in relation to the amount of capital introduced by the owner, the type of finance that may be available, how much it will cost, how it will be repaid, and how the bank would wish to see it secured.

   Mr. Cox will be prepared to answer Mr. Stirling's questions and discuss the subject areas mentioned above. In particular Mr. Cox should be aware of any alternative sources of finance, e.g. loans from the family (Desmond?) and any other savings that he may have. He should also be prepared to outline how he wishes the business to develop over the next twelve months.

**section three
social and public sector
organizations and finance**

Chapter Twenty Four
Public Sector Finance

So far we have examined in detail the financial needs and operations of individuals and business organizations, which comprise what we call the *Private Sector*. In this Chapter we will consider the *Public Sector,* its financial objectives, sources of finance, and its expenditure. But first, it is important to define what we mean by the "Public Sector".

The Public Sector

The Central Government of the UK is responsible for a number of bodies which comprise the Public Sector. These are organizations which serve the needs of the public and are held in public ownership. They include:

* **Central Government Departments,** e.g. Defence, Transport, Health and Social Security, Energy, Environment, Education and Science
* **Local Authorities** (dealt with in detail in Chapter 25)
* **Public Utilities,** e.g. Electricity Supply Industry, Passenger Transport Executives
* **Health Authorities**
* **Public Corporations,** e.g. British Rail, British Coal, the BBC, the Post Office

This wide range of organizations operates at local, regional and national levels, providing services for the public, some of them free, some of the services are charged on a commercial basis.

Financial Objectives of the Public Sector

Organizations in the Public Sector are accountable to the public: they serve the public and they use public funds. Whereas the individual and the business organization aim to increase their wealth through efficiency and *profit,* Public Sector organizations should be seen as an efficient means of *spending* public money raised through taxes and borrowing. An important objective of any Public Sector organization is, therefore, to ensure that it is spending efficiently. If it is not, then the issue may become political: the Central Government may hold the purse strings, but the electorate provides the gold. It should also be noted that the objectives of Public Sector organizations are motivated by political and economic pressures which may dictate, for instance, the rate of growth of expenditure, or the size of financial surpluses or deficits.

It is also useful to compare public utilities and other public corporations with large quoted public companies. Both generally have some form of rate of return objective as a target. These are important for the Public Sector bodies because the Government from time to time will privatise a public utility or corporation, e.g. British Telecom or British Gas. They will sell off these institutions to the public who will subscribe for shares which are then quoted and traded on the Stock Exchange. In order to attract such public investment the bodies concerned will need to show that they have been performing well and are meeting the set rates of return. Thus public utilities and public corporations need to have financial objectives similar to those of public limited companies (in the 'private' sector).

Sources of Central Government Finance

How does the Central Government raise the money it needs for its spending programmes? Spending is either 'current' (regular and recurrent) or 'capital' (long term investment); both types are funded from specific sources, listed below.

Current Expenditure is met from:
- taxes on income (e.g. Income Tax)
- taxes on expenditure (e.g. VAT)
- National Insurance Contributions
- miscellaneous income (rent, dividends, interest)

Capital Expenditure is met from:
- short term loans from the London Money Markets (Treasury Bills)
- issue of Government 'gilt-edged' Stock on the Stock Exchange
- investment by the public in National Savings Schemes such as National Savings Certificates, Premium Savings Bonds
- privatisation (sale of public corporations to the general public, e.g. British Telecom, British Gas)
- taxes on capital

Fig 24.1 on the next page sets out the sources of Government income, and the way in which it is spent.

Central Government Expenditure: The Budget

A prominent lady politician has frequently compared the management of the State with the management of a household. The comparison is apt: the Greek word for household management is 'economics', and this science of obtaining maximum return from limited resources is consistently applied by Central Government to its spending. Central Government clearly cannot spend without restriction: the result is too much money in the system and consequent inflation. Central Government is therefore, like the individual, faced with 'opportunity cost': it asks itself questions such as should the money available be spent on motorways, hospitals or opera houses? The areas of public expenditure are therefore the subject of much political debate.

Public awareness of Government spending decisions is focussed on the annual Budget in which the Chancellor of the Exchequer announces how the Government intends to raise money in direct and indirect taxation. The Budget, contrary to the impression one gets from the media, involves more than the Chancellor spending a weekend or two with a pocket calculator working out how to pay the nation's 'housekeeping' bills. It is one step in a long complex process which takes over 12 months to complete, and which we will now examine in detail.

❑ **Public Expenditure Survey**
   In the spring of the year preceding the Budget, officials from the Treasury and other Central Government Departments work together in compiling the Public Expenditure Survey. This is a three year, inflation-adjusted forecast for revenue and capital expenditure by Central and Local government bodies, public corporations and nationalised industries.

❑ **White Paper**
   As soon as the Public Expenditure Survey is completed, it is passed to the Cabinet for approval and published as a White Paper.

❑ **Departmental Spending Requirements: Appropriations**
   The groundwork for the Budget is done by the Central Government's Departments which work out the spending estimates for the following year from the Public Expenditure Survey. These estimates are passed to the Treasury in December preceding the Budget and placed before the Cabinet for approval as departmental 'Appropriations'. They then go before Parliament for incorporation into the Consolidated Fund (Appropriation) Act in the summer following the Budget.

Public Money: Income and Expenditure 1987-1988

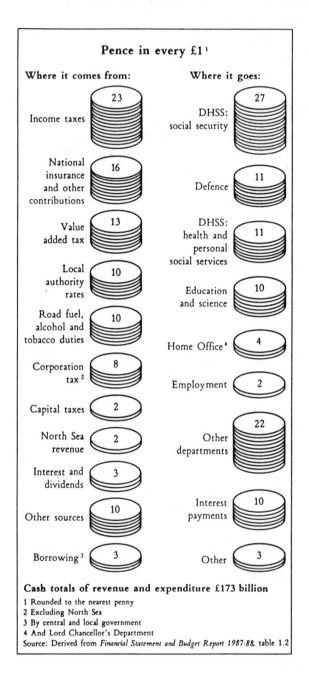

Pence in every £1 [1]

Where it comes from:		Where it goes:	
Income taxes	23	DHSS: social security	27
National insurance and other contributions	16	Defence	11
Value added tax	13	DHSS: health and personal social services	11
Local authority rates	10	Education and science	10
Road fuel, alcohol and tobacco duties	10	Home Office [4]	4
Corporation tax [2]	8	Employment	2
Capital taxes	2	Other departments	22
North Sea revenue	2		
Interest and dividends	3		
Other sources	10	Interest payments	10
Borrowing [3]	3	Other	3

Cash totals of revenue and expenditure £173 billion

1 Rounded to the nearest penny
2 Excluding North Sea
3 By central and local government
4 And Lord Chancellor's Department
Source: Derived from *Financial Statement and Budget Report 1987-88*, table 1.2

Fig 24.1
Source: *Economic Progress Report*

❑ **The Budget**

The Budget is the means by which the Treasury raises finance for its planned expenditure. In recent years it has also determined the size of the Budget deficit, i.e. the amount of money which will *not* be covered by taxes and will need to be financed from other sources, such as borrowing. At present, however, the Chancellor is in the enviable position of having a budget surplus, i.e. an excess of income over expenditure which will enable him to repay some of the Government's borrowing from the public.

The Chancellor of the Exchequer places his or her proposals before Parliament in March or April of each year; they are then debated and possibly amended by Parliament before being consolidated into the Finance Act in August.

Central Government Accounts and Audit

Accounts

The Bank of England acts as banker to the Government and maintains a number of accounts on its behalf:

- **The Consolidated Fund** receives all revenue from taxes and miscellaneous items, and provides funds for all Central Government Departments

- **The National Loans Fund** receives all loans granted and is the source for repayments

- **The Exchange Equalisation Account** is for all foreign currency dealings entered into by the Bank of England on behalf of the government to maintain the stability of the pound

Audit

The Exchequer and Audit Department, a branch of the Civil Service, carries out the necessary inspection of accounts, regulation of forecasting techniques and prevention of wastage of public funds. Critics of the system would point out that this form of audit is internal (i.e. carried out by a Government Department) and lacks the impartiality of an outside body.

Chapter Summary

❑ The Public Sector's financial objectives are to seek efficiency in expenditure and, in the case of public corporations and utilities, to achieve a set rate of return.

❑ The Government raises finance for public spending from a number of sources, including taxation and borrowing.

❑ The process leading up to the Chancellor's Budget is long and complex, involving all Central Government Departments.

❑ Because of its importance to the individual's spending power, the Budget receives more public attention than the equally important expenditure plans.

In the next Chapter we will turn to a more regional view of the Public Sector and examine the financing of Local authorities which, like central Government, place great emphasis on the accurate estimation of expenditure.

✍️ Student Activities

1. Research your College Library (under the supervision of your lecturer) for newspaper and magazine articles detailing the most recent public expenditure plans and the budget and reactions to them. From this source material extract the following information:

   - How the Chancellor intends to raise money by way of direct and indirect taxes and other means.
   - How the Chancellor intends to spend the money raised.

   From the articles you have read, comment on:

   (a) How these measures are likely to affect the 'person in the street'. Will he/she be better off?

   (b) Does the Budget favour the better-off as opposed to the lower paid, or vice versa? How far is this a reflection of the thinking of the political party in power?

   Present your findings in the form of a written report addressed to your lecturer.

2. Obtain the prospectus and/or publicity material for a public sector organization which the Government is intending to 'privatise' (or has 'privatised'). You are a clerical worker in 'Omnifinance plc', a financial services company, which among other activites, gives investment advice. Write a letter for your own signature from your local office (make up an address) to Michael Idas, 23 Chepstow Crescent, Eastford, telling him:

   - how to obtain shares in the new company
   - how much it will cost him, and when he will have to pay
   - how successful the enterprise has been while under public sector management
   - why the enterprise is being 'privatised'
   - the benefits he will receive by subscribing for shares

3. Devise and conduct a public opinion poll in your locality (under your lecturer's supervision) on the subject of "How to pay for public services".

   The poll should investigate the following areas:

   "Does the public know the source(s) of the funds for Government expenditure?"
   Is the public aware of the use of funds raised from taxes, privatisations and government borrowing? This area could be investigated by asking where the public thinks the money from premium bonds, the issue of British Gas shares, VAT, National Insurance, income tax, is invested.

   "Does the public think it is being taxed enough?"
   This area could be extended to cover issues such as:
   - are the right things being taxed?
   - is tax fairly levied on the poor and the rich alike?
   - would the public be prepared to pay more tax to cover services such as Health and Education?

   The findings should be

   (a) the subject of a written report addressed to your lecturer
   (b) debated in a class session

Chapter Twenty Five
Local Authority Finance

Local Authority is a term applied to local governing councils which operate both in the county areas and also in urban areas. In the county areas the Local Authority is normally structured in three tiers:

- the County Council
- the Borough or District Councils
- the Parish Councils

In the urban areas, on the other hand, only *one* level of council exists: in London there are separate Borough Councils (such as Brent or Westminster) and in other urban areas there are Metropolitan Borough Councils (such as Birmingham or Liverpool).

Local Authorities taken as a whole have a wide range of services to administer. These include education, environmental health, planning, refuse collection, social services, transport, fire services, libraries and recreational facilities. In this chapter we will see how the Local Authorities finance their operations, and also how they prepare and present their accounts to the public.

Financial Objectives: Budgeting for Expenditure

As we have seen earlier, sole traders, partnerships and limited companies are in business to make a profit. They will choose a market for their product or service, price their product according to that market, and produce enough to meet estimated demand. Expenditure of the business will, therefore, be reduced as far as possible to meet this demand and maximise profit.

Local Authorities, on the other hand, do not have the profit motive as a major objective. They do not rely for their survival on the level of demand in a competitive market. Therefore, they approach the subject of expenditure quite differently: they carefully budget for how much they need to spend on administration and services; then they tackle the problem of how they are going to raise those funds.

The budgeting process of a Local Authority is normally divided into four separate budgets:

The Revenue Budget is a compilation of projections of likely expenditure and income of the Local Authority services during the coming year. It is also responsible for setting the Community Charge.

The Capital Budget sets targets for spending on long term assets such as roads and schools. Its time span is normally five years, although it can be longer. It is reviewed each year, i.e. a further year is added to the five year plan, making it a 'rolling' budget.

The Manpower Budget controls the level of staffing, the most expensive item for any Local Authority, which are essentially labour-intensive organizations.

The Cash Flow Budget, like the cash budget of an individual or business organization, projects and monitors the amount of money that is likely to be received or paid out over a given period. One important function is the management of repayment and interest for Local Authority Loan Debt.

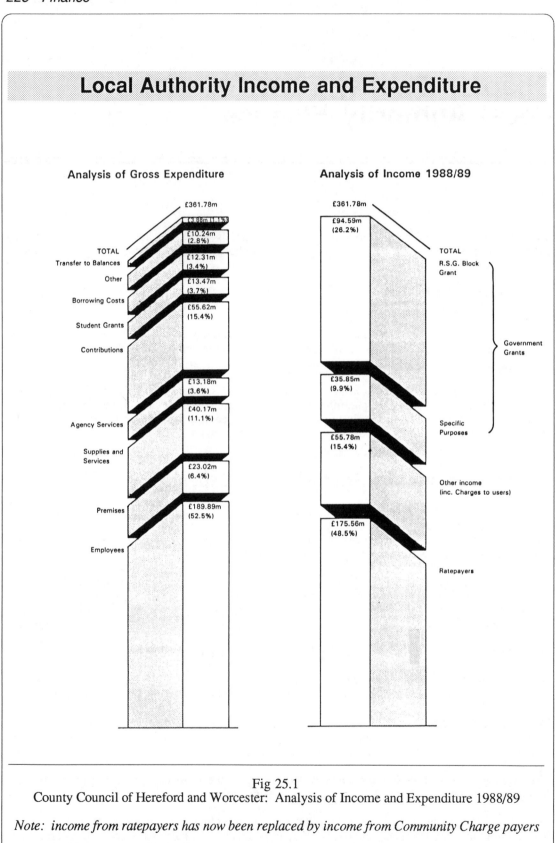

Fig 25.1
County Council of Hereford and Worcester: Analysis of Income and Expenditure 1988/89

Note: income from ratepayers has now been replaced by income from Community Charge payers

Sources of Local Authority Finance

Local Authority spending is of two types:

* *capital* expenditure for major projects such as roads and hospitals
* *revenue* expenditure for day-to-day running costs

❏ Capital Expenditure

The sources of finance for *capital* expenditure are:

* loan debt
* contributions from Local Authority revenue
* specific Central Government grants
* sale of existing capital items
* internally accumulated funds (Capital and Renewals Funds)
* leasing

❏ Revenue expenditure

There are four main sources of finance for *revenue* expenditure:

* Central Government grants: Revenue Support Grant (also known as the Standard Spending Grant)
* redistributed income from the Uniform Business Rate (a levy on business property) collected by Local Authorities on behalf of Central Government
* local taxes: the Community Charge in England, Wales and Scotland
* fees and charges for local services

We will now look at the most important of these sources of finance: Central Government grants, charges for local services, local taxes, and Local Authority borrowing.

❏ Central Government Grants

Central Government grants are of two types:

* Specific Grants
* Revenue Support Grant

Specific Grants
The Specific Grants, as the title suggests, are intended to assist specific requirements such as housing, police and transport.

Revenue Support Grant
Central Government calculates each year the amount of revenue expenditure which it considers each local authority *should* incur in providing what it calls the *standard level of service*. This is known as a *Standard Spending Assessment* (SSA). You may well ask how the Government performs this calculation. The answer lies in the application of complex formulae to all areas of revenue expenditure, based on population and other factors relevant to the area, to produce a total revenue spending figure.

The table below sets out the total Local Authority spending estimated by the Government for England.

Total of Standard Spending Assessments for England

£m.

Education	14 752.5
Social Services	3 591.9
Police	2 124.5
Fire and Civil Defence	876.6
Highway Maintanence	1 578.0
Other Services (eg Flood Defence)	4 502.1
Interest on Local Authority Debt	2 379.7
TOTAL STANDARD SPENDING	29 805.3

The Central Government then allocates a share of this total of Standard Spending Assessments to Local Authorities as the *Revenue Support Grant* in proportion to the adult population in each Authority. The grant is therefore *fixed* by Central Government. It is then up to each Local Authority to spend the grant as it thinks appropriate, and as efficiently - or inefficiently - as the financial management of the Authority allows.

The Revenue Support Grant will not cover all the revenue expenditure undertaken by Local Authority. The difference is made up from

• fees and charges for local services
• payment by Central Government of money raised from the Uniform Business Rate
• local taxation: the Community Charge in England, Wales and Scotland

We will deal with these sources of income in turn.

❏ Charges for Local Services

A certain proportion, typically 25%, of a Local Authority's income comes from charges for services provided. Some services give a social benefit, others are more commercial in nature and may compete with private enterprise. Socially oriented income includes rent from council housing and elderly persons' homes, while income from more commercial sources includes revenue from car parks and caravan sites, lotteries and leisure centres.

❏ Uniform Business Rate (National Non-Domestic Rate)

Central Government taxes business premises and property by means of the *Uniform Business Rate* (UBR) also known as the *National Non-Domestic Rate*. All business property has been valued for taxation purposes by the Inland Revenue and given a *rateable value* expressed in £s. Rateable value is a hypothetical annual rental value; it is *not* the market value of the property. A factory unit, for instance, may be given a rateable value of £50,000. The tax due to Central Government is calculated by applying a standard multiplier (the Uniform Business Rate) to the rateable value. This multiplier is currently 34.8p in the £, but will be raised annually in line with inflation. The rates due on the factory unit will therefore be:

£50 000 (rateable value) x 34.8p (Uniform Business Rate multiplier) = £17 400 per year

The Uniform Business Rate is collected by the Local Authorities and passed over to a central pool which Central Government then reallocates to Local Authorities to help fund their revenue expenditure. The allocation is made on the basis of the figure for the adult population in the Local Authority area, a figure which is also used for the calculation of the Community Charge (see below).

❏ Local Taxation: the Community Charge

General Rates: a Historical Note

Before April 1990 in England and Wales (and April 1989 in Scotland), local taxation was raised by Local Authorities by means of the *General Rates*. This levy was essentially a tax on the occupation of property, whether for domestic or business purposes. Each property was given a rateable value (in the same way as business property is now assessed for Uniform Business Rate) and the rates calculated by applying so many pence in the £ to that rateable value. Thus a property was taxed according to its size rather than on the number of occupants. Whatever the advantages and disadvantages of the rating system (a subject for lively political debate!), it was replaced for domestic properties in April 1990 in England and Wales (April 1989 in Scotland) by the Community Charge, or Poll Tax as it is commonly known, which is a local taxation on individuals of 18 years of age and over. In April 1990, Uniform Business Rate became the basis for local business taxation.

Types of Community Charge

The Community Charge is a tax levied by a Local Authority on adults in its area to raise money for its revenue expenditure.

There are three types of Community Charge:

* *Personal Community Charge*, a flat rate tax payable by all adults, unless they are exempt
* *Standard Community Charge*, a tax on second homes, holiday cottages and empty properties - this is fixed by each Local Authority and can be up to twice the Personal Community Charge
* *Collective Community Charge*, paid by landlords of buildings with short-stay residents (eg hostels); the landlord charges residents a daily contribution ($\frac{1}{365}$ of the annual Personal Community Charge) and passes on the money (less 5% commission) to the Local Authority

Community Charge Register

The Community Charge is levied on the basis of each Local Authority's Community Charge Register, a computer database of names and addresses of individuals of 18 and over resident in that Authority. The Register was compiled from a canvass taken in 1989 and is updated each time an individual moves and notifies the Authority. It is an offence for anyone of 18 and over to avoid registration for the tax.

Rebates

With the exception of students (see below) rebates are available to payers of the Personal Community Charge. These are means-tested benefits and may result in rebates of up to 80%.

Students

Full-time students in further and higher education are a special category of charge payer who, unless they are exempt (see below), pay only 20% of the full Personal Community Charge.

Exemptions

The following categories of adults are exempt from the Personal Community Charge:
* prisoners who are detained by the order of a court (except those detained for non-payment of the Community Charge or a fine)
* visiting armed forces and foreign diplomats
* members of international headquarters and defence organizations
* the severely mentally impaired
* long term hospital patients and patients in homes
* members of religious communities
* low-paid care workers
* students under 20 and in full-time further (but not higher) education or still at school
* persons of no fixed abode and residents of certain hostels

Payment of the Community Charge

The annual Community Charge is payable by ten instalments. Other payment periods, e.g. weekly, annually, monthly (12 instalments), may be made by mutual agreement between the chargepayer and the Authority concerned.

❏ Controls over Local Authority Spending

The sources of funding for Local Authority revenue spending are set out in the diagram below. Note that the levels of the Government sources of funding - the Revenue Support Grant and the Uniform Business Rate - are outside the control of the Local Authority.

Money contributed by the Government (fixed amounts)	**Money raised from within the Local Authority (amounts decided upon by Local Authority)**
Revenue Support Grant	Community Charge
Redistributed Uniform Business Rate	Fees and Charges for Local Services

Community Charge "Capping"

It therefore follows that if a Local Authority wishes to spend more than the Government considers that it should (ie more than the *standard level of service* which forms the basis for the calculation of the Revenue Support Grant) the extra money will have to be found from

- fees and charges for local services
- the Community Charge set by the Local Authority

In the main, the extra money will be obtained from the Community Charge. In order to prevent Local Authorities from spending too much and consequently levying a very high Community Charge, the Government has the power to "charge cap." This process involves the Secretary of State for the Environment setting formulae for limits on expenditure in relation to the Standard Spending Assessment. The Authority concerned must submit revised expenditure figures in order to comply with the imposed spending limits. As a *consequence* of this the Community Charge will be set at a lower level. The process of "charge capping" might therefore be more accurately termed "expenditure capping."

Setting the Community Charge

The Community Charge calculation is shown on the Community Charge Bill sent to every chargepayer by the Local Authority. An example is illustrated in fig 25.2 on the next page. Note the following details:

- the right-hand column of figures shows the *Government's estimate* for the standard level of service for Authorities in the area in terms of £ per adult (ie spending per adult head of population)
- the left-hand column of figures shows the *Authority's plans* for spending in £ per adult
- from these spending totals are deducted the fixed Government income from Revenue Support Grant and Uniform Business Rates
- the difference shown at the bottom of the left-hand column is the Community Charge arrived at by the Local Authority and charged to the adult population living within the Authority
- the figure of £297.94 at the foot of the right-hand column equates to the National average figure of £278 mentioned in the first paragraph and is the same on Community Charge bills for all Authorities

Community Charge Bill

Glebelands District Council
75 Orchard Road
Knightworth
GB6 52Z
Tel 0897 892700

Treasurer John Minor, I P F A

Date of Issue 21 March 199–

> to
> Mr R Williams
> 87 Kenilworth Close
> Knightworth GB8 65X

Account No 10000376457823

You are shown in the Glebelands District Council's Community Charge Register as being subject to a
Personal Community Charge
The Community Charge helps to pay for spending by the local authorities in your area. The rest of their spending is supported by the Government Revenue Support Grant, by rates paid by businesses, by other Government grants, by fees, charges and other income. Revenue Support Grant is calculated on the basis that a standard level of service can be broadly provided anywhere in England for a Community Charge of £278.00
The Community Charge for your area is made up as follows:

	Your Authority's Plans £ per head	Government Standard Level of service £ per Head
Wyvern County Council	664.17	628.91
Glebelands District Council	91.83	81.39
Knightworth Parish Council	5.31	
	761.31	710.30
Less Revenue Support Grant	- 139.85	- 139.85
Less Business Rates	- 292.51	- 292.51
Charge before Adjustments	328.95	277.94
Adjustments	0.00	
PERSONAL COMMUNITY CHARGE	328.95	

PAYMENT INSTRUCTIONS
You may send the amount stated above to the Treasurer's Department at the above address (cheques crossed and made payable to Glebelands District Council), or you may pay by standing order or direct debit through your bank (see overleaf).

Fig.25.2
Community Charge Bill sent to a Personal Community Charge Payer

Forms of Local Authority Borrowing

As we saw earlier, Local Authorities also finance their operations from loans that they raise.

Local Authority Mortgages
A Local Authority Mortgage is a loan evidenced in the form of a signed and sealed legal document. Mortgages are available from:

- local investors
- large institutions (e.g. pension funds, insurance companies)
- Public Works Loan Board (P.W.L.B.)

The period of mortgage loans can vary from 10 to 80 years; repayment can be in instalments, or at maturity, i.e. the end of the loan.

Local Authority Stock Issues
Local Authority Stock is issued and traded on the Stock Exchange, and thus can be bought by the public in the same way as public limited company shares and Government Stock. Stock is only issued by the larger Local Authorities.

Local Authority Bonds
Local Authority Bonds are sold directly 'over the counter' to private investors, and can take the form of 'local', 'yearling' and 'negotiable' bonds. They are issued for periods of up to a year (hence 'yearling') and may be renewed as they mature.

Temporary Loans
Financial institutions, large companies and other Local Authorities sometimes have short-term surpluses of cash which they place with money brokers. These funds are then lent by the brokers to similar institutions with a cash requirement. Local Authorities can borrow such funds for periods from one day to one year; they will issue 'deposit receipts' in return for the loans.

Local Authority Loan Administration: the Loans Fund

As you will see from fig. 25.1, a Local Authority has many services to finance, and it is therefore clear that it would be administratively difficult to apply any particular loan to any particular service. The Local Government Act 1972 has therefore provided that a Local Authority may set up a Loans Fund, often known as a 'Consolidated Loans Fund'.

A Loans Fund is a 'pool' of money into which all money raised from borrowing is paid, and out of which the Local Authority draws money to finance capital expenditure and repay borrowing. The departments (individual services) which borrow money from the Loans Fund are known as the 'borrowing accounts'; these are required to repay the loans to the Loans Fund over a period related to the life of the asset purchased.

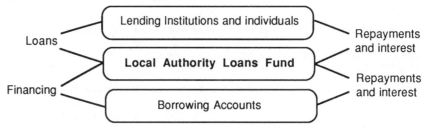

The Loans Fund is, therefore, a very useful arrangement as it enables the Local Authority to average out the cost of its many forms of borrowing in terms of interest rates and administrative expenses. The interest cost is passed on as a standard rate to each borrowing account, and is repaid along with the loan principal amount of the loan.

Financial Control of a Local Authority

When examining finance for individuals and business organizations we have seen that financial control is important for efficiency and profitability. Local Authorities also aim to be efficient, and not wasteful with the resources they have at their disposal, largely because they are accountable to Central Government and the chargepayers for those resources. Local Authorities are therefore subject to both internal and external controls, some of them set down in law.

❏ Internal Financial Control of a Local Authority

There is no legally defined structure for the financial organization of a Local Authority, but the following hierarchy is fairly typical:

The Finance Committee directs financial policy and makes recommendations to the Council. Its functions include the supervision of borrowing, investment, banking operations, and expenditure.

The Director of Finance, also known as the Treasurer is an important figure in Local Authority finance. His position may be compared with that of a Finance Director of a large public limited company. He has overall control of the day-to-day running of the Finance Division, and is directly responsible to the Finance Committee.

The Finance Department is subdivided into operational divisions such as collection of revenue, expenditure, wages and salaries. Its accounting functions include budgetary control (the recording of transactions) and financial planning (the planning of future needs).

Internal Audit is carried out by a separate section of the Finance Department, and is required by law. Its function is to monitor and ensure the efficiency and accuracy of the Local Authority's accounting system, compliance with law and council policies, and the prevention and detection of fraud.

❏ External Financial Control: the Audit Commission

External audit of Local Authorities, like internal audit, is required by law, principally the Local Government Finance Act 1982, which established the Audit Commission. This independent body, which has the motto of the three E's - economy, efficiency, effectiveness - aims to achieve 'value for money' from the Local Authorities. It does this by appointing either a District Auditor or an Approved Auditor.

District Auditors are members of the Audit Inspectorate, which is part of the Civil Service. They each have responsibility for a certain geographical area.

Approved Auditors are members of a recognised Accounting Body, approved by the Secretary of State. These bodies include The Institute of Chartered Accountants in England and Wales, The Chartered Association of Certified Accountants, and The Chartered Institute of Public Finance and Accounting (CIPFA).

The Audit Commission publishes data which which enables useful comparison to be made of performance and the efficiency of the provision of services by Local Authorities with similar geographic locations and demographic patterns.

Duties of an External Auditor
An approved or district auditor must examine the accounts for a number of reasons:

- most importantly to ensure that there is a minimum amount of waste and inefficiency
- to ensure that the accounts are drawn up in accordance with accepted accounting practices
- to ensure consistency in the running of the accounts
- to report on any instance of waste or fraud
- to check that internal audit is adequate

The Internal Accounts of a Local Authority

The published accounts of a Local Authority, which we shall describe in the next section, are prepared from the day-to-day accounting records. These may be summarised as follows:

Cash Accounts are comparable with the 'bank' account maintained by a business in its Cash Book. These accounts record all receipts and payments passed through the bank; separate accounts are kept for capital and revenue transactions.

Income Accounts and Expenditure Accounts record separately, in addition to the Cash Account, income received, on a cash payment or credit basis, and all payments made by the Local authority in respect of capital items, goods and services, and wages and salaries.

Revenue Accounts are compiled from Income and Expenditure accounts, and are basically the Profit & Loss accounts of individual services or departments. They show:
- income: government grants, charges and fees
- expenditure: salaries, running expenses (not capital items), interest and repayment of loans
- any surplus or deficit

Capital Accounts are also compiled from the Income and Expenditure accounts, but record capital items in specified services or departments. They are comparable to the fixed asset accounts of businesses.

The Published Accounts of a Local Authority

The Local Government Planning and Land Act 1980 states that all Local Authorities must produce an Annual Report, and that the Report must contain the relevant accounts. The District or Borough Council and the County Council therefore both publish Accounts as at 31 March each year, the accounts being set out according to a CIPFA Code of Practice issued in June 1987.

As we have seen when examining the aims of the Audit Commission, the present emphasis in viewing the accounts of Local Authorities is on efficiency. The Accounts will therefore contain a number of 'performance indicators' which tell the reader how well the Local Authority is performing in comparison with the year's budget and the previous year's figures. The most important items in the Accounts will be:

- the Finance Director's Report on the Accounts
- the Auditor's Report on the Accounts
- details of revenue income and expenditure by service, including performance indicators
- a Revenue Account Summary
- a Capital Account Summary by service, showing sources of finance
- general statistics and performance indicators for services
- a manpower summary
- a Consolidated Balance Sheet (see fig. 25.3)
- a Consolidated Statement of Revenue and Capital Movements

Additionally, if the Authority is a Housing Authority, it will also present a Housing Revenue Account, as it will be directly responsible for administering local housing. The Code of Practice mentioned above states that the Annual Report should be readily available to the public. It will be distributed to:

- town halls, county halls, public libraries
- the local press (with a press release)
- interested groups who have requested a copy
- employees of the Local Authority

Students are strongly recommended to obtain a set of Local Authority accounts for closer study. A balance sheet of a County Council is set out in fig. 25.3.

CONSOLIDATED BALANCE SHEET

The balance sheet summarises the state of the County Councils affairs at 31 March 1989 and incorporates the balances of the County Fund but excludes the Superannuation and Trust Funds.

	£000	31.3.89 £000	31.3.88 £000
Fixed Assets		88,687	92,227
Deferred Charges		170	192
Long-term debtors		1,108	1,100
Total Non-Current Assets		**89,965**	**93,519**
Current Assets			
Stocks	2,569		2,602
Debtors	20,678		15,719
Temporary Investments	27,292		15,179
Cash in hands of accounting officers	333		313
		50,872	33,813
Less Current Liabilities			
Creditors	25,450		27,299
Temporary Loans	612		3,754
Cash overdrawn	13,849		9,173
		39,911	40,226
Net Current Liabilities		**10,961**	**(6,413)**
		100,926	87,106
Financed by:			
Long-term borrowing			
Public Works Loan Board	43,751		37,403
Other Local Authorities	4,993		5,276
Other mortgages & bonds	3,840	52,584	4,344
Deferred capital receipts		54	55
Capital receipts unapplied		17,326	12,030
Reserve Funds			
Further Education Colleges Reserve	372		306
Property Maintenance Reserve	230		260
Holme Lacy House Reserve	150		144
Road Maintenance Reserve	178		874
D.S.S.	337		—
Schools Capitation Reserve	499		482
Short Life Assets Reserve	2,141		3,102
Redditch Burden Reserve	132		132
Direct Labour Organisation Reserve	1,294		1,066
Other Reserves	430	5,763	309
Revenue balances		25,199	21,323
		100,926	87,106

Fig.25.3
County Council of Hereford and Worcester
Consolidated Balance Sheet as at 31 March 1989

Chapter Summary

❏ Local Authorities, which include the County Council, District and Borough Councils, and Parish Councils in the counties, Metropolitan councils in urban areas, and the London Boroughs, do not aim to make a profit.

❏ Budgets have to be prepared for both revenue and capital spending.

❏ Sources of finance include government grants, charges for services, the Community Charge, and borrowing from institutions and individuals.

❏ Local Authorities are under tight financial control and publish Annual Accounts, the form of which is different from those of business organizations.

❏ The present aim for a Local Authority is to give 'value for money'.

 ## Student Activities

1. Obtain a "Financial Information for Community Charge Payers" leaflet from the Treasurer's Department of your local charging authority.

    As an exercise in the presentation of financial information

    (a) draw up pie charts showing the breakdown of local authority spending and sources of income

    (b) draw up bar charts showing the increase or decrease in spending from the previous to the present year

    If possible use a computer spreadsheet or database with graphics facilities to prepare this visual information

2. Obtain the Annual Report and Accounts of your local County Council (or equivalent), and compare them with the Annual Report and Accounts of a public limited company. Pay particular attention to:

    (a) The overall appearance and presentation - are shareholders and ratepayers given the same style of document?

    (b) The items reported in the financial statements - how do they differ?

    (c) The apparent financial objectives of the two bodies - how do they differ, and in what ways are they the same? (Look at the Chairman's/Treasurer's Report.)

    (d) The auditors - who are they in each case; are they public sector or private sector accountants?

Assignment Thirteen

Explaining the Community Charge

GENERAL OBJECTIVES COVERED
B, E, F.

SKILLS DEVELOPED
Learning and studying, working with others, communicating, numeracy, design and visual discrimination.

SITUATION
You work as a member of a Special Projects team in the Public Relations Department of the Kingsdown District Council. As part of your work you visit schools and further education colleges in your area to explain what the Local Council is, and how it affects the ordinary resident in the Borough of Kingsdown. You are aware that although most of the pupils and students do not yet pay the Community Charge, they will soon do so, and will need an explanation of how it will affect them.

You have been commissioned to design an information package which will comprise
• a pamphlet explaining *why* and *how* the Community Charge is levied
• visual aids and a script for a talk on the subject
• a video on the subject - this can be sent out to the schools and colleges where talks are not practicable

To help you, the Treasurers Department has provided you with a blank Community Charge Bill which you are allowed to photocopy (see page 240 overleaf)

STUDENT TASKS
These tasks are best carried out in groups of three or four. Any or all of the tasks may be completed as part of the Assignment.

1. Design a pamphlet which explains in *simple* terms
    (a) What a Local Authority is.
    (b) The services that a Local Authority provides, and what they cost
    (c) How the Local Authority raises money for this expenditure.
    (d) What the Community Charge is, and who pays it, and how it affects different types of student
    (e) How to interpret a Community Charge Bill (a sample bill would be a useful illustration here).

2. On the basis of the subject matter presented in Task 1, prepare a talk suitable for school and college students. You will need a script and visual aids such as flip charts, handouts and overhead projector slides. Give the talk as a trial run to your colleagues in the Public Relationsl Department (to your fellow students in the College context) and ask them for verbal and/or written comments on its effectiveness.

3. Using the script and visual aids prepared in Task 2, record a video presentation of your talk, and play it back to your colleagues (fellow students) and ask for their verbal and/or written comments. If this video is successful, it can be sent out to the schools and further education colleges in the area.

Community Charge Bill

Kingsdown District Council
56 Osborne Road
Kingsdown
KG6 52Z
Tel 0797 792700

Treasurer Nigel Lowson, I P F A

Date of Issue

to

Account No

You are shown in the Kingsdown District Council's Community Charge Register as being subject to a

The Community Charge helps to pay for spending by the local authorities in your area. The rest of their spending is supported by the Government Revenue Support Grant, by rates paid by businesses, by other Government grants, by fees, charges and other income. Revenue Support Grant is calculated on the basis that a standard level of service can be broadly provided anywhere in England for a Community Charge of £
The Community Charge for your area is made up as follows:

	Your Authority's Plans £ per head	Government Standard Level of service £ per Head
Wyvern County Council		
Kingsdown District Council		
Lea Green Parish Council	____	____
	____	____
Less Revenue Support Grant		
Less Business Rates		
Charge before Adjustments	____	____
Adjustments	____	
PERSONAL COMMUNITY CHARGE	____	

PAYMENT INSTRUCTIONS
You may send the amount stated above to the Treasurer's Department at the above address (cheques crossed and made payable to Kingsdown District Council), or you may pay by standing order or direct debit through your bank (see overleaf).

Sample Community Charge Bill sent to a Personal Community Charge Payer

Chapter Twenty Six
Finance for Social Organizations

We have seen in our studies of Finance that an individual needs to make the most *efficient* use of financial resources, and a business aims to maximise *profit*. These aims are naturally and rightly self-centred. The aim of a social organization, on the other hand, is to provide benefits for the *social* good. But what do we mean by 'social' and 'social organization'? "Social" also has connotations of providing a benefit for the community.

A social organization is the voluntary co-operation of individuals with a mutual interest to arrange social activities for the benefit of themselves and/or others.

For example, an angling club can arrange a good day's fishing, and a literary association can organise a stimulating poetry reading. On a more informal basis a group of individuals can arrange a holiday. In all cases the activity will be enjoyed and *financed* by the members.

In this Chapter we will examine the affairs of the Crown Heath Cricket Club, a typical social organization which, as we will see, is dependent solely on the drive and enthusiasm of its members and the support of the local village community to enable it to operate and to expand its activities.

Crown Heath Cricket Club: The Present Situation

The village of Crown Heath is very much a farming community; it boasts a fine old church, three pubs and a well-known cricket team. The team's activities are made possible by the Crown Heath Cricket Club, which is fortunate in being able to rent a clubhouse, equipped with a bar, from the Parish Council. The Club owns the furniture and fittings (£2,000 at cost) and sports equipment (£1,000 at cost).

The setting of the clubhouse by the village green is ideal for the team's many fixtures; yet the scene is far from idyllic: the building is cramped, a new changing room is needed, and a recent visit by a Fire Officer has pointed to major deficiencies in the building's fire doors. Before seeing how the situation is to be remedied, it is important to examine the Club's financial control and accounting records.

Financial Control of the Club

The officers of the Club include the Chairman, Secretary and the Treasurer, who is a local bank manager. Between them they run the affairs of the Club, aiming to cover expenses comfortably, but not setting out to make a profit. The Club has its own bank account, and the bank mandate allows any two of the officers to sign cheques. The accounting records are, of necessity, very simple.

Accounting Records of the Club

Cash Book: Receipts and Payments Account

The cash book used, often called the *Receipts and Payments Account* is a simple version of the cash book used by businesses (see Chapter 9); it records amounts paid into and out of the bank account, and cash held by the Club. It is normally ruled off at the end of a financial year and does not therefore record refinements such as accruals and prepayments (see Chapter 14), or distinguish between capital and revenue expenditure.

The Receipts and Payments Account is very often the *only* accounting record kept by social organizations which meet infrequently or only handle small amounts of money. A more accurate method of accounting is preferable for the latter social organisation: the Treasurer of the Crown Heath Cricket Club produces final accounts as follows:

- income and expenditure account (profit and loss account)
- balance sheet

We will examine this process in detail for an accounting year ending on 31 December 19-8.

Receipts and Payments Account

First, a summary is made of the Cash Book at the end of the financial year:

Crown Heath Cricket Club
Receipts and Payments Account for the Year ended 31 December 19-8

RECEIPTS	£	PAYMENTS	£
Bank balance at 1 January	231	Rent	200
Subscriptions	875	Heating oil	900
Bar takings	2 700	Electricity	127
Donations	500	Bar expenses	1 250
Sale of Programmes	310	Printing of Programmes	175
		Sports equipment	510
		Groundsman's wages	1 050
		Sundry expenses	35
		Bank balance at 31 Dec.	369
	4 616		4 616

As we have seen, Treasurers of some social organizations go no further than this accounting summary. What are its shortcomings, and how can it be improved?

- The acquisition of assets, here sports equipment of £510, is recorded along with other expenses and does not appear on a balance sheet. The members *do not known what they own.*

- The summary ignores the fact that subscriptions of £875 include £70 paid by members in advance *for next year.*

- The summary ignores the fact that rent of £50 has been paid for the first quarter of *next year* (a prepayment).

Thus the Receipts and Payments Account is not an entirely true picture of the Club's affairs *for the year*. The Treasurer therefore converts this cash book summary into a more accurate view of the year's income and expenditure, an Income and Expenditure Account, comparable to a business' Trading and Profit and Loss Account.

Income and Expenditure Account

In drafting this account, the Treasurer must make the following adjustments:

- Adjust for prepayments (deduct £50 from the rent of £200 = £150).
  Note: an adjustment would be made for any accruals (expenses outstanding) by adding to the yearly total.

- Adjust the subscriptions by deducting advance payments of £70 from the total of £875 = £805.
  Note: subscriptions outstanding are ignored for the year's accounts - they are often paid late, if at all.

- Provide for depreciation on furniture and fittings and sports equipment, say £75 in total.

- Exclude any asset purchase not part of normal running expenses, here sports equipment of £510.

- Net the contributions from fund raising activities, here:

  (a) bar takings £2 700 less bar expenses £1 250 = bar profit £1 450
  (b) sale of programmes £310 less printing costs £175 = profit £135

  Note: if the bar is run throughout the year, the Treasurer may keep a separate 'Bar Trading Account'. This is prepared on the same basis as the trading account of a business.

The revised account will appear as set out below, but note:

- expenditure is recorded on the left and income on the right
- a surplus (as here) is referred to as an 'excess of income over expenditure' and a deficit as an 'excess of expenditure over income'

Crown Heath Cricket Club
Income and Expenditure Account for the year ended 31 December 19-8

EXPENDITURE	£	INCOME	£
Rent	150	Subscriptions	805
Heating oil	900	Profit on bar	1 450
Electricity	127	Profit on programmes	135
Groundsman's wages	1 050	Donations	500
Sundry expenses	35		
Provision for depreciation	75		
Excess of income over expenditure	553		
	2 890		2 890

The £553 surplus for the year has largely been spent on sports equipment (£510) which then appears in the balance sheet, illustrated on the next page.

The balance sheet is presented in the traditional horizontal form, the customary format for a social organization.

Balance Sheet

Crown Heath Cricket Club
Balance Sheet as at 31 December 19-8

	£	£	£		£
FIXED ASSETS	Cost	Dep'n	Net		
Furniture & fittings	2 000	1 100	900	ACCUMULATED FUND	2 045
Sports Equipment	1 000	250	750	Surplus of income over	
	3 000	1 350	1 650	expenditure	553
					2 598
CURRENT ASSETS				CURRENT LIABILITIES	
Bar Stocks		835		Subscriptions paid in	
Prepayment of Rent		50		advance	70
Bank		369		Creditors	356
Cash		120	1 374		
			3 024		3 024

A social organization does not have 'capital' as such. Instead, the term *Accumulated Fund* or *General Fund* is used to describe the difference between the total assets and total liabilities of the organization. In the case of the Crown Heath Cricket Club the Accumulated Fund of £2 045 represents the members' 'stake' in the Club at the beginning of the financial year.

Fund Raising Efforts: Sources of Finance

The Treasurer presents the accounts, audited by an outsider (an accountant living in the village) at the Annual General Meeting of the Club on 10 April 19-9. The members can see clearly from the Income and Expenditure Account what income has been received, and expenditure incurred. They know from the balance sheet exactly what the Club owes and what assets it owns.

On the face of it, the financial state of the Club is healthy. But, as was mentioned earlier, two large items of capital expenditure are required: an extension to the changing room costing £8 000, and new fire doors costing £500 to be installed within the next twelve months. The Treasurer mentions that the Rural District Council will give a grant of 50% of the cost of the extension, as long as 25% of the total extension costs, i.e. £2 000, has been raised by the members themselves by the time the grant application is submitted. The Club therefore needs £2 500, i.e. £2,000 plus £500.

How is the money to be raised? The following points are decided at the meeting:

*   the fire doors are more urgent and should have priority
*   subscriptions can only cover revenue ('running') expenses
*   borrowing from commercial sources is not feasible: there is no tangible security or steady source of repayment

Fund raising by the members is the obvious solution. There are various suggestions, each of which it is hoped will raise £500:

*   a sponsored cricket match
*   a midsummer party
*   a car boot sale on the village green
*   a 'buy a brick' campaign (specifically for the extension)
*   a 'casino night' at the clubhouse

Members volunteer to run the various events and schemes. Because of the popularity of the Club in the neighbourhood, they are hopeful of raising the £2 500 required. A visit to the Club in twelve months' time may well reveal that the money has been raised, but also that more funds are required for a different purpose. So this short-term cycle of fund raising and renewal, typical of many social organizations, continues, and as long as it does, so the social organization will survive.

Chapter Summary

❏ We have examined in this Chapter the fortunes of one particular type of social organization - the social sports club - which has large sums of money passing through its hands, and like a business organization needs tight accounting control and a well organized financial planning process.

❏ Unlike a business organization, however, it does not base its activities on the profit motive, but operates for the social benefit of its members and the general public.

In the next Chapter we will see that some business organizations, usually the larger ones, do bear social considerations in mind, but usually with the ultimate goal of profitability.

Student Activities

1.　You are Fund Raising Secretary of the Friends of Monkswood Hospital. The 'Friends' constitute a charitable organization which raises money to help buy kidney machines. Your committee has decided to hold a Craft Fair in Monkswood Town Hall. You are given the following information by the Treasurer:

Hire of Hall and wages of hall staff	£400.00
Advertising in local papers	£18.50
Entry fee to general public	£0.50

There are two types of stall:

• The commercial stalls, manned by local craftsmen, who sell for their own profit:
　stall fee £15, plus 10% of takings, which are expected to average £150 per stall.

• The charity stalls, manned by the Friends, who give all their takings to the Charity:
　stall fee nil, average takings expected to be £50.

You expect that there will be six commercial stall holders and four charity stalls.

The committee has also decided to hold a raffle, and to spend £50 (to come from the Craft Fair budget) on prizes. They ask for your recommendation for the price of tickets, which are printed in books of ten.

You are to draft a memorandum to the committee. This will include:

(a)　A calculation supported by a break-even graph to show how many members of the public, each paying a 50p entry fee, are needed, *in addition* to stall income, to cover the cost of raffle prizes, hiring and staffing the hall, and advertising the Fair. Also calculate the extra profit you would make if the number attending the Fair was firstly 250, and secondly 500. Ignore any profit on the raffle.

(b)　A suggested pricing policy for the raffle tickets, noting how many tickets the Friends will need to sell to break-even on the £50 cost of prizes. A committee member has suggested a 10% discount on books of ten tickets. Whole books are expected to account for 20% of sales.

(c)　Suggestions, in view of the profit forecasts, for improving the income from the Fair as a whole.

2. You have recently taken over as the Treasurer of the Hallow Male Voice Choir. The accounts of the previous year (to 31 December 19-8) have been prepared, but only as a Receipts and Payments Account as follows:

Hallow Male Voice Choir
Receipts and Payments Account for the year to 31 December 19-8

RECEIPTS	£	PAYMENTS	£
Bank balance as at 1 Jan. 19-8	112	Concert costs	1 250
Subscriptions	750	Conductor's fee	300
Music Festival prize	500	Music purchase	450
Concert ticket sales	825	Printing of programmes	60
Fund raising activities (raffles)	427	Bank balance as at 31 Dec 19-8	554
	2 614		2 614

Additionally, you note that:

• £65 of subscriptions, included in the £750, are paid in advance for 19-9.

• The Club owes £40 for programme printing.

• Your committee wants you to set up a 'Concert Account' which will net the concert costs with the concert ticket sales.

• Stocks of music held, including that recently bought, are valued at cost of £1 125. All music used is owned by the Club and lent to members free of charge.

Your committee ask you to:

(a) Prepare an Income and Expenditure Account for the year and a Balance Sheet, showing an Accumulated Fund, at the year-end.

(b) Write accompanying notes, commenting on and explaining the sources of income, and how they have been spent, and concluding with recommendations for improving income by fund raising or by other means.

3. Form into groups of three or four students. You decide to go on a holiday to Austria for a week. Collect information from travel agencies and banks, and discuss the following, comparing relative costs:

• means of transport, e.g. package tour, train, hiring a car;

• where you will stay, e.g. hotel, chalet self-catering, camping;

• other financial considerations, e.g. insurance;

• means of taking money, e.g. currency, travellers cheques, eurocheques.

You will then come to the following decisions:

(a) How much you can afford individually (consider how you are going to raise the money) and consequently the overall budget figure to which you will work.

(b) What form the holiday will take, a decision based on your first discussions and the budget figure arrived at.

Present your findings in the form of an oral presentation to the class.

Assignment Fourteen

The Severn Social Club

GENERAL OBJECTIVES COVERED
B, C, E, F.

SKILLS DEVELOPED
Working with others, communicating, numeracy, identifying and tackling problems.

SITUATION
The Severn Social Club is an organization strictly for the under-25s. It arranges social events such as discos, dances, and short holidays abroad for its members. It is entirely self-supporting, and has earned itself a good reputation in the area as it also helps raise money for charity through its annual sponsored walk.

The Club has a major problem: the present Treasurer, who is retiring as Treasurer on 31 March 19-8, the end of the Club's financial year, has left the accounts in a poor state and the Club's bank account overdrawn by £5.10.

STUDENT TASKS
You are to divide into groups of four or five to form the Committee of the Severn Social Club. You are to allocate between you the roles of Chairperson, a new Treasurer, Secretary and Membership Secretary. You hold an informal meeting on 10 April. The new Treasurer discovers in the previous Treasurer's box file containing all the accounting records, the following items:

- A bank statement (illustrated) for the last financial year of the Club. The previous Treasurer has annotated the items on the statement with details of the transactions.

- The following invoices relating to the financial year ending March 19-8: a printing bill of £23.50 and an advertising bill of £7.50, both overdue, and both for publicity.

- An invoice for second-hand disco equipment bought by the Club for £1 000 on 1 July 19-7. The equipment was a good buy, so you consider £1 000 also to be the present value of the equipment.

- An envelope marked 'Sponsored Walk Proceeds' containing £12.50 in cash. You suspect that the previous Treasurer has forgotten to pay the money into the bank. This cash and the disco equipment appear to be the only assets held by the Club.

- A list which shows that there were 120 members at 31 March 19-8. The subscription is £5 per year. The Treasurer has scribbled a note to the effect that, during the year, £50 of subscriptions were paid in advance.

In your groups you should undertake the following tasks:

1. The Chairperson is to chair a formal meeting, for which the following agenda has been drawn up:

    (a) the financial situation of the Club as at 31 March 19-8
    (b) money raising over the next twelve months
    (c) social events for the year

    (d) fund raising for charity
    (e) ways of attracting new members
    (f) any other business

As a result of the meeting you have held, further tasks are allocated by mutual consent.

2.   The Treasurer, in view of the sparse accounting data, is to draw up a Receipts and Payments Account, and an Income and Expenditure account for the past financial year, together with a Balance Sheet showing the Accumulated Fund as at 31 March 19-8. These accounts must be verified and checked by the other committee members before being passed to the auditor (lecturer) after the next meeting (see below), and to the members at the AGM on 1 September 19-8.

3.   The Secretary will write up the minutes of the meeting and circulate them to members for approval.

4.   The Membership Secretary will draft a letter to send to students at colleges in the area to encourage them to join the Club. The letter should be circulated to committee members for their approval.

5.   After the completion of these tasks, a further meeting will be held with the following agenda:

    (a) approval of the minutes of the previous meeting
    (b) approval of the Treasurer's accounts to be presented to the AGM on 1 September 19-8
    (c) approval of the letter to attract new members
    (d) any other business

IN ACCOUNT WITH

National Bank plc

Branch Worcester

TITLE OF ACCOUNT..... SEVERN SOCIAL CLUB

ACCOUNT NUMBER.... 21097318

STATEMENT NUMBER 5

DATE	PARTICULARS	PAYMENTS £	RECEIPTS £	BALANCE £
19-7				
1 Apl	Balance b/f			219.15 Cr
8 Apl	Credit ⎱ subscriptions		510.00	729.15 Cr
18 Apl	Credit ⎰		50.00	779.15 Cr
21 Apl	Credit ⎰		40.00	819.15 Cr
7 May	Chq 329710 disco hire	150.00		669.15 Cr
9 May	Chq 329711 advert for dance	17.50		651.65 Cr
9 May	Chq 329712 hall hire and drink	250.00		401.65 Cr
13 May	Credit dance receipts		612.00	1 013.65 Cr
21 Jun	Chq 329713 sponsored walk expenses	25.00		988.65 Cr
28 Jun	Credit sponsored walk takings		509.75	1 498.40 Cr
1 Jul	Chq 329714 disco purchase	1 000.00		498.40 Cr
5 Jul	Chq 329715 donation to hospital	500.00		1.60 Dr
19-8				
5 Jan	Credit subscriptions		50.00	48.40 Cr
17 Jan	Chq 329716 treasurers expenses	25.00		23.40 Cr
12 Mar	Chq 329717 publicity (advert)	28.50		5.10 Dr
31 Mar	Balance c/f			5.10 Dr

Chapter Twenty Seven
Social Implications of Business Decisions

In our studies of Finance we have identified in turn the financial objectives of individuals, business organizations, the public sector and social organizations. Clearly, these objectives are different. We could generalise and say that individuals and businesses are self-oriented, aiming to achieve personal gain, whereas the public sector and social organizations have the public welfare at heart, and strive towards general social improvement. It would be naïve to assume that businesses are motivated solely by profit: as we will see in the situations presented in this Chapter, it is evident that many businesses, organizations and individuals within them are very mindful of social needs. As we will see, businesses sometimes reach a compromise between maximising profit and benefiting the workforce and society at large. Often this will work indirectly to the benefit and profit of the business.

We will now look at three quite different situations: a business introducing new technology and threatening redundancies, a manufacturing business which has made a substantial loss which will affect the workforce, and a large corporation which decides to use a proportion of its profits to benefit the public. All the organizations described are fictional, but are true to life.

Case Study: Wyvern Building Society

Situation

The Wyvern Building Society is a medium sized regional building society, based in the West Midlands, with a branch network spread over an eighty mile radius around its headquarters in Birmingham. The staff are loyal and hardworking. Conditions of service have been favourable, with low interest-rate mortgages and non-contributory pensions among the major perks.

But time cannot stand still for the Wyvern Building Society. The senior management has been worried for some time: competition for deposits in the High Street has been fierce, with other building societies, banks and money shops offering high rates of interest and a fast, efficient, highly automated service. The Wyvern by comparison offers a more personal service, but its computer equipment is slow and outdated. A team of consultants working for a major computer firm has studied the branch network and has come up with the following recommendations:

1. To centralise most of the Society's administration and loan management in the Birmingham headquarters, a large freehold building owned by the Society. The reorganization would save an estimated £750 000 a year, but would mean the shedding of 30 jobs and relocation of some staff to the Birmingham area, where the cost of living is higher.

2. Installation of electronic terminals at all of the Society's branches for staff operation, and cash dispensers for public use at each branch, linked to other financial institutions' machines via the LINK network. This will cost around £2m, but it will also make savings in the form of 20 jobs lost and increased efficiency.

These proposals are 'leaked' to the staff's union who threaten industrial action if the following demands are not met:

- no redundancies as a result of the introduction of electronic equipment
- no relocations to more expensive areas
- adequate staff training for new equipment

The loss of jobs as a result of technological innovation has been a cause of concern to staff in the financial services industry as much as it has to workers in traditional British industries. Whether the machine introduced is a computer or a robot, the result is often the same: loss of jobs, loss of earnings, increased unemployment.

Solution

The Wyvern Building Society, like many business organizations is faced with a dilemma: whether to improve efficiency and profitability but to incur job losses and staff dissatisfaction, or to maintain the status quo, but lose competitive edge. The British 'spirit of compromise' works strongly in such situations, and the Wyvern management puts forward proposals which make concessions to both sides. These are accepted by the Union.

1.   To go ahead with the relocation of administration and management to Birmingham, but offering generous relocation payments with an improved 'City' living allowance (an increment to salary).

2.   To go ahead with the installation of electronic equipment at the Wyvern's branches, with a promise of adequate staff training.

3.   Not to serve any redundancy notices, but to offer early retirement to the staff; this, together with natural wastage (staff leaving for family reasons and going for other jobs), should achieve the reduction of 50 jobs over 2 years.

To the cynically minded, the case of Wyvern Building Society may seem like a fairy story, but in fact similar problems are constantly arising in the service industries, such as banking and insurance, where similar compromise solutions are frequently worked out. Very few redundancies are to be found in these areas, possibly because the service industries are making sufficient profit to enable them to afford a 'social conscience'. However, our next case is based on a firm in the manufacturing industry, and the circumstances here are less happy.

Case Study: Dynawash PLC

Situation

'Dynawash' is a household name in advanced washing machine technology. Dynawash PLC, a quoted public limited company, is a major employer, providing 520 jobs in a depressed area in South Wales. The company was set up with the help of Government grants in a Regional Development Area, and its advanced products have made considerable headway in the UK and export markets.

The auditors have just finished their annual audit and the news, as suspected, is not good. During the last year the company's sales turnover was £156m, but because of increased foreign competition and technical problems with the products, a net loss of £500,000 has been recorded.

The first problem is one of communication. How is the bad news to be transmitted, and to whom?

- **The management** will be only too aware of the situation through internal meetings.

- **The workforce** will have distributed to them a specially printed and highly simplified version of the Annual Report, making ample use of pie and bar charts to present figures. This will be in addition to the far more rapid 'grapevine'.

- **The press** will be given a press release. This will inform the financial press in the City and also the local press of the year's losses and their possible consequences.

- **The shareholders** will be advised at a later stage through the Annual Report and Accounts, but will find out more immediately from press reports.

- **The local community** will be told by the employees and the local press.

Solutions

We are not suggesting any one solution for Dynawash, but instead will propose a series of scenarios, to leave you to come to a decision as to which is preferable or more probable.

Collapse and Liquidation

Rumour in the City of London, fuelled by press reports of the loss, leads to widespread selling of the company's shares, which plummet from 128p to 21p at the close of trading on the Stock Exchange. The company's bank, which has been concerned for some time, starts the insolvency process by calling in the debt and preparing to realise its security. There is little hope for the workforce who foresee closure of the plant within a week. 520 job losses seem inevitable.

Takeover

The directors of Dynawash have taken the initiative and approached Techno PLC, a domestic appliance manufacturing group, which has shown an interest in Dynawash in the past. The directors have presented the management accounts and Techno is happy to buy a controlling interest, as the shares are now a bargain. It may mean some streamlining and minor job losses, but the majority of jobs will be saved.

Management Buy-out

The management have convinced a Venture Capital Company, by means of a persuasive business plan, that they can turn the company around. The Venture Capital Company injects loans and takes shares, as do the directors themselves. Between them, they decide that 20% of the workforce will have to be laid off, but may be taken on again later.

The Government Steps in?

As Dynawash was originally set up with generous capital grants from the Welsh Development Agency, the directors again approach this body for assistance. They argue that additional grants could enable them to return the company to profitable trading and avoid the otherwise inevitable job losses. The

- If they invest, will they be in danger of losing more public money, or will it enable them to recoup existing losses?

- Should they impose special conditions if they invest? For example, should they insist on cutbacks in certain areas, causing limited job losses?

- Should they cut their losses entirely and suggest the plant be closed, on the grounds that it would be cheaper in the long run for the State to pay unemployment and supplementary benefit to the workers?

Conclusion

As you will appreciate from the variety of solutions proposed above, there is no clear 'right' answer. The business decision involves, as ever, a compromise between efficiency and social considerations. Whereas in the case of the Wyvern Building Society the decision rested within the business organization, in the case of Dynawash PLC the decision, assisted by the powers of persuasion of the directors, lies largely in the hands of the creditors.

Case Study: Chemindustries UK

Situation

Our final scene is the London boardroom of Chemindustries UK, the UK subsidiary of an American chemicals and pharmaceuticals corporation. The directors are discussing the advertising budget for the next year. There is a strong difference of opinion between the American and UK directors. Both want to promote the image of Chemindustries, a name virtually unknown in the UK. The Americans favour a widespread TV and newspaper coverage, whereas the British favour a mix of advertising and sponsorship. With the fixed sum of £10m, the British argue that the way to promote Chemindustries into the national consciousness is by sponsoring national and community events. In other words, by sponsorship they will provide a form of social benefit which would otherwise have been paid for out of the public sector purse. Their proposals include:

- Sponsorship of TV snooker: Chemindustries carbon fibre is used in snooker cues.

- Sponsorship of Agricultural and Horticultural Shows: their agrochemical division supplies a wide range of fertilizers and crop control chemicals.

- Chemindustries Scholarships: the funding of University study and research in Chemistry.

- Sponsorship of a concert series in London: a major opportunity to provide entertainment and promote the name of Chemindustries in the capital.

Solution

After much heated discussion, the board agrees to spend 50% of the advertising budget on the sponsorship proposal. They will monitor the success of the campaign and review the situation in six months' time, and again in twelve months, when the following year's budget will be decided. They consider that £5m is better spent on providing social benefits than in increasing the profits of advertising agencies.

Chapter Summary

❑ These three different case studies present different problems. In the first two case studies they involve making a decision: should resources be used to increase profit (or reduce loss), or to provide a social benefit? In the last case it is a question of whether profit should be used for the social good, or to benefit other commercial organizations.

❑ In the cases of Wyvern Building Society and Chemindustries UK, the decision rests with the business organization which is able to make a reasonable compromise, because it has the necessary funds.

❑ In the more distressing case of Dynawash PLC the decision rests with the company's creditors and outside bodies. Their decision is more likely to be based on the benefit *they* will receive from the deal that is decided upon.

✍ Student Activities

1.   Form into two groups within the class. One group is the works committee of Fineware Porcelain Ltd. and the other the Board of Directors. The issue under discussion is the recent announcement by the company of a net profit for the year of £512 000. the works committee want a pay rise of 8% as they consider the workforce should benefit from the profit. The management, on the other hand, want to invest in new kilns which will mean an eventual reduction of three in the workforce of 52. They consider a pay rise of 4% quite sufficient and in line with the national average of pay settlements.

Discuss the issues within your groups and then join together for a formal debate: 'This House considers that profit should only be used for the benefit of the shareholders'. Bring into your discussion the recent legislation for participation by employees in the profits of the employer.

2.   Investigate the use of sponsorship in your locality in areas such as sport and the arts.

Consider:

(a) whether this is an effective form of advertising for the sponsor

(b) how the sponsor benefits from the sponsorship

(c) how the public has benefitted from this form of private funding

(d) the extent to which public sector funds have been saved

(e) any further forms of sponsorship which would be useful in your locality

Present your findings in the form of a report to your lecturer.

index